Sunset

BEST HOME PLANS

Country Living

Loaded with Victorian charm, this gracious country home features a
two-story, turreted bay and a rounded front porch. See plan
AX-90307 on page 82.

Sunset Publishing Corporation ■ **Menlo Park, California**

Photographers: Breland & Farmer Designers, Inc.: 5 top right; **Mark Englund:** 4 bottom, 5 bottom; **Philip Harvey:** 10 top, back cover; **Kershner Communications:** 5 top left; **Stephen Marley:** 11 top left and right; **Russ Widstrand:** 10 bottom; **Tom Wyatt:** 11 bottom.

Cover: Pictured is plan J-91068 on page 114. Cover design by Susan Bryant and Naganuma Design & Direction. Photography by Mark Englund.

Editor, Sunset Books: Elizabeth L. Hogan

First printing September 1992

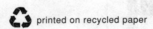 printed on recycled paper

A Dream Come True

Planning and building a house is one of life's most creative and rewarding challenges. Whether you're seriously considering building a new home or you're just dreaming about it, this book offers a wealth of inspiration and information to help you get started.

On the following pages, you'll learn how to plan and manage a home-building project—and how to ensure its success. Then you'll discover more than 200 proven home plans, designed for families just like yours by architects and professional designers. Peruse the pages and study the floor plans; you're sure to find a home that's just right for you. When you're ready to order blueprints, you can simply call or mail in your order, and you'll receive the plans within days.

Enjoy the adventure!

Expansive four-bedroom ranch is filled with important extras—a three-car garage, a sunken living room, a fireplace and wet bar in the family room, and a master bedroom suite with a walk-in dressing room. See plan H-3701-1A on page 161.

Contents

Country Charm

Today's American families have embraced one style of architecture more than any other: country. Perhaps it's the perennial appeal of a simple way of life. Or maybe it represents a return to the traditions and ways that nurtured our forefathers. Whatever the reason, you're sure to find a wealth of inspiration and information among the hundreds of country-style home plans in this book.

Although many have a nostalgic appeal on the outside, the homes are thoroughly up-to-date on the inside, with all the amenities you expect to find in a new home. Even if you're just dreaming about building a home, these plans can show you just how charming your dream home can be.

The two keys to success in building are capable project management and good design. The next few pages will walk you through some of the most important aspects of project management: you'll find an overview of the building process, directions for selecting the right plan and getting the most from it, and methods for successfully working with a builder and other professionals.

The balance of the book presents professionally designed stock plans for country houses in a wide range of configurations and expressions. Once you find a plan that will work for you—perhaps with a few modifications made later to personalize it for your family—you can order construction blueprints for a fraction of the cost of a custom design, a savings of many thousands of dollars (see pages 12–15 for information on how to order).

Gracious country manor includes a stately entrance, generous family and entertaining areas, and an elegant master suite. See plan DD-4458 on page 19.

Wraparound front porch lends nostalgic charm to this country classic. Inside, a large country kitchen opens to the family room. See plans H-3711-1/1A and -2/2A on page 81.

Compact country home, a classic story-and-a-half design, features a screened-in back porch and a deluxe master bedroom. See plan E-1626 on page 96.

Contemporary style joins with country vernacular in this outstanding home design. Inside is an impressive master suite and a vaulted foyer. See plan B-88015 on page 87.

The Art of Building

As you embark on your home-building project, think of it as a trip—clearly not a vacation but rather an interesting, adventurous, at times difficult expedition. Meticulous planning will make your journey not only far more enjoyable but also much more successful. By careful planning, you can avoid—or at least minimize—some of the pitfalls along the way.

Start with realistic expectations of the road ahead. To do this, you'll want to gain an understanding of the basic house-building process, settle on a design that will work for you and your family, and make sure your project is actually doable. By taking those initial steps, you can gain a clear idea of how much time, money, and energy you'll need to invest to make your dream come true.

The Building Process

Your role in planning and managing a house-building project can be divided into two parts: prebuilding preparation and construction management.

■ **Prebuilding preparation.** This is where you should focus most of your attention. In the hands of a qualified contractor whose expertise you can rely on, the actual building process should go fairly smoothly. But during most of the prebuilding stage, you're generally on your own. Your job will be to launch the project and develop a talented team that can help you bring your new home to fruition.

When you work with stock plans, the prebuilding process usually goes as follows:

First, you research the general area where you want to live, selecting one or more possible home sites (unless you already own a suitable lot). Then you choose a basic house design, with the idea that it may require some modification. Finally, you analyze the site, the design, and your budget to determine if the project is actually attainable.

If you decide that it is, you purchase the land and order blue-prints. If you want to modify them, you consult an architect, designer, or contractor. Once the plans are finalized, you request bids from contractors and arrange any necessary construction financing.

After selecting a builder and signing a contract, you (or your contractor) then file the plans with the building department. When the plans are approved, often several weeks—or even months—later, you're ready to begin construction.

■ **Construction management.** Unless you intend to act as your own contractor, your role during the building process is mostly one of quality control and time management. Even so, it's important to know the sequence of events and something about construction methods so you can discuss progress with your builder and prepare for any important decisions you may need to make along the way.

Decision-making is critical. Once construction begins, the builder must usually plunge ahead, keeping his carpenters and subcontractors progressing steadily. If you haven't made a key decision—which model bathtub or sink to install, for example—it can bring construction to a frustrating and expensive halt.

Usually, you'll make such decisions before the onset of building, but, inevitably, some issue or another will arise during construction. Being knowledgeable about the building process will help you anticipate and circumvent potential logjams.

Selecting a House Plan

Searching for the right plan can be a fun, interactive family experience—one of the most exciting parts of a house-building project. Gather the family around as you peruse the home plans in this book. Study the size, location, and configuration of each room; traffic patterns both inside the house and to the outdoors; exterior style; and how you'll use the available space. Discuss the pros and cons of the various plans.

Browse through pictures of homes in magazines to stimulate ideas. Clip the photos you like so you can think about your favorite options. When you visit the homes of friends, note special features that appeal to you. Also, look carefully at the homes in your neighborhood, noting their style and how they fit the site.

Mark those plans that most closely suit your ideals. Then, to narrow down your choices, critique each plan, using the following information as a guide.

■ **Overall size and budget.** How large a house do you want? Will the house you're considering fit your family's requirements? Look at the overall square footage and room sizes. If you have a hard time visualizing room sizes, measure some of the rooms in your present home and compare.

It's often better for the house to be a little too big than a little too small, but remember that every extra square foot will cost more money to build and maintain.

■ **Number and type of rooms.** Beyond thinking about the number of bedrooms and baths you want, consider your family's life-style and how you use space. Do you want both a family room and a living room? Do you need a formal dining space? Will you require some extra rooms, or "swing spaces," that can serve multiple purposes, such as a home office–guest room combination?

■ **Room placement and traffic patterns.** What are your preferences for locations of formal living areas, master bedroom, and children's rooms? Do you prefer a kitchen that's open to family areas or one that's private and out of the way? How much do you use exterior spaces and how should they relate to the interior?

Once you make those determinations, look carefully at the floor plan of the house you're considering to see if it meets your needs and if the traffic flow will be convenient for your family.

■ **Architectural style.** Have you always wanted to live in a Victorian farmhouse? Now is your chance to create a house that matches your idea of "home" (taking into account, of course, styles in your neighborhood). But don't let your preference for one particular architectural style dictate your home's floor plan. If the floor plan doesn't work for your family, keep looking.

■ **Site considerations.** Most people choose a site before selecting a plan—or at least they've zeroed in on the basic type of land where they'll situate their house. It sounds elementary, but choose a house that will fit the site.

When figuring the "footprint" of a house, you must know about any restrictions that will affect your home's height or proximity to the property lines. Call the local building department (look under city or county listings in the phone book) and get a very clear description of any restrictions, such as setbacks, height limits, and lot coverage, that will affect what you can build on the site (see "Working with City Hall," at right).

When you visit potential sites, note trees, rock outcroppings, slopes, views, winds, sun, neighboring homes, and other factors. All will impact on how your house works on a particular site.

Once you've narrowed down the choice of sites, consult an architect or building designer (see page 8) to help you evaluate how some potential houses will work on the sites you have in mind.

Is Your Project Doable?

Before you purchase land, make sure your project is doable. Although it's too early at this stage to pinpoint costs, making a few phone calls will help you determine whether your project is realistic. You'll be able to learn if you can afford to build the house, how long it will take, and what obstacles may stand in your way.

To get a ballpark estimate of cost, multiply a house's total

Working with City Hall

For any building project, even a minor one, it's essential to be familiar with building codes and other restrictions that can affect your project.

■ **Building codes,** generally implemented by the city or county building department, set the standards for safe, lasting construction. Codes specify minimum construction techniques and materials for foundations, framing, electrical wiring, plumbing, insulation, and all other aspects of a building. Although codes are adopted and enforced locally, most regional codes conform to the standards set by the national Uniform Building Code, Standard Building Code, or Basic Building Code. In some cases, local codes set more restrictive standards than national ones.

■ **Building permits** are required for home-building projects nearly everywhere. If you work with a contractor, the builder's firm should handle all necessary permits.

More than one permit may be needed; for example, one will cover the foundation, another the electrical wiring, and still another the heating equipment installation. Each will probably involve a fee and require inspections by building officials before work can proceed. (Inspections benefit *you,* as they ensure that the job is being done satisfactorily.) Permit fees are generally a percentage (1 to 1.5 percent) of the project's estimated value, often calculated on square footage.

It's important to file for the necessary permits. Failure to do so can result in fines or legal action against you. You can even be forced to undo the work performed. At the very least, your negligence may come back to haunt you later when you're ready to sell your house.

■ **Zoning ordinances,** particular to your community, restrict setbacks (how near to property lines you may build), your house's allowable height, lot coverage factors (how much of your property you can cover with structures), and other factors that impact design and building. If your plans don't conform to zoning ordinances, you can try to obtain a variance, an exception to the rules. But this legal work can be expensive and time-consuming. Even if you prove that your project won't negatively affect your neighbors, the building department can still refuse to grant the variance.

■ **Deeds and covenants** attach to the lot. Deeds set out property lines and easements; covenants may establish architectural standards in a neighborhood. Since both can seriously impact your project, make sure you have complete information on any deeds or covenants before you turn over a spadeful of soil.

square footage (of livable space) by the local average cost per square foot for new construction. (To obtain local averages, call a contractor, an architect, a realtor, or the local chapter of the National Association of Home Builders.) Some contractors may even be willing to give you a preliminary bid. Once you know approximate costs, speak to your lender to explore financing.

It's a good idea to discuss your project with several contractors (see page 8). They may be aware of problems in your area that could limit your options—bedrock that makes digging basements difficult, for example. These conversations are actually the first step in developing a list of contractors from which you'll choose the one who will build your home.

Recruiting Your Home Team

A home-building project will inject you and your family into the building business, an area that may be unfamiliar territory. Among the people you'll be working with are architects, designers, landscapers, contractors, and subcontractors.

Design Help

A qualified architect or designer can help you modify and personalize your home plan, taking into account your family's needs and budget and the house's style. In fact, you may want to consider consulting such a person while you're selecting a plan to help you articulate your needs.

Design professionals are capable of handling any or all aspects of the design process. For example, they can review your house plans, suggest options, and then provide rough sketches of the options on tracing paper. Many architects will even secure needed permits and negotiate with contractors or subcontractors, as well as oversee the quality of the work.

Of course, you don't necessarily need an architect or designer to implement minor changes in a plan; although most contractors aren't trained in design, some can help you with modifications.

An open-ended, hourly-fee arrangement that you work out with your architect or designer allows for flexibility, but it often turns out to be more costly than working on a flat-fee basis. On a flat fee, you agree to pay a specific amount of money for a certain amount of work.

To find architects and designers, contact such trade associations as the American Institute of Architects (AIA), American Institute of Building Designers (AIBD), American Society of Landscape Architects (ASLA), and American Society of Interior Designers (ASID). Although many professionals choose not to belong to trade associations, those who do have met the standards of their respective associations. For phone numbers of local branches, check the Yellow Pages.

■ **Architects** are licensed by the state and have degrees. They're trained in all facets of building design and construction. Although some can handle interior design and structural engineering, others hire specialists for those tasks.

■ **Building designers** are generally unlicensed but may be accredited by the American Institute of Building Designers. Their backgrounds are varied: some may be unlicensed architects in apprenticeship; others are interior designers or contractors with design skills.

■ **Draftspersons** offer an economical route to making simple changes on your drawings. Like building designers, these people may be unlicensed architect apprentices, engineers, or members of related trades. Most are accomplished at drawing up plans.

■ **Interior designers,** as their job title suggests, design interiors. They work with you to choose room finishes, furnishings, appliances, and decorative elements. Part of their expertise is in arranging furnishings to create a workable space plan. Some interior designers are employed by architectural firms; others work independently. Financial arrangements vary, depending on the designer's preference.

Related professionals are kitchen and bathroom designers, who concentrate on fixtures, cabinetry, appliances, materials, and space planning for the kitchen and bath.

■ **Landscape architects, designers, and contractors** design outdoor areas. Landscape architects are state-licensed to practice landscape design. A landscape designer usually has a landscape architect's education and training but does not have a state license. Licensed landscape contractors specialize in garden construction, though some also have design skills and experience.

■ **Soils specialists and structural engineers** may be needed for projects where unstable soils or uncommon wind loads or seismic forces must be taken into account. Any

structural changes to a house require the expertise of a structural engineer to verify that the house won't fall down.

Services of these specialists can be expensive, but they're imperative in certain conditions to ensure a safe, sturdy structure. Your building department will probably let you know if their services are required.

General Contractors

To build your house, hire a licensed general contractor. Most states require a contractor to be licensed and insured for worker's compensation in order to contract a building project and hire other subcontractors. State licensing ensures that contractors have met minimum training standards and have a specified level of experience. Licensing does not guarantee, however, that they're good at what they do.

When contractors hire subcontractors, they're responsible for overseeing the quality of work and materials of the subcontractors and for paying them.

■ **Finding a contractor.** How do you find a good contractor? Start by getting referrals from people you know who have built or remodeled their home. Nothing beats a personal recommendation. The best contractors are usually busily moving from one satisfied client to another prospect, advertised only by word of mouth.

You can also ask local real estate brokers and lenders or even your building inspector for names of qualified builders. Experienced lumber dealers are another good source of names.

In the Yellow Pages, look under "Contractors–Building, General"; or call the local chapter of the National Association of Home Builders.

■ **Choosing a contractor.** Once you have a list of names of prospective builders, call several of them. On the telephone, ask first whether they handle your type of job and can work within your schedule. If they can, arrange a meeting with each one and ask them to be prepared with references of former clients and photos of previous jobs. Better still, meet them at one of their current work sites so you can get a glimpse of the quality of their work and how organized and thorough they are.

Take your plan to the meeting and discuss it enough to request a rough estimate (some builders will comply, while others will be reluctant to offer a ballpark estimate, preferring to give you a hard bid based on complete drawings). Don't hesitate to probe for advice or suggestions that might make building your house less expensive.

Be especially aware of each contractor's personality and how well you communicate. Good chemistry between you and your builder is a key ingredient for success.

Narrow down the candidates to three or four. Ask each for a firm bid, based on the exact same set of plans and specifications. For the bids to be accurate, your plans need to be complete and the specifications as precise as possible, calling out particular appliances, fixtures, floorings, roofing material, and so forth. (Some of these are specified in a stock-plan set; others are not.)

Call the contractors' references and ask about the quality of their work, their relationship with their clients, their promptness, and their readiness to follow up on problems. Visit former clients to check the contractor's work firsthand.

Be sure your final candidates are licensed, bonded, and insured for worker's compensation, public liability, and property damage. Also, try to determine how financially solvent they are (you can call their bank and credit references). Avoid contractors who are operating hand-to-mouth.

Don't automatically hire the contractor with the lowest bid if you don't think you'll get along well or if you have any doubts about the quality of the person's work. Instead, look for both the most reasonable bid and the contractor with the best credentials, references, terms, and compatibility with your family.

A word about bonds: You can request a performance bond that guarantees that your job will be finished by your contractor. If the job isn't completed, the bonding company will cover the cost of hiring another contractor to finish it. Bonds cost from 2 to 6 percent of the value of the project.

Your Building Contract

A building contract (see below) binds and protects both you and your contractor. It isn't just a legal document. It's also a list of the expectations of both parties. The best way to minimize the possibility of misunderstandings and costly changes later on is to write down every possible detail. Whether the contract is a standard form or one composed by you, have an attorney look it over before both you and the contractor sign it.

The contract should clearly specify all the work that needs to be done, including particular materials and work descriptions, the time schedule, and method of payment. It should be keyed to the working drawings.

A Sample Building Contract

Project and participants. Give a general description of the project, its address, and the names and addresses of both you and the builder.

Construction materials. Identify all construction materials by brand name, quality markings (species, grades, etc.), and model numbers where applicable. Avoid the clause "or equal," which allows the builder to substitute other materials for your choices. For materials you can't specify now, set down a budget figure.

Time schedule. Include both start and completion dates and specify that work will be "continuous." Although a contractor cannot be responsible for delays caused by strikes and material shortages, your builder should assume responsibility for completing the project within a reasonable period of time.

Work to be performed. State all work you expect the contractor to perform, from initial grading to finished painting.

Method and schedule of payment. Specify how and when payments are to be made. Typical agreements specify installment payments as particular phases of work are completed. Final payment is withheld until the job receives its final inspection and is cleared of all liens.

Waiver of liens. Protect yourself with a waiver of liens signed by the general contractor, the subcontractors, and all major suppliers. That way, subcontractors who are not paid for materials or services cannot place a lien on your property.

Personalizing Stock Plans

The beauty of buying stock plans for your new home is that they offer tested, well-conceived design at an affordable price. And stock plans dramatically reduce the time it takes to design a house, since the plans are ready when you are.

Because they were not created specifically for your family, stock plans may not reflect your personal taste. But it's not difficult to make revisions in stock plans that will turn your home into an expression of your family's personality. You'll surely want to add personal touches and choose your own finishes.

Ideally, the modifications you implement will be fairly minor. The more extensive the changes, the more expensive the plans. Major changes take valuable design time, and those that affect a house's structure may require a structural engineer's approval.

If you anticipate wholesale changes, such as moving a number of bearing walls or changing the roofline significantly, you may be better off selecting another plan. On the other hand, reconfiguring or changing the sizes of some rooms can probably be handled fairly easily.

Some structural changes may even be necessary to comply with local codes. Your area may have specific requirements for snow loads, energy codes, seismic or wind resistance, and so forth. Those types of modifications are likely to require the services of an architect or structural engineer.

Plan Modifications

Before you pencil in any changes, live with your plans for a while. Study them carefully—at your building site, if possible. Try to picture the finished house: how rooms will interrelate, where the sun will enter and at what angle, what the view will be from each window. Think about traffic patterns, access to rooms, room sizes, window and door locations, natural light, and kitchen and bathroom layouts.

Typical changes might involve adding windows or skylights to

bring in natural light or capture a view. Or you may want to widen a hallway or doorway for roomier access, extend a room, eliminate doors, or change window and door sizes. Perhaps you'd like to shorten a room, stealing the gained space for a large closet. Look closely at the kitchen; it's not difficult to reconfigure the layout if it makes the space more convenient for you.

Above all, take your time—this is your home and it should reflect your taste and needs. Make your changes now, during the planning stage. Once construction begins, it will take crowbars, hammers, saws, new materials, and, most significantly, time to alter the plans. Because changes are not part of your building contract, you can count on them being expensive extras once construction begins.

Specifying Finishes

One way to personalize a house without changing its structure is to substitute your favorite finishes for those specified on the plan.

Would you prefer a stuccoed exterior rather than the wood siding shown on the plan? In most cases, this is a relatively easy change. Do you like the look of a wood shingle roof rather than the composition shingles shown on the plan? This, too, is easy. Perhaps you would like to change the windows from sliders to casements, or upgrade to high-efficiency glazing. No problem. Many of those kinds of changes can be worked out with your contractor.

Inside, you may want hardwood where vinyl flooring is shown. In fact, you can—and should—choose types, colors, and styles of floorings, wall coverings, tile, plumbing fixtures, door hardware, cabinetry, appliances, lighting fixtures, and other interior details, for it's these materials that will personalize your home. For help in making selections, consult an architect or interior designer (see page 8).

Each material you select should be spelled out clearly and precisely in your building contract.

Finishing touches can transform a house built from stock plans into an expression of your family's taste and style. Clockwise, from far left: Colorful tilework and custom cabinetry enliven a bathroom (Design: Osburn Design); highly organized closet system maximizes storage space (Architect: David Jeremiah Hurley); low-level deck expands living space to outdoor areas (Landscape architects: The Runa Group, Inc.); built-ins convert the corner of a guest room into a home office (Design: Lynn Williams of The French Connection); French country cabinetry lends style and old-world charm to a kitchen (Design: Garry Bishop/Showcase Kitchens).

What the Plans Include

Complete construction blueprints are available for every house shown in this book. Clear and concise, these detailed blueprints are designed by licensed architects or members of the American Institute of Building Designers (AIBD). Each plan is designed to meet standards set down by nationally recognized building codes (the Uniform Building Code, Standard Building Code, or Basic Building Code) at the time and for the area where they were drawn.

Remember, however, that every state, county, and municipality has its own codes, zoning requirements, ordinances, and building regulations. Modifications may be necessary to comply with such local requirements as snow loads, energy codes, seismic zones, and flood areas.

Although blueprint sets vary depending on the size and complexity of the house and on the individual designer's style, each set may include the elements described below and shown at right.

■ **Exterior elevations** show the front, rear, and sides of the house, including exterior materials, details, and measurements.

■ **Foundation plans** include drawings for a full, partial, or daylight basement, crawlspace, pole, pier, or slab foundation. All necessary notations and dimensions are included. (Foundation options will vary for each plan. If the plan you choose doesn't have the type of foundation you desire, a generic conversion diagram is available.)

■ **Detailed floor plans** show the placement of interior walls and the dimensions of rooms, doors, windows, stairways, and similar elements for each level of the house.

■ **Cross sections** show details of the house as though it were cut in slices from the roof to the foundation. The cross sections give the home's construction, insulation, flooring, and roofing details.

■ **Interior elevations** show the specific details of cabinets (kitchen, bathroom, and utility room), fireplaces, built-in units, and other special interior features.

■ **Roof details** give the layout of rafters, dormers, gables, and other roof elements, including clerestory windows and skylights. These details may be shown on the elevation sheet or on a separate diagram.

■ **Schematic electrical layouts** show the suggested locations for switches, fixtures, and outlets. These details may be shown on the floor plan or on a separate diagram.

■ **General specifications** provide instructions and information regarding excavation and grading, masonry and concrete work, carpentry and woodwork, thermal and moisture protection, drywall, tile, flooring, glazing, and caulking and sealants.

Other Helpful Building Aids

In addition to the construction information on every set of plans, you can buy the following guides.

■ **Reproducible blueprints** are helpful if you'll be making changes to the stock plan you've chosen. These blueprints are original line drawings produced on erasable, reproducible paper for the purpose of modification. When alterations are complete, working copies can be made.

■ **Itemized materials list** details the quantity, type, and size of materials needed to build your home. (This list is extremely helpful in obtaining an accurate construction bid. It's not intended for use to order materials.)

■ **Mirror-reverse plans** are useful if you want to build your home in the reverse of the plan that's shown. Because the lettering and dimensions read backwards, be sure to buy at least one regular-reading set of blueprints.

■ **Description of materials** gives the type and quality of materials suggested for the home. This form may be required for obtaining FHA or VA financing.

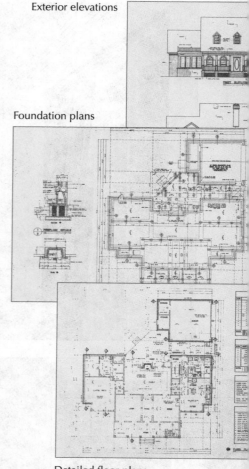

Exterior elevations

Foundation plans

Detailed floor plans

■ **How-to diagrams** for plumbing, wiring, solar heating, framing and foundation conversions show how to plumb, wire, install a solar heating system, convert plans with 2 by 4 exterior walls to 2 by 6 construction (or vice versa), and adapt a plan for a basement, crawlspace, or slab foundation. These diagrams are not specific to any one plan.

NOTE: Due to regional variations, local availability of materials, local codes, methods of installation, and individual preferences, detailed heating, plumbing, and electrical specifications are not included on plans. The duct work, venting, and other details will vary, depending on the heating and cooling system you use and the type of energy that operates it. These details and specifications are easily obtained from your builder or local supplier.

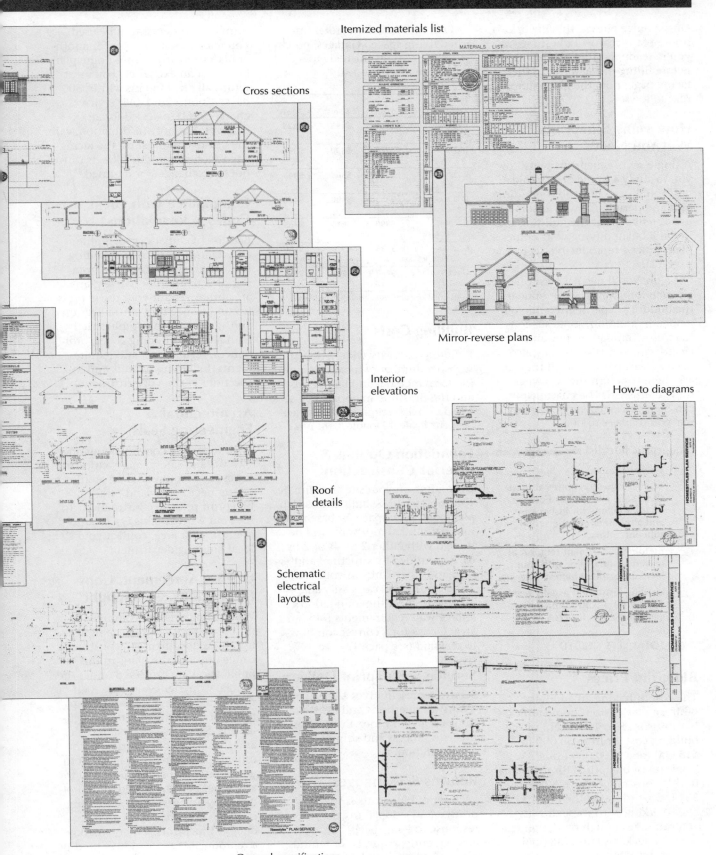

Itemized materials list

Cross sections

Mirror-reverse plans

Interior
elevations

How-to diagrams

Roof
details

Schematic
electrical
layouts

General specifications

Before You Order

Once you've chosen the one or two house plans that work best for you, you're ready to order blueprints. Before filling in the form on the facing page, note the information that follows.

How Many Blueprints Will You Need?

A single set of blueprints will allow you to study a home design in detail. You'll need more for obtaining bids and permits, as well as some to use as reference at the building site. If you'll be modifying your home plan, order a reproducible set (see page 12).

Figure you'll need at least one set each for yourself, your builder, the building department, and your lender. In addition, some subcontractors—foundation, plumber, electrician, and HVAC—may also need at least partial sets. If they do, ask them to return the sets when they're finished. The chart below can help you calculate how many sets you're likely to need.

Blueprint Checklist

_____ **Owner's set(s)**

_____ **Builder usually requires at least three sets: one for legal documentation, one for inspections, and a minimum of one set for subcontractors.**

_____ **Building department requires at least one set. Check with your local department before ordering.**

_____ **Lending institution usually needs one set for a conventional mortgage, three sets for FHA or VA loans.**

_____ **TOTAL SETS NEEDED**

Blueprint Prices

The cost of having an architect design a new custom home typically runs from 5 to 15 percent of the building cost, or from $5,000 to $15,000 for a $100,000 home. A single set of blueprints for the plans in this book ranges from $250 to $535, depending on the house's size. Working with these drawings, you can save enough on design fees to add a deck, a swimming pool, or a luxurious kitchen.

Pricing is based on "total finished living space." Garages, porches, decks, and unfinished basements are not included.

Price Code (Size)	1 Set	4 Sets	7 Sets*
A (under 1,500 sq. ft.)	$250	$295	$325
B (1,500–1,999 sq. ft.)	$285	$330	$360
C (2,000–2,499 sq. ft.)	$320	$365	$395
D (2,500–2,999 sq. ft.)	$355	$400	$430
E (3,000–3,499 sq. ft.)	$390	$435	$465
F (3,500–3,999 sq. ft.)	$425	$470	$500
G (4,000 sq. ft. and up)	$460	$505	$535

*This price also applies to reproducible blueprints.

Building Costs

Building costs vary widely, depending on a number of factors, including local material and labor costs and the finishing materials you select. For help estimating costs, see "Is Your Project Doable?" on page 7.

Foundation Options & Exterior Construction

Depending on your site and climate, your home will be built with a slab, pier, pole, crawlspace, or basement foundation. Exterior walls will be framed with either 2 by 4s or 2 by 6s, determined by structural and insulation standards in your area. Most contractors can easily adapt a home to meet the foundation and/or wall requirements for your area. Or ask for a conversion how-to diagram (see page 12).

Service & Blueprint Delivery

Service representatives are available to answer questions and assist you in placing your order. Every effort is made to process and ship orders within 48 hours.

Returns & Exchanges

Each set of blueprints is specially printed and shipped to you in response to your specific order; consequently, requests for refunds cannot be honored. However, if the prints you order cannot be used, you may exchange them for another plan from any Sunset home plan book. For an exchange, you must return all sets of plans within 30 days. A nonrefundable service charge will be assessed for all exchanges; for more information, call the toll-free number on the facing page. Note: Reproducible sets cannot be exchanged or returned.

Compliance with Local Codes & Regulations

Because of climatic, geographic, and political variations, building codes and regulations vary from one area to another. These plans are authorized for your use expressly conditioned on your obligation and agreement to comply strictly with all local building codes, ordinances, regulations, and requirements, including permits and inspections at time of construction.

Architectural & Engineering Seals

With increased concern about energy costs and safety, many cities and states now require that an architect or engineer review and "seal" a blueprint prior to construction. To find out whether this is a requirement in your area, contact your local building department.

License Agreement, Copy Restrictions & Copyright

When you purchase your blueprints, you are granted the right to use those documents to construct a single unit. All the plans in this publication are protected under the Federal Copyright Act, Title XVII of the United States Code and Chapter 37 of the Code of Federal Regulations. Each designer retains title and ownership of the original documents. The blueprints licensed to you cannot be used by or resold to any other person, copied, or reproduced by any means. The copying restrictions do not apply to reproducible blueprints. When you buy a reproducible set, you may modify and reproduce it for your own use.

Blueprint Order Form

Complete this order form in just three easy steps. Then mail in your order or, for faster service, call toll-free.

1. Blueprints & Accessories

BLUEPRINT CHART

Price Code	1 Set	4 Sets	7 Sets	Reproducible Set*
A	$250	$295	$325	$325
B	$285	$330	$360	$360
C	$320	$365	$395	$395
D	$355	$400	$430	$430
E	$390	$435	$465	$465
F	$425	$470	$500	$500
G	$460	$505	$535	$535

Prices subject to change

*A reproducible set is produced on erasable paper for the purpose of modification. It is only available for plans with prefixes AG, AGH, AH, AHP, APS, B, CAR, CPS, DD, DG, DW, E, EOF, GL, GSA, H, HFL, J, KLF, LRD, M, NW, OH, PH, S, SDG, UDG, V.

Mirror-Reverse Sets: $40 surcharge. From the total number of sets you ordered above, choose the number you want to be reversed. *Note: All writing on mirror-reverse plans is backwards. Order at least one regular-reading set.*

Itemized Materials List: One set $40; each additional set $10. Details the quantity, type, and size of materials needed to build your home.

Description of Materials: Sold in a set of two for $40 (for use in obtaining FHA or VA financing).

Typical How-To Diagrams: One set $12.50; two sets $23; three sets $30; four sets $35. General guides on plumbing, wiring, and solar heating, plus information on how to convert from one foundation or exterior framing to another. *Note: These diagrams are not specific to any one plan.*

2. Sales Tax & Shipping

Determine your subtotal and add appropriate local state sales tax, plus shipping and handling (see chart below).

SHIPPING & HANDLING

	1 Set	4 Sets/ Reproducible Set	7 Sets
Regular U.S. (4–6 working days)	$12.50	$15.00	$17.50
Express U.S. (2 working days)	$25.00	$27.50	$30.00
Regular Canada (2–3 weeks)	$12.50	$15.00	$17.50
Express Canada (4–6 working days)	$25.00	$35.00	$45.00
Overseas/Airmail (7–10 working days)	$50.00	$60.00	$70.00

3. Customer Information

Choose the method of payment you prefer. Include check, money order, or credit card information, complete name and address portion, and mail to:

Sunset/HomeStyles Plan Service
275 Market Street, Suite 521
Minneapolis, MN 55405

FOR FASTER SERVICE CALL 1-800-547-5570

SS02

COMPLETE THIS FORM

Plan Number _____ **Price Code** _____

Foundation _____
(Review your plan carefully for foundation options—basement, pole, pier, crawlspace, or slab. Many plans offer several options; others offer only one.)

Number of Sets: $_____
☐ One Set   (See chart at left)
☐ Four Sets
☐ Seven Sets
☐ One Reproducible Set

Additional Sets _____ $_____
    ($35 each)

Mirror-Reverse Sets _____ $_____
    ($40 surcharge)

Itemized Materials List $_____
Only available for plans with prefixes AH, AHP, AX, B, C, CAR, CDG*, CPS, DD*, DG, DW, E, GSA, H, HFL, I, J, K, LRD, N, NW,* P, PH, R, S, SD*, U, UDG, VL, W. *Not available on all plans. Please call before ordering.

Description of Materials $_____
Only available on plans with prefixes AHP, C, DW, H, HFL, J, K, KY, N, P, PH, VL.

Typical How-To Diagrams $_____
☐ Plumbing   ☐ Wiring   ☐ Solar Heating   ☐ Foundation & Framing Conversion

SUBTOTAL $_____

SALES TAX $_____

SHIPPING & HANDLING $_____

GRAND TOTAL $_____

☐ Check/money order enclosed (in U.S. funds)
☐ VISA   ☐ MasterCard   ☐ AmEx   ☐ Discover

Credit Card # _____ **Exp. Date** _____

Signature _____

Name _____

Address _____

City _____ **State** ____ **Country** _____

Zip _____ **Daytime Phone** (____)_____

☐ Please check if you are a contractor.

Mail form to: Sunset/HomeStyles Plan Service
275 Market Street, Suite 521
Minneapolis, MN 55405

Or Fax to: (612) 338-1626

FOR FASTER SERVICE CALL 1-800-547-5570

SS02

Photo by Gil Ford

Spacious and Stately

- Covered porches front and rear.
- Downstairs master suite with spectacular bath.
- Family/living/dining areas combine for entertaining large groups.
- Classic Creole/plantation exterior.

Plan E-3000

Bedrooms: 4	Baths: 3½

Space:

Upper floor:	1,027 sq. ft.
Main floor:	2,008 sq. ft.

Total living area:	**3,035 sq. ft.**
Porches:	429 sq. ft.
Basement:	2,008 sq. ft.
Garage:	484 sq. ft.
Storage:	96 sq. ft.

Exterior Wall Framing:	2x6

Typical Ceiling Heights:

Upper floor:	8'
Main floor:	9'

Foundation options:
Standard basement.
Crawlspace.
Slab.
(Foundation & framing conversion diagram available — see order form.)

Blueprint Price Code:	E

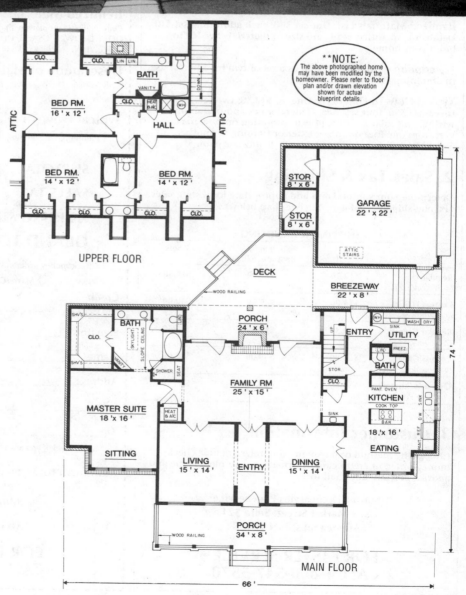

NOTE: The above photographed home may have been modified by the homeowner. Please refer to floor plan and/or drawn elevation shown for actual blueprint details.

UPPER FLOOR

MAIN FLOOR

TO ORDER THIS BLUEPRINT,
CALL TOLL-FREE 1-800-547-5570
(prices and details on pp. 12-15.)

Plan E-3000

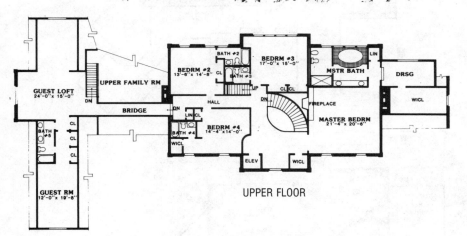

UPPER FLOOR

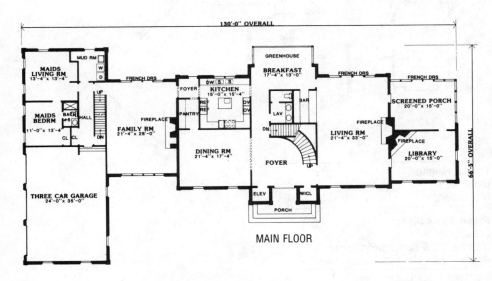

MAIN FLOOR

Unsurpassed Elegance

- Nothing has been compromised in this gracious, all brick, Georgian styled colonial.
- Some of its many highlights: an elevator in the foyer, a private library with fireplace, full servant accommodations, four conventional bedrooms, an interior bridge above the family room that leads to a guest loft and bedroom, and a lovely breakfast room with greenhouse.
- The second floor may be accessed by stairways off the foyer and family room; both family room and living room offer fireplaces and French doors to the rear of the home.
- Each sleeping room has its own private bath; the master bedroom also features a romantic fireplace and large luxury tub.

Plan AX-98747

Bedrooms: 4-6	Baths: 6 ½
Space:	
Upper floor	3,612 sq. ft.
Main floor	4,470 sq. ft.
Total Living Area	**8,082 sq. ft.**
Basement	3,850 sq. ft.
Garage	840 sq. ft.
Exterior Wall Framing	2x4

Foundation options:

Partial Basement

(Foundation & framing conversion diagram available—see order form.)

Blueprint Price Code	**G**

European Exterior Excitement

- The elegant exterior of this home exudes a European flair with its shuttered windows and stucco finish with quoin details.
- A curving staircase highlights the 17′ vaulted entry to create a dramatic entrance.
- Graceful archways lead into the dining and living room. Note the 15′ coffered ceiling in the living room.
- The den is located in a quiet corner of the home directly off the entry and includes built-in cabinetry.
- A large cooking island and walk-in pantry are featured in the spacious kitchen.
- The adjoining nook is encircled by windows and provides a sunny breakfast area.
- A second staircase is featured in the family room and routes traffic upstairs to the bedrooms, bypassing the formal area of the house.
- The master bedroom includes a sitting area with private viewing deck and a luxurious bath with a his and her walk-in closet.

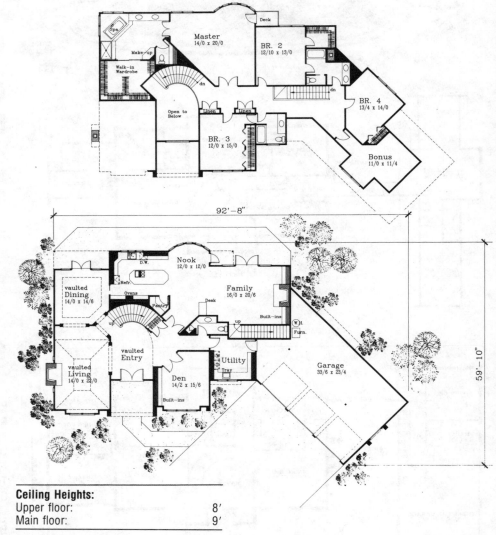

Plan CDG-2014

Bedrooms: 4-5 +	Baths: 3½
Space:	
Upper floor:	2,269 sq. ft.
Main floor:	2,175 sq. ft.
Bonus area:	125 sq. ft.
Total living area:	**4,569 sq. ft.**
Garage:	782 sq. ft.
Exterior Wall Framing:	**2x4**

Ceiling Heights:	
Upper floor:	8′
Main floor:	9′

Foundation options:
Crawlspace.
(Foundation & framing conversion diagram available — see order form.)

Blueprint Price Code:	G

***TO ORDER THIS BLUEPRINT,
CALL TOLL-FREE 1-800-547-5570***
(prices and details on pp. 12-15.)

Plan CDG-2014

Exquisitely Done

- The circular front steps, stately two-story entryway and three-car side garage give an indication of the exquisite interior features you'll find.
- The foyer with sweeping stairway opens to flanking formal living areas and a massive family room to the rear with vaulted ceiling and masonry fireplace.
- The roomy gourmet kitchen and bayed breakfast room also feature a nearby wet bar and pantry; attached is a skylit screened porch with built-in barbeque.
- A library sits next to the beautiful master suite with coffered ceiling and spacious bath with huge garden tub and curved shower.
- Three additional bedrooms share the upper level with a balcony that overlooks the foyer below.

Plan DD-4458

Bedrooms: 4	Baths: 3½

Space:

Upper floor	1,067 sq. ft.
Main floor	3,391 sq. ft.
Total Living Area	**4,458 sq. ft.**
Garage	774 sq. ft.
Exterior Wall Framing	2x4

Foundation options:

Basement
Crawlspace
Slab
(Foundation & framing conversion diagram available—see order form.)

Blueprint Price Code	G

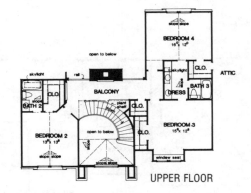

UPPER FLOOR

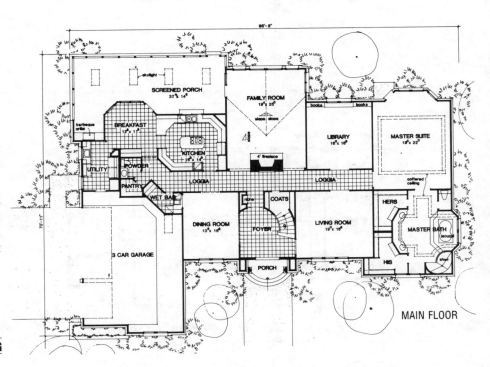

MAIN FLOOR

Plan DD-4458

Arched Elegance

- Gracious arched windows and entry portico create a rhythm and style on this brick-clad exterior.
- An elegant curved staircase with balcony bridge overhead lend interest to the raised entry foyer.
- Two steps down to the left of the foyer lies the cathedral — vaulted living room with fireplace and formal dining room defined with column separation.
- The quiet main floor master wing features another bay window, coved ceiling, walk-in closets, and well-planned private bath.
- The island kitchen overlooks the bay-windowed breakfast wall of the adjacent family room.

Plan DD-3639

Bedrooms: 4 +		Baths: 3½
Space:		
Upper floor:		868 sq. ft.
Main floor:		2,771 sq. ft.
Total living area:		3,639 sq. ft.
Basement:		1,730 sq. ft.
Garage:		approx. 790 sq. ft.
Exterior Wall Framing:		2x4
Ceiling Heights:		
Upper floor:		8'
Main floor:		9'

Foundation options:
Standard basement.
Slab.
(Foundation & framing conversion diagram available — see order form.)

Blueprint Price Code:	F

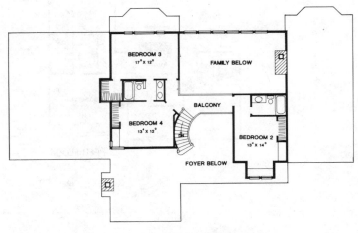

UPPER FLOOR

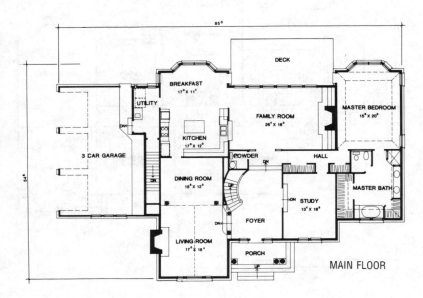

MAIN FLOOR

Plan DD-3639

Handsome Hill-Hugging Haven

- Multiple octagonal rooms allow this dramatic home to take full advantage of surrounding views.
- A dazzling two-story entry greets guests from the three-car garage motor courtyard.
- Once inside the front door, a soaring dome ceiling catches the eye past the octagonal stairway.
- A sunken living and dining room

with cathedral and domed ceiling face out to the rear deck and views.
- The octagonal island kitchen and breakfast nook are sure to please.
- The main floor den features a second fireplace and front-facing window seat.
- The entire second floor houses the master bedroom suite with a sensational master bath.

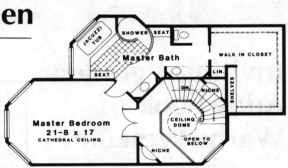

UPPER FLOOR

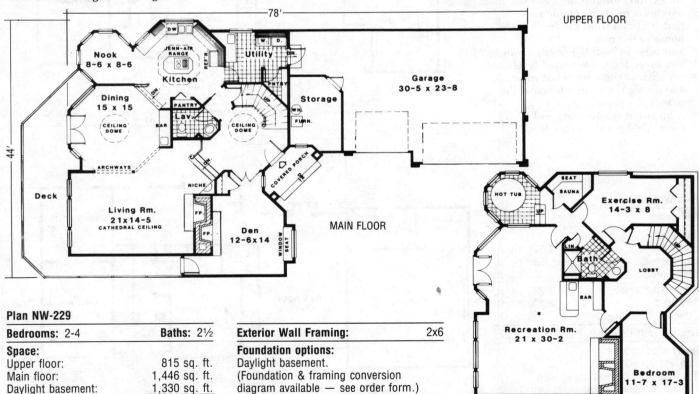

MAIN FLOOR

Plan NW-229

Bedrooms: 2-4	Baths: 2½

Space:

Upper floor:	815 sq. ft.
Main floor:	1,446 sq. ft.
Daylight basement:	1,330 sq. ft.
Total living area:	**3,591 sq. ft.**

Exterior Wall Framing: 2x6

Foundation options:
Daylight basement.
(Foundation & framing conversion diagram available — see order form.)

Blueprint Price Code: F

BASEMENT

**TO ORDER THIS BLUEPRINT,
CALL TOLL-FREE 1-800-547-5570**
(prices and details on pp. 12-15.)

Plan NW-229

Inviting Veranda Adds Look of Warm Welcome

- An exciting interior bridge overlooks the huge family room that stretches from the front of the home to the rear.
- Stairways in both the family room and foyer access the upper level.
- An open kitchen, breakfast room, and dining room stretch across the rear of the home.
- A luxurious master suite and bonus room highlight the upper level.

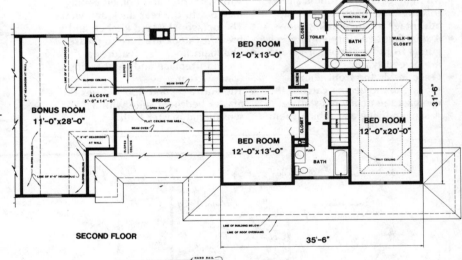

SECOND FLOOR

Plan W-3219

Bedrooms: 4-5	Baths: 3

Space:

Upper floor:	1,120 sq. ft.
Main floor:	1,689 sq. ft.
Bonus room:	429 sq. ft.
Total living area:	**3,238 sq. ft.**
Basement:	1,130 sq. ft.
Garage and storage:	540 sq. ft.

Exterior Wall Framing:	2x4

Foundation options:
Standard basement.
(Foundation & framing conversion diagram available — see order form.)

Blueprint Price Code:	E

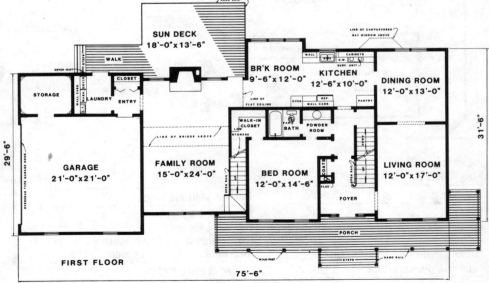

FIRST FLOOR

TO ORDER THIS BLUEPRINT, CALL TOLL-FREE 1-800-547-5570
(prices and details on pp. 12-15.)

Plan W-3219

Striking Traditional Farmhouse

- This eye-catching design will attract compliments wherever it is built, with its wide front porch, decorative columns and gables.
- The interior is equally fascinating, with an abundance of space for formal entertaining and casual family living.
- A large kitchen and eating area are at the heart of the home, and a spacious family room with a fireplace opens onto a secluded back porch.
- For formal occasions, the living and dining rooms adjoin each other to create a fine space for entertaining.
- The master suite is fit for royalty, with its bright sitting area, majestic bath and enormous walk-in closet.
- The upstairs bedrooms are also roomy, and one boasts a private bath. All three feature walk-in closets.

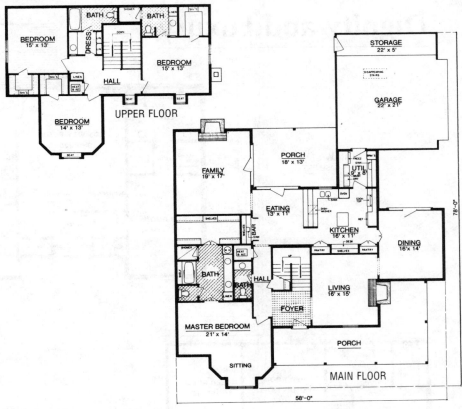

Plan E-3101		
Bedrooms: 4		**Baths:** 2½
Space:		
Upper floor		1,074 sq. ft.
Main floor		2,088 sq. ft.
Total Living Area		**3,162 sq. ft.**
Basement	(approx.)	2,088 sq. ft.
Garage		462 sq. ft.
Storage		110 sq. ft.
Porches		598 sq. ft.

Exterior Wall Framing   2x6
Foundation options:
Standard basement
Crawlspace
Slab
(Foundation & framing conversion diagram available—see order form.)
Blueprint Price Code   E

TO ORDER THIS BLUEPRINT,
CALL TOLL-FREE 1-800-547-5570
(prices and details on pp. 12-15.)

Plan E-3101

Dignity and Luxury

PLAN W-3135
WITH BASEMENT

37'-8"

BATH

WHIRLPOOL TUB

WALK-IN CLOSET

AREA

WALK-IN CLOSET

ACTIVITY ROOM
20'-0"x20'-0"

BED ROOM
13'-6"x19'-0"

DOWN   UP

OPEN RAIL

FOYER

1/2 BATH

STOOP

STEP

COATS

SUN DECK
26'-0"x12'-0"

WALK

BR'K ROOM
13'-6"x11'-0"

PANTRY

LAUNDRY

STORAGE

ENTRY

KITCHEN
13'-6"x11'-0"

STEP

GARAGE
21'-0"x21'-0"

DINING ROOM
13'-6"x13'-6"

71'-2"

FIRST FLOOR

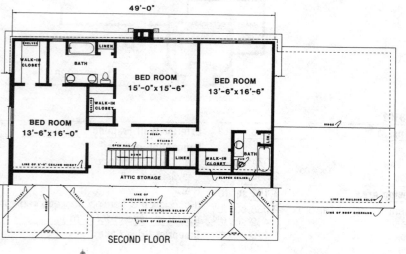

49'-0"

SHELVES

WALK-IN CLOSET

LINEN

BATH

WALK-IN CLOSET

BED ROOM
15'-0"x15'-6"

BED ROOM
13'-6"x16'-6"

BED ROOM
13'-6"x16'-0"

OPEN RAIL

DISAP. STAIRS

LINEN

WALK-IN CLOSET

BATH

LINEN

LINE OF 6'-8" CEILING HEIGHT

ATTIC STORAGE

SLOPED CEILING

RIDGE

LINE OF RECESSED ENTRY

LINE OF BUILDING BELOW

LINE OF BUILDING BELOW

LINE OF ROOF OVERHANG

LINE OF ROOF OVERHANG

SECOND FLOOR

First floor:	1,860 sq. ft.
Second floor:	1,271 sq. ft.
Total living area:	3,131 sq. ft.
Garage & storage:	545 sq. ft.
Deck & walk:	344 sq. ft.
Stoop:	34 sq. ft.
Basement:	1,771 sq. ft.

***TO ORDER THIS BLUEPRINT,
CALL TOLL-FREE 1-800-547-5570***
(prices and details on pp. 12-15.)

Blueprint Price Code E

Plan W-3135

Plan S-82290

Bedrooms: 3-4	Baths: 3

Space:

Upper floor:	935 sq. ft.
Main floor:	2,540 sq. ft.

Total living area:	3,475 sq. ft.
Basement:	1,125 sq. ft.
Garage:	689 sq. ft.

Exterior Wall Framing:	2x6

Ceiling Heights:

Upper floor:	8'
Main floor:	9'

Foundation options:
Standard basement.
Crawlspace.
(Foundation & framing conversion diagram available — see order form.)

Blueprint Price Code: E

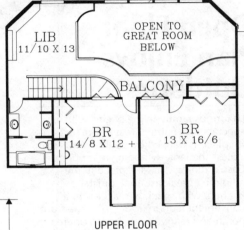

UPPER FLOOR

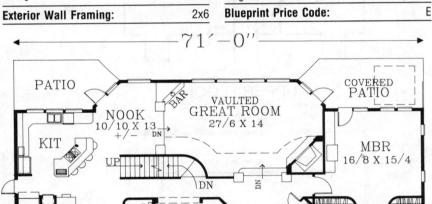

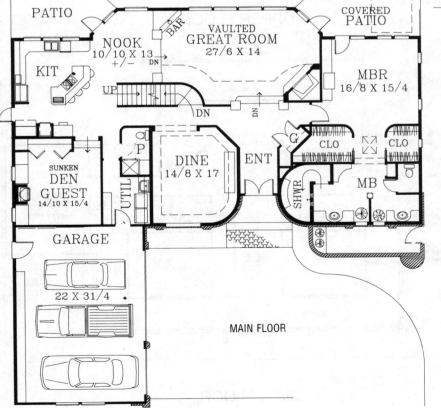

MAIN FLOOR

Elegant Curves

- A sleek exterior character is created with a curved brick wing-wall and entry.
- The elegant curves are thematically continued inside with a curved staircase, balcony overlooking the Great Room, dining room, master bedroom, and even a curved shower in the master bath.
- The Great Room features a corner fireplace, a wet bar, and access to the covered patio.
- The island kitchen serves a breakfast bar, a nook, and the formal dining room.
- A sunken guest room offers privacy for working, TV watching, or overnight visitors.

Plan S-82290

TO ORDER THIS BLUEPRINT, CALL TOLL-FREE 1-800-547-5570
(prices and details on pp. 12-15.)

25

Open Floor Plan Enjoys Outdoors

- Luxurious family living begins with a spectacular central Great Room; a fireplace is flanked by double doors that access the large wrapping rear porch.
- Casual dining can take place in the adjoining breakfast nook or island kitchen, with snack bar; access to a convenient laundry room, plus the front porch and rear veranda is also offered in the kitchen.
- Formal dining and living rooms flank the foyer.
- For privacy, you'll find the master suite on the main floor; it features a spacious walk-in closet and large bath with dual vanities, whirlpool tub and separate shower.
- Two extra bedrooms, each with personal dressing areas, share the upper level.

Plan VL-3038

Bedrooms: 3	**Baths:** 2 ½

Space:

Upper floor	836 sq. ft.
Main floor	2,202 sq. ft.
Total Living Area	**3,038 sq. ft.**
Exterior Wall Framing	2x4

Foundation options:

Crawlspace

Slab

(Foundation & framing conversion diagram available—see order form.)

Blueprint Price Code	E

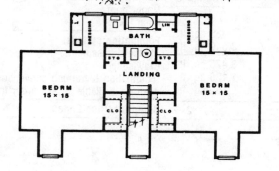

UPPER FLOOR

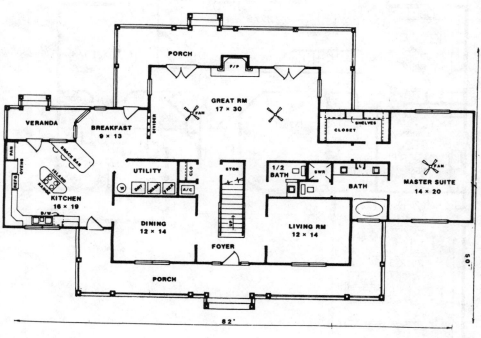

MAIN FLOOR

Plan VL-3038

Designed to Stand the Test of Time

- This dignified and stately home is planned to provide gracious, comfortable living for generations of families to come.
- An efficient foyer leads into formal living and dining rooms, or directly into a spacious family room.
- The kitchen, eating and utility areas are large, providing plenty of space for family activities and chores.
- The majestic master suite includes a luxurious master bath and a huge walk-in closet.
- The efficient second floor provides three secondary bedrooms and two full baths.

Plan E-2901

Bedrooms: 4	Baths: 3½
Space:	
Upper floor	970 sq. ft.
Main floor	1,984 sq. ft.
Total Living Area	**2,954 sq. ft.**
Basement (approx.)	1,984 sq. ft.
Garage	462 sq. ft.
Storage	112 sq. ft.
Porches & balcony	260 sq. ft.
Exterior Wall Framing	2x6

Foundation options:
Standard basement
Crawlspace
Slab
(Foundation & framing conversion diagram available—see order form.)

Blueprint Price Code	D

UPPER FLOOR

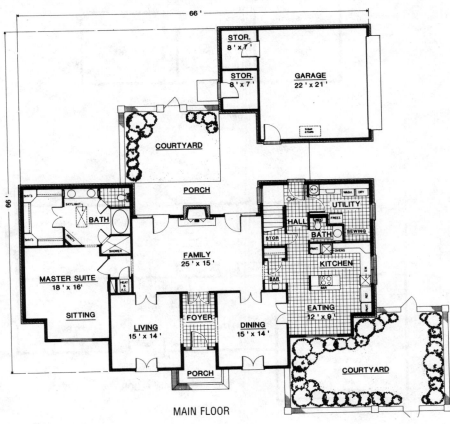

MAIN FLOOR

Plan E-2901

Early American with Four Bedrooms

- **Time-tested traditional shows the symmetry of design that keeps this style always popular.**
- **Basically rectangular two-story with simple, straight roofline offers big space for economical costs.**
- **Main floor presents spacious family room and living room.**
- **Large island kitchen adjoins a bright, bay-windowed dinette area.**
- **Formal dining room is large enough for a good-sized dinner party.**
- **A study behind the garage is available for an exercise or hobby room, or perhaps a home office or work room.**
- **Upstairs, the spacious master suite includes a deluxe bath and large walk-in closet.**

Plan A-118-DS

Bedrooms: 4	Baths: 2½

Space:

Upper floor:	1,344 sq. ft.
Main floor:	1,556 sq. ft.
Total living area:	**2,900 sq. ft.**
Basement:	approx. 1,556 sq. ft.
Garage:	576 sq. ft.

Exterior Wall Framing:	2x4

Foundation options:
Standard basement only.
(Foundation & framing conversion diagram available — see order form.)

Blueprint Price Code:	D

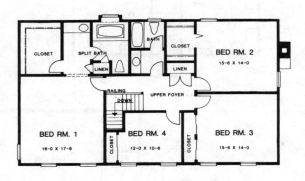

UPPER FLOOR

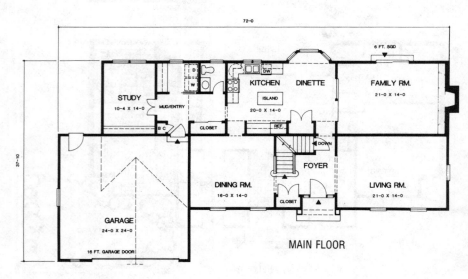

MAIN FLOOR

Plan A-118-DS

Classic Country Design

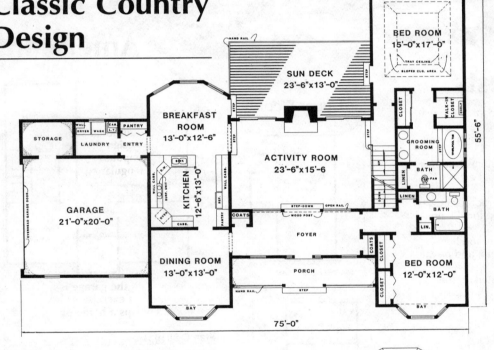

SUN DECK
23'-6"x13'-0"

BREAKFAST ROOM
13'-0"x12'-6"

STORAGE

LAUNDRY   ENTRY   PANTRY

KITCHEN
12'-6"x13'-0"

GARAGE
21'-0"x20'-0"

ACTIVITY ROOM
23'-6"x15'-6

BED ROOM
15'-0"x17'-0"
TRAY CEILING
SLOPED CLG. AREA

CLOSET   WALK-IN CLOSET

GROOMING ROOM

BATH

LINEN

STEP-DOWN   OPEN RAIL
WOOD POST

FOYER

DINING ROOM
13'-0"x13'-0"

COATS

PORCH

BAY

HAND RAIL   STEP

COATS   CLOSET   CLOSET

BED ROOM
12'-0"x12'-0"

BAY

BATH

LIN.

55'-6"

75'-0"

PLAN W-2837
WITH BASEMENT

First floor: 2,131 sq. ft.
Second floor: 747 sq. ft.

Total living area: 2,878 sq. ft.
Garage & Storage: 504 sq. ft.
Porch: 120 sq. ft.
Sun Deck: 295 sq. ft.
Basement: 916 sq. ft.

LINE ROOF OVERHANG
LINE OF BUILDING BELOW

RIDGE

ATTIC STORAGE

BED ROOM
11'-6"x 13'-0"

BED ROOM
11'-6"x 13'-0"

ATTIC STORAGE

CLOSET   CLOSET

POWDER ROOM   BATH

SLOPED CEILING   SLOPED CEILING

DORMER   DORMER   DORMER

ATTIC STORAGE

VALLEY

LINE OF BUILDING BELOW
LINE OF ROOF OVERHANG

SECOND FLOOR

Blueprint Price Code D

Plan W-2837

**TO ORDER THIS BLUEPRINT,
CALL TOLL-FREE 1-800-547-5570**
(prices and details on pp. 12-15.)   **29**

Welcome Guests

- A view to a large two-story Great room at the rear of this distinguished brick home, with a hearth and sliders to an adjoining outdoor deck, welcomes arriving guests.
- The front dining room and study both feature bay windows; the study can be used as an extra bedroom or guest room.
- A second stairway off the breakfast room accesses a home office or bonus space; an optional bath could also be built in.
- The main floor master suite offers his and her walk-in closets, a splashy master bath, and private access to the rear deck.
- Three secondary bedrooms are located off the second floor balcony that overlooks the Great room and foyer.

Upper Floor

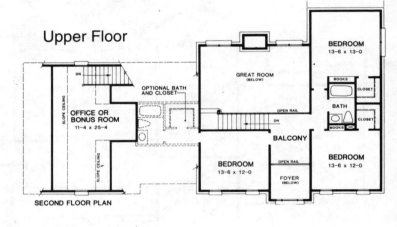

Main Floor

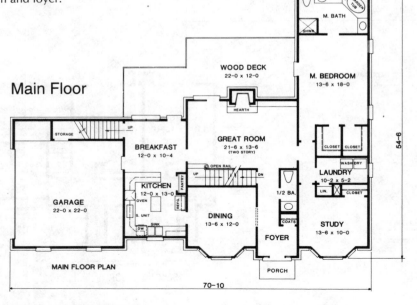

Plan C-9010

Bedrooms: 4-5	Baths: 2 ½-3 ½
Space:	
Upper floor	761 sq. ft.
Main floor	1,637 sq. ft.
Bonus room	347 sq. ft.
Optional bath & closet	106 sq. ft.
Total Living Area	**2,851 sq. ft.**
Basement	1,637 sq. ft.
Garage	572 sq. ft.
Exterior Wall Framing	2x4
Foundation options:	
Standard Basement	
Crawlspace	
(Foundation & framing conversion diagram	
available—see order form.)	
Blueprint Price Code	D

Plan C-9010

Distinctive Facade

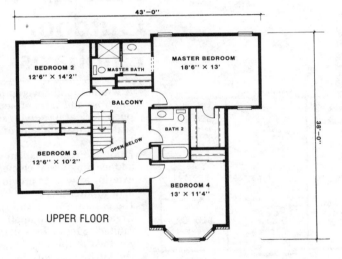

BEDROOM 2
12'6'' × 14'2''

MASTER BEDROOM
18'6'' × 13'

MASTER BATH

BALCONY

BATH 2

BEDROOM 3
12'6'' × 10'2''

OPEN BELOW

BEDROOM 4
13' × 11'4''

43'-0''

38'-0''

UPPER FLOOR

Plan GL-2704

Bedrooms: 4	Baths: 2½

Finished space:	
Upper floor:	1,231 sq. ft.
Main floor:	1,473 sq. ft.

Total living area:	2,704 sq. ft.
Garage:	528 sq. ft.

Features:
Large island kitchen.
Separate formal and informal dining areas.
Spacious family room with fireplace.

Exterior Wall Framing:	2x6

Foundation options:
Standard basement only.
(Foundation & framing conversion
diagram available — see order form.)

Blueprint Price Code:	D

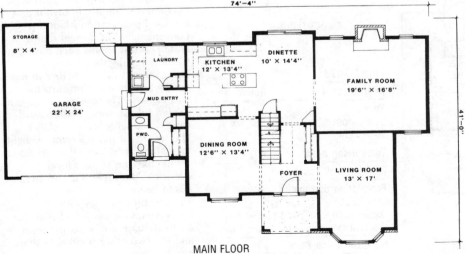

STORAGE
8' × 4'

LAUNDRY

KITCHEN
12' × 13'4''

DINETTE
10' × 14'4''

FAMILY ROOM
19'6'' × 16'8''

MUD ENTRY

GARAGE
22' × 24'

PWD.

DINING ROOM
12'6'' × 13'4''

FOYER

LIVING ROOM
13' × 17'

74'-4''

41'-0''

MAIN FLOOR

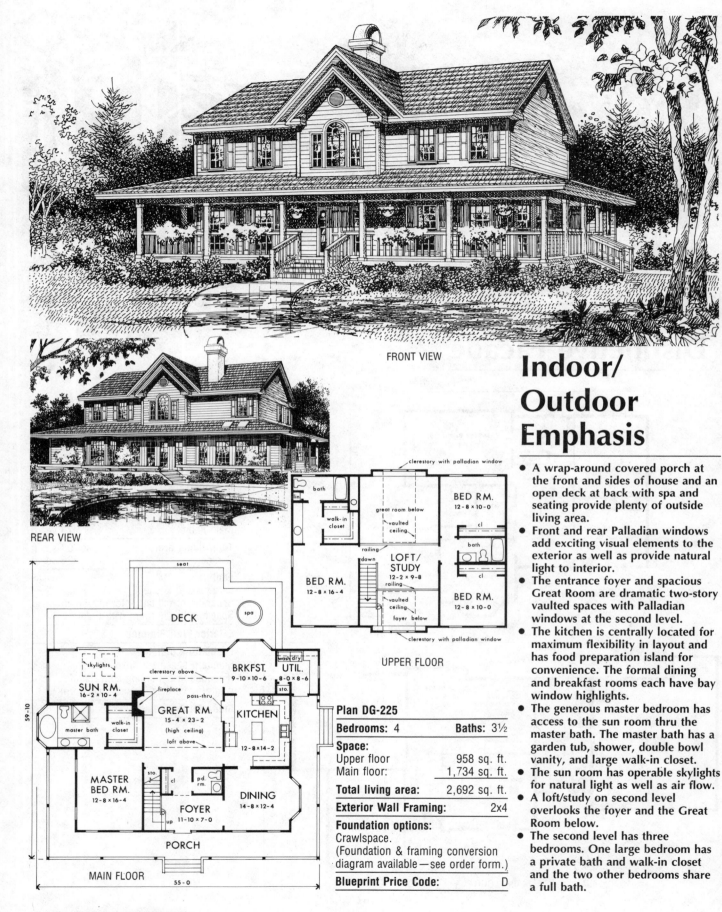

FRONT VIEW

REAR VIEW

seat

DECK

spa

skylights

clerestory above

SUN RM.
16-2 × 10-4

fireplace

pass-thru

GREAT RM.
15-4 × 23-2

(high ceiling)

loft above

BRKFST.
9-10 × 10-6

UTIL.
8-0 × 8-6

wash dry

sto.

KITCHEN

12-8 × 14-2

master bath

walk-in closet

MASTER BED RM.
12-8 × 16-4

sto.

cl

pd. rm.

FOYER
11-10 × 7-0

up

DINING
14-8 × 12-4

PORCH

MAIN FLOOR

59-10

55-0

---

clerestory with palladian window

bath

lin

walk-in closet

great room below

vaulted ceiling

BED RM.
12-8 × 10-0

cl

bath

cl

railing

BED RM.
12-8 × 16-4

down

LOFT/ STUDY
12-2 × 9-8

railing

vaulted ceiling

foyer below

BED RM.
12-8 × 10-0

clerestory with palladian window

UPPER FLOOR

Plan DG-225

Bedrooms: 4	Baths: 3½

Space:

Upper floor	958 sq. ft.
Main floor:	1,734 sq. ft.

Total living area:	**2,692 sq. ft.**

Exterior Wall Framing:	2x4

Foundation options:
Crawlspace.
(Foundation & framing conversion diagram available—see order form.)

Blueprint Price Code:	D

Indoor/ Outdoor Emphasis

- A wrap-around covered porch at the front and sides of house and an open deck at back with spa and seating provide plenty of outside living area.
- Front and rear Palladian windows add exciting visual elements to the exterior as well as provide natural light to interior.
- The entrance foyer and spacious Great Room are dramatic two-story vaulted spaces with Palladian windows at the second level.
- The kitchen is centrally located for maximum flexibility in layout and has food preparation island for convenience. The formal dining and breakfast rooms each have bay window highlights.
- The generous master bedroom has access to the sun room thru the master bath. The master bath has a garden tub, shower, double bowl vanity, and large walk-in closet.
- The sun room has operable skylights for natural light as well as air flow.
- A loft/study on second level overlooks the foyer and the Great Room below.
- The second level has three bedrooms. One large bedroom has a private bath and walk-in closet and the two other bedrooms share a full bath.

Plan DG-225

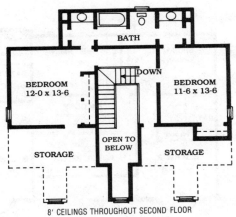

8' CEILINGS THROUGHOUT SECOND FLOOR

◀74'▶

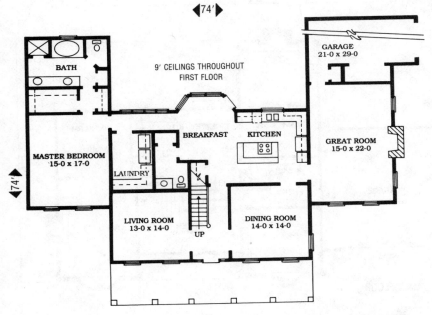

Gulf-Style Plantation Home

This stately home is designed for those who love the look of the older houses found along the coastal regions of the Gulf of Mexico. A large breakfast area is planned for those who like spaciousness in this popular area, and a well-planned utility room is conveniently located near the kitchen and the master bedroom. Please note the tremendous amount of storage space both upstairs and down in this gracious house.

First floor:	2,026 sq. ft.
Second floor:	663 sq. ft.
Total living area:	2,689 sq. ft.

PLAN V-2689
WITHOUT BASEMENT
(CRAWLSPACE FOUNDATION)

Blueprint Price Code D

Plan V-2689

Stately Facade, Gracious Interior

- With its stately and imposing exterior, this home will draw admiring glances in any neighborhood, and the interior is equally as impressive.
- A spacious, two-story-high foyer greets guests and carries them to the living room, library or into the more informal parts of the home.
- A roomy dinette/kitchen combination recalls the days of country kitchens. With the huge adjoining family room, there's plenty of space for family activities and chores.
- For formal occasions, the living and dining rooms provide abundant space for eating and entertaining.
- Upstairs, the master suite is truly magnificent, with its bay window, double-door entry, deluxe bath and large walk-in closet.
- Three other bedrooms share another full bath.

Plan A-170-DS

Bedrooms: 4	Baths: 2½
Space:	
Upper floor	1,164 sq. ft.
Main floor	1,476 sq. ft.
Total Living Area	**2,640 sq. ft.**
Basement (approx.)	1,476 sq. ft.
Garage	484 sq. ft.
Exterior Wall Framing	2x4

Foundation options:
Standard Basement
(Foundation & framing conversion diagram available—see order form.)

Blueprint Price Code	**D**

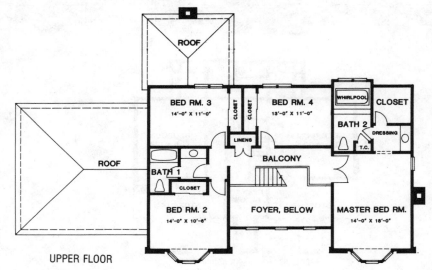

UPPER FLOOR

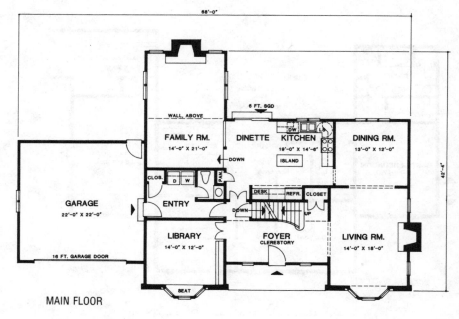

MAIN FLOOR

Plan A-170-DS

Loaded with Features

- A traditional feeling pervades this modern design, with its gabled roof, large front porch and two rear decks.
- Inside, you'll find an open-concept plan which lends a feeling of spaciousness throughout the home.
- The dining room off the entry can easily be converted to a den or even to a guest bedroom if formal dining isn't part of your family's routine.
- The large kitchen/nook/family room combination offers plenty of space for casual dining as well as for all sorts of family activities.
- The upper-level master suite features a double-door entry, luxurious bath, large closet and private balcony with an exterior spiral staircase.
- Two additional bedrooms share a second full bath, and a bonus room provides space for play, study, hobbies, exercise or for another sleeping room.

Plan S-62586

Bedrooms: 3-5	Baths: 2½
Space:	
Upper floor	1,056 sq. ft.
Main floor	1,416 sq. ft.
Bonus area	144 sq. ft.
Total Living Area	**2,616 sq. ft.**
Basement (approx.)	1,416 sq. ft.
Garage (2-car version)	476 sq. ft.
(3-car version, approx.)	676 sq. ft.
Exterior Wall Framing	2x6

Foundation options:
Standard Basement
Crawlspace
(Foundation & framing conversion diagram available—see order form.)

Blueprint Price Code	**D**

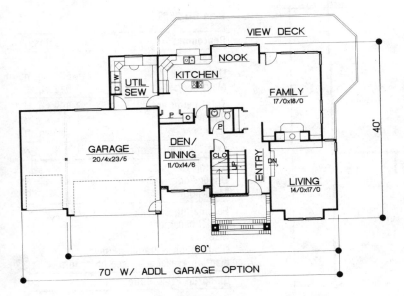

MAIN FLOOR

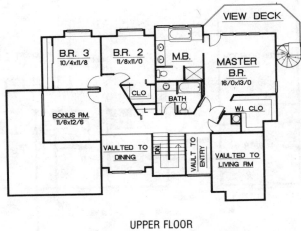

UPPER FLOOR

Plan S-62586

Established Character

- A charming front porch with support pillars, palladian windows, dormers, and brick all give this home an established character.
- The formal living and dining rooms overlook the rear deck with plenty of glass and feature a tall fireplace rising up to meet the vaulted ceiling.
- The kitchen has a work island overlooking the octagonal morning room and the informal family living space.
- There are two bedrooms on the main floor and two more on the upper floor.
- The main floor master suite overlooks the rear yard. It features a large walk-in closet and exciting private bath with separate shower and tub under the palladian window.

UPPER FLOOR

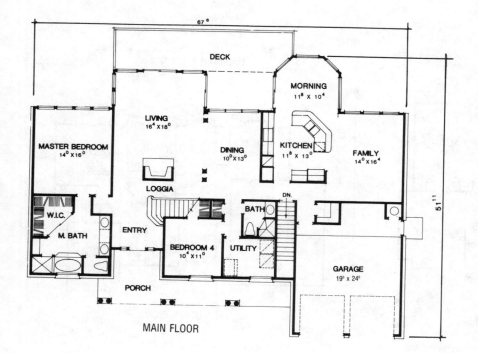

MAIN FLOOR

Plan DD-2509

Bedrooms: 4	Baths: 3
Space:	
Upper floor:	588 sq. ft.
Main floor:	2,011 sq. ft.
Total living area:	2,599 sq. ft.
Basement:	1,444 sq. ft.
Garage:	456 sq. ft.
Exterior Wall Framing:	2x4
Ceiling Heights:	
Upper floor:	8'
Main floor:	9'

Foundation options:
Partial basement.
Slab.
(Foundation & framing conversion diagram available — see order form.)

Blueprint Price Code: D

TO ORDER THIS BLUEPRINT, CALL TOLL-FREE 1-800-547-5570

Plan DD-2509

Nostalgic Remembrance

- A covered front porch with round columns and dormers with roundtop windows gives a nostalgic remembrance of homes of yesteryear.
- The floor plan blends in modern conveniences and dramatics such as vaulted ceilings, a lavish master bath and an island cooktop in the kitchen.
- The foyer opens to the formal dining room, separated by four stylish columns.
- The foyer also offers a view into the exciting Great Room with cathedral ceiling, fireplace and sliders to the rear deck and skylit sunroom.
- The second floor bedrooms share a dormer-lit bath and overlook the Great Room with arched window below.

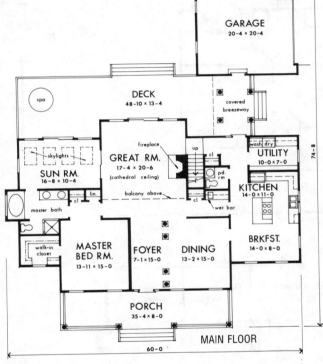

MAIN FLOOR

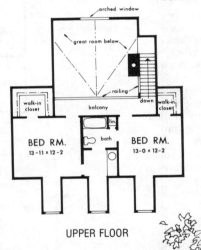

UPPER FLOOR

Plan DG-212	
Bedrooms: 3	**Baths:** 2½

Space:	
Upper floor	735 sq. ft.
Main floor:	1,852 sq. ft.
Total living area:	2,587 sq. ft.
Garage:	413 sq. ft.
Exterior Wall Framing:	2x4

Foundation options:
Crawlspace.
(Foundation & framing conversion diagram available — see order form.)

Blueprint Price Code: D

TO ORDER THIS BLUEPRINT,
CALL TOLL-FREE 1-800-547-5570
(prices and details on pp. 12-15.)

Luxurious Space

- This design manages to look both cozy and impressive at the same time, with its covered porch, gables and large divided-pane windows.
- The interior is loaded with features, starting with the interesting angled foyer area which provides easy access to all parts of the home.
- The large and interesting kitchen/ breakfast/family room area provides abundant space for family activities and household tasks, especially with the adjacent laundry/mudroom area.
- The formal living room boasts a vaulted ceiling, fireplace and bright windows at two corners.
- Upstairs, a gorgeous master suite includes a private master bath with a skylight, and a large closet.
- Two other bedrooms share another full bath. The second floor also features a den or fourth bedroom as well as a loft area which can be used as a sitting room, library, playroom or studio.

Plan B-87115-L

Bedrooms: 3-4	Baths: 2½
Space:	
Upper floor	1,186 sq. ft.
Main floor	1,369 sq. ft.
Total Living Area	**2,555 sq. ft.**
Basement	1,369 sq. ft.
Garage	572 sq. ft.
Exterior Wall Framing	2x4

Foundation options:

Standard Basement
(Foundation & framing conversion diagram available—see order form.)

Blueprint Price Code	D

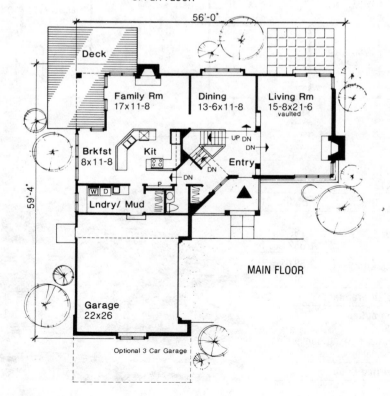

UPPER FLOOR

MAIN FLOOR

TO ORDER THIS BLUEPRINT,
CALL TOLL-FREE 1-800-547-5570

Plan B-87115-L

Clean Lines, Brick Accents

Clean, symmetric lines accented with brick provide an attractive exterior to this innovative design.

The vaulted entry is highlighted by an open stairway with a sweeping, elongated base. It creates a spectacular first impression. An open railing is designed between the stairs and vaulted living room to emphasize the expansive feel and look of the interior.

The vaulted dining room is a step up from the living room and is highlighted by a convenient wet bar for entertaining.

A corner window, pantry, and curved island counter are all features of this efficient kitchen.

Angling off the nook you will discover the family room set off by a handsome fireplace. A handy den is accessible just off the family room for studies and office work.

Double doors usher you into the beautiful master suite upstairs. It features a marvelous bath with tiled shower and spa tub, plus an enormous walk-in closet.

Both children's bedrooms are generously sized, and include built-in desks set under the windows.

Main floor:	1,475 sq. ft.
Upper floor:	1,060 sq. ft.
Total living area:	2,535 sq. ft.

UPPER FLOOR

Master 15/0 x 15/6
Bedrm. 3 11/0 x 14/0
Bedrm. 2 11/6 x 14/0
lin.
dn

PLAN R-2122
WITHOUT BASEMENT
(CRAWLSPACE FOUNDATION)

47'-0"
56'-6"

PATIO
Vaulted Dining 12/0 x 13/6
Kit. 10/6 x 15/6
Nook
Family 14/6 x 15/6
Vaulted Living 14/6 x 19/0
Den 11/6 x 10/6
Garage 20/4 x 21/8

MAIN FLOOR

Blueprint Price Code D

Plan R-2122

39

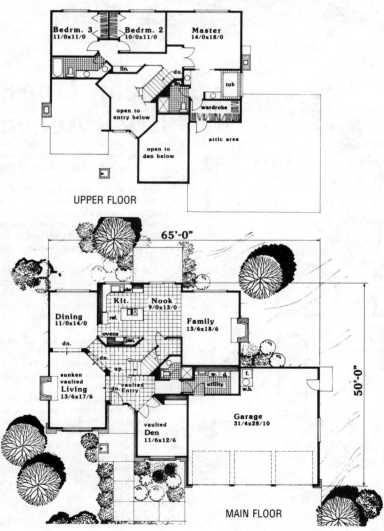

Bedrm. 3
11/0x11/0

Bedrm. 2
10/0x11/0

Master
14/0x18/0

lin.

dn.

tub

wardrobe

open to
entry below

attic area

open to
den below

UPPER FLOOR

65'-0"

50'-0"

Kit.

Nook
9/0x13/0

Dining
11/0x14/0

ovens

ref.

pan.

Family
13/6x18/6

dn.

dn.

up.

w.

utility

f.

w.h.

sunken
vaulted
Living
13/6x17/6

vaulted
dn. Entry

Garage
31/4x28/10

vaulted
Den
11/6x12/6

MAIN FLOOR

Timeless Beauty

- Graceful arches and the warmth of brick reflect the ageless beauty of this impressive design.
- The attractive vaulted entry provides easy access to all parts of the home, and a powder room is close at hand.
- Off the entry, a sunken living room boasts a handsome fireplace and a vaulted ceiling, and the room also opens to the dining room a step up through an arched entryway.
- The vaulted den provides space for an impressive home office or study.
- The large, informal kitchen/nook/family room area provides great space for family life.
- The master suite upstairs includes a deluxe private bath and large walk-in closet. Two other bedrooms and another full bath finish off the second floor.

Plan R-2102

Bedrooms: 3	Baths: 2½
Space:	
Upper floor	933 sq. ft.
Main floor	1,546 sq. ft.
Total Living Area	**2,479 sq. ft.**
Garage	903 sq. ft.
Exterior Wall Framing	2x4

Foundation options:
Crawlspace
(Foundation & framing conversion diagram available—see order form.)

Blueprint Price Code	C

Striking Design for Sloping Lot

The brick accents, beautiful windows and stairway up to the entry are striking, and there are many extra features in this 2,467 sq. ft. home. The upstairs has two bedrooms plus a bath, and the hallway is lined with book shelves.

For the homemaker, there is a large kitchen with an island, a separate pantry, a built-in desk, and even a nook which looks out to a nice patio.

Then, for the "piece de resistance", see the master bedroom suite. The bedroom is vaulted and the bath includes a spa, double vanity and a long walk-in wardrobe.

To top off all these wonderful features, there is a three-car garage, which also includes a storage area.

MAIN FLOOR

50'-0"
47'-6"

Patio
Nook
Kitchen 10/0x15/6
Family 17/0x13/6
spa
Mstr.Bath
d.
w.
pantry
up
Dining 10/6/10/0
vaulted Master 17/8x17/4
Foyer
Den/Br.4 11/0x12/4
vaulted Living 13/0x16/0
DRIVEWAY below

Exterior walls are 2x6 construction.

Garage

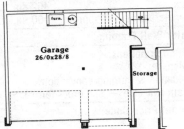

furn. wh
up
Garage 26/0x28/8
Storage

UPPER FLOOR

Br.2 10/0x11/10
Br.3 13/6x10/2
books
dn.
open to below

PLAN R-4036
WITHOUT BASEMENT
(CRAWLSPACE FOUNDATION)

Main floor:	2,002 sq. ft.
Upper floor:	465 sq. ft.
Total living area: (Not counting garage)	2,467 sq. ft.
Storage:	60 sq. ft.

Blueprint Price Code C

Plan R-4036

TO ORDER THIS BLUEPRINT, CALL TOLL-FREE 1-800-547-5570
(prices and details on pp. 12-15.)

Move-up Masterpiece

- This traditional two-story with stately dual gables, turned garage and covered front porch offers everything the move-up family has long strived for in their dream home.
- The formal living and dining rooms are quietly placed to the left of the plan.
- The main family living room opens

to the island kitchen, breakfast room, study and rear deck, with garage access through the utility mud room as well.

- The upper floor houses three more bedrooms, including a master suite with third fireplace, walk-in closet and private bath with corner tub under glass.

UPPER FLOOR

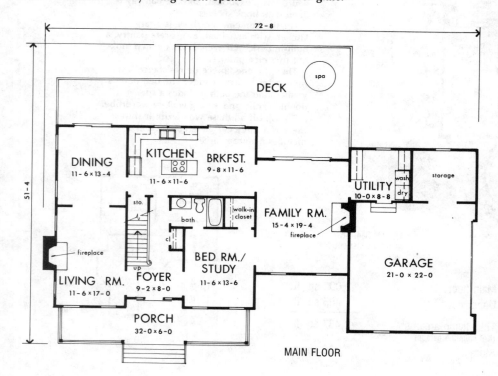

MAIN FLOOR

Plan DG-210

Bedrooms: 4	Baths: 3

Space:

Upper floor	1,003 sq. ft.
Main floor:	1,451 sq. ft.
Total living area:	**2,454 sq. ft.**
Garage:	462 sq. ft.
Storage area:	approx. 100 sq. ft.

Exterior Wall Framing:	2x4

Foundation options:
Crawlspace.
(Foundation & framing conversion diagram available — see order form.)

Blueprint Price Code:	C

Plan DG-210

PLAN U-8503-T

Specify basement, crawlspace or slab foundation.
Both 2x4 and 2x6 options included in blueprints.

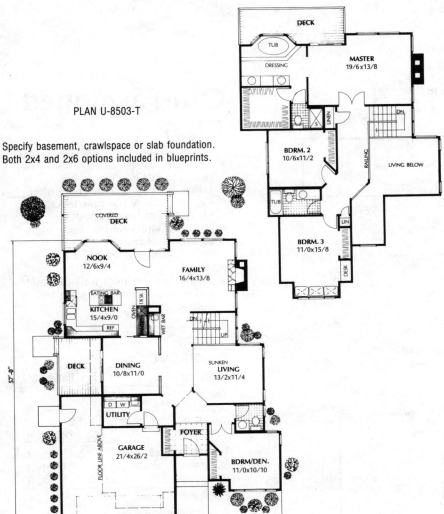

Tantalizing Design

Interesting roof lines and delicately arched windows tantalize the neighbors of this exquisite two-story. Careful planning combines rich accents with function to create a fantastic layout. You can enjoy a dream world in the master suite with a private deck. All-in-all, this is a home that makes the most out of living.

First floor:	1,349 sq. ft.
Second floor:	1,090 sq. ft.
Total living area:	**2,439 sq. ft.**
(Not counting basement or garage)	
Basement (optional):	1,241 sq. ft.

Blueprint Price Code C

Plan U-8503-T

TO ORDER THIS BLUEPRINT, CALL TOLL-FREE 1-800-547-5570
(prices and details on pp. 12-15.)

43

Old-Fashioned Charm

- A trio of dormers add old-fashioned charm to this modern design.
- Living and dining rooms both offer vaulted ceilings and flow together for feeling of spaciousness.
- The open kitchen/nook/family room arrangement features a sunny alcove, walk-in pantry and a wood stove.
- Master suite includes walk-in closet and deluxe bath with spa tub and shower.

UPPER FLOOR

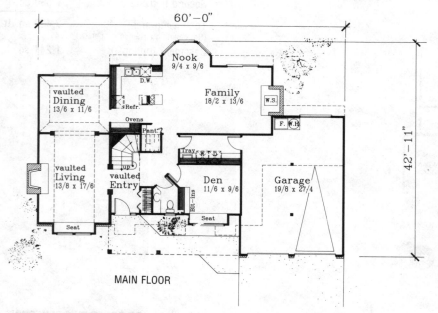

MAIN FLOOR

Plan CDG-2004	
Bedrooms: 3	**Baths:** 2½

Space:	
Upper floor:	928 sq. ft.
Main floor:	1,317 sq. ft.
Bonus area:	192 sq. ft.
Total living area:	**2,437 sq. ft.**
Basement:	882 sq. ft.
Garage:	537 sq. ft.

Exterior Wall Framing:	2x4

Foundation options:
Daylight basement.
Crawlspace.
(Foundation & framing conversion diagram available — see order form.)

Blueprint Price Code:	C

Plan CDG-2004

Attractive Design for Any Setting

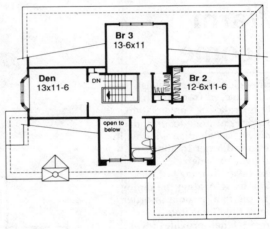

Br 3 13-6x11

Den 13x11-6

DN

Br 2 12-6x11-6

open to below

55'-4"

Deck

Brkfst 8x10

Family 13-4x13-8

Master Suite 19-6x12 vaulted

Kit 10x12

Dining 13x11-6

DN UP

W D

Living Rm 19-4x12

48'-6"

Garage 22-8x22

Plan B-89004

Bedrooms: 3	**Baths:** 2½

Finished space:

Upper floor:	769 sq. ft.
Main floor:	1,637 sq. ft.

Total living area:	2,406 sq. ft.
Basement:	1,637 sq. ft.
Garage:	498 sq. ft.

Features:
Upstairs den available for library,
   study, computer or hobby room.
Roomy living room features fireplace.
Deluxe downstairs master suite.

Exterior Wall Framing:	2x4

Foundation options:
Standard basement only.
(Foundation & framing conversion
diagram available — see order form.)

Blueprint Price Code:	C

Plan B-89004

A Warm Welcome

- A warm welcome awaits guests on the wide covered front porch, perfect for relaxing conversation.
- A two-story entrance foyer and stairway has a Palladian window in a clerestory dormer to allow natural light to penetrate.
- You can take advantage of the flexibility by relocating the dining room to the family room in order to enlarge the Great Room.
- U-shaped kitchen provides ideal layout for food preparation, spaciously opening to the family room and breakfast eating area.
- A sun room accessed from the Great Room and master bath can act as a passive solar energy collector with proper southern exposure.
- The master bedroom has a fireplace, walk-in closet, a double bowl vanity with separate bath area and private door to the sun room.
- Two secondary bedrooms, each with walk-in closets, and a bath built for two are found on the upper floor.
- Also note the large bonus room above the garage.

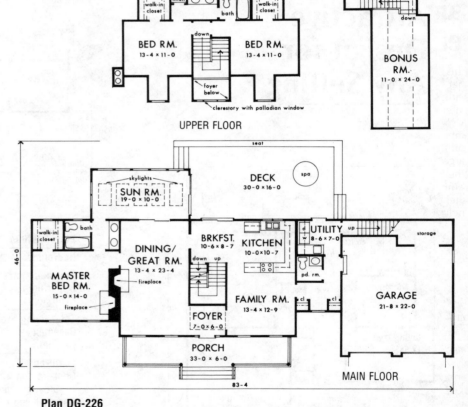

Plan DG-226

Bedrooms: 3	Baths: 2½

Space:

Upper floor:	554 sq. ft.
Main floor:	1,578 sq. ft.
Bonus room:	264 sq. ft.
Total living area:	2,396 sq. ft.
Basement:	1,204 sq. ft.
Garage:	477 sq. ft.

Exterior Wall Framing: 2x4

Foundation options:
Standard basement.
Crawlspace.
(Foundation & framing conversion diagram available — see order form.)

Blueprint Price Code: C

TO ORDER THIS BLUEPRINT, CALL TOLL-FREE 1-800-547-5570
(prices and details on pp. 12-15.)

Plan DG-226

Family Room
Features Cathedral Ceiling

- This dignified plan features an interior that is as impressive as the exterior, with abundant space for both formal entertaining and casual living.
- A spacious foyer provides a great first impression, which is continued by the formal dining room at the right or the large living room at the left.
- The kitchen/dinette combination is reminiscent of the great country kitchens of the past, and the kitchen includes a pantry and built-in desk.

- Also note the mudroom and laundry area.
- The family room may well be the highlight of this plan, with its striking cathedral ceiling, fireplace and bright walls of windows protruding into the backyard.
- Upstairs, a roomy master suite features a private bath and large walk-in closet.
- Three other bedrooms share another full bath. The front bedroom features a high ceiling and a Palladian window.

UPPER FLOOR

Plan A-2105-DS	
Bedrooms: 4	**Baths:** 2½
Space:	
Upper floor	1,044 sq. ft.
Main floor	1,350 sq. ft.
Total Living Area	**2,394 sq. ft.**
Basement	1,350 sq. ft.
Garage	484 sq. ft.
Exterior Wall Framing	2x4
Foundation options:	
Standard Basement	
(Foundation & framing conversion diagram available—see order form.)	
Blueprint Price Code	C

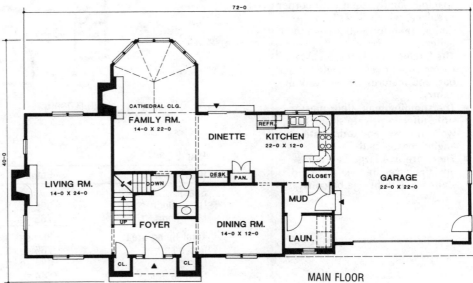

MAIN FLOOR

Plan A-2105-DS

You Asked For It!

- Our most popular plan in recent years, E-3000, has now been downsized for affordability, without sacrificing character or excitement.
- Exterior appeal is created with a covered front porch with decorative columns, triple dormers and rail-topped bay windows.
- The floor plan has combined the separate living and family rooms available in E-3000 into one spacious family room with corner fireplace, which flows into the dining room through a columned gallery.
- The kitchen serves the breakfast eating room over an angled snack bar, and features a huge walk-in pantry.
- The stunning main-floor master suite offers a private sitting area, a walk-in closet and a dramatic, angled master bath.
- There are two large bedrooms upstairs accessible via a curved staircase with bridge balcony.

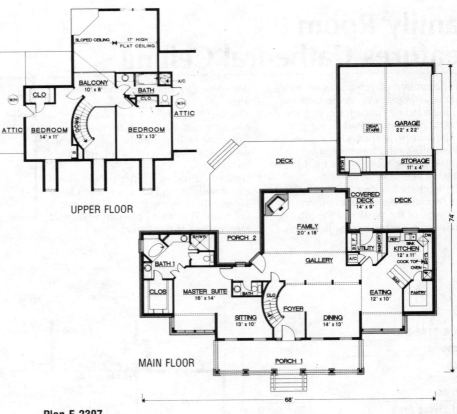

UPPER FLOOR

MAIN FLOOR

Plan E-2307

Bedrooms: 3	Baths: 2½

Space:

Upper floor:	595 sq. ft.
Main floor:	1,765 sq. ft.
Total living area:	**2,360 sq. ft.**
Basement:	1,765 sq. ft.
Garage:	484 sq. ft.
Storage area:	44 sq. ft.

Exterior Wall Framing: 2x6

Foundation options:
Standard basement.
Crawlspace.
Slab.
(Foundation & framing conversion diagram available — see order form.)

Blueprint Price Code: C

Plan E-2307

Main Floor Master Suite

- A traditional design with a contemporary interior, this home offers plenty of space and features for today's family.
- A large living room is brightened by a beautiful bay window.

- A spacious family room features an impressive fireplace.
- The kitchen/nook combination is roomy and efficient, with a pantry and adjoining laundry and half-bath.

- The downstairs master suite is luxurious, with a private, skylighted bath and large walk-in closet.
- Upstairs, three bedrooms share another full bath.

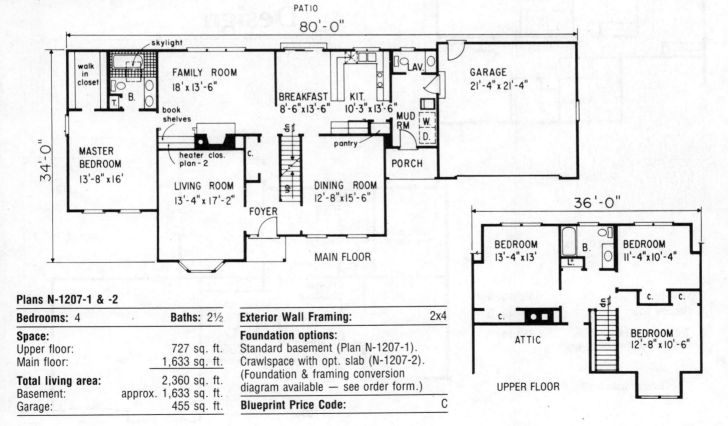

Plans N-1207-1 & -2

Bedrooms: 4	Baths: 2½

Space:

Upper floor:	727 sq. ft.
Main floor:	1,633 sq. ft.
Total living area:	**2,360 sq. ft.**
Basement:	approx. 1,633 sq. ft.
Garage:	455 sq. ft.

Exterior Wall Framing: 2x4

Foundation options:
Standard basement (Plan N-1207-1).
Crawlspace with opt. slab (N-1207-2).
(Foundation & framing conversion diagram available — see order form.)

Blueprint Price Code: C

***TO ORDER THIS BLUEPRINT,
CALL TOLL-FREE 1-800-547-5570***
(prices and details on pp. 12-15.)

Plans N-1207-1 & -2

Four-Bedroom Traditional Design

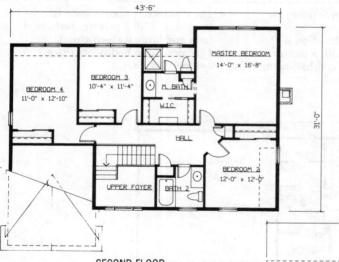

SECOND FLOOR

43'-6"

BEDROOM 4
11'-0" x 12'-10"

BEDROOM 3
10'-4" x 11'-4"

M. BATH

W.I.C.

MASTER BEDROOM
14'-0" x 16'-8"

31'-0"

HALL

UPPER FOYER

BATH 2

BEDROOM 2
12'-0" x 12'-0"

PLAN GL-2359
WITH BASEMENT

First floor: 1,306 sq. ft.
Second floor: 1,053 sq. ft.

Total living area: 2,359 sq. ft.
(Not counting basement or garage)

Exterior walls are 2x6 construction.

64'-0"

DINING ROOM
12'-0" x 15'-0"

KITCHEN
9'-0" x 15'-0"

DINETTE
8'-6" x 13'-0"

FAMILY ROOM
14'-0" x 18'-0"

REF.

LIVING ROOM
14'-0" x 17'-0"

FOYER

MUD AREA

2nd floor above

44'-0"

PWD.

LAUNDRY

GARAGE
23'-10" x 21'-10" +

PORCH

FIRST FLOOR

**TO ORDER THIS BLUEPRINT,
CALL TOLL-FREE 1-800-547-5570**
(prices and details on pp. 12-15.)

Blueprint Price Code C

Plan GL-2359

Distinctive Design At Home in Any Neighborhood

UPPER FLOOR

Dimensions: 32'–2", 35'–0"

- BEDROOM 3 10'8" × 11'
- BEDROOM 2 10'10" × 11'
- W.I.C.
- BALCONY
- BATH 2
- MASTER BATH
- UPPER FOYER
- MASTER BEDROOM 13' × 14'2"
- W.I.C.

Plan GL-2359-3

Bedrooms: 3	Baths: 3

Finished space:	
Upper floor:	904 sq. ft.
Main floor:	1,455 sq. ft.

Total living area:	2,359 sq. ft.
Garage:	491 sq. ft.

Features:
Great country kitchen/dinette/family room combination.
Spacious living/dining area.
Impressive two-story foyer.
Front-facing study ideal for home office.

Exterior Wall Framing:	2x6

Foundation options:
Standard basement only.
(Foundation & framing conversion diagram available — see order form.)

Blueprint Price Code:	C

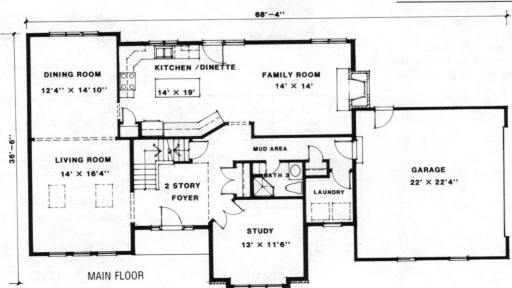

MAIN FLOOR

Dimensions: 68'–4", 36'–6"

- DINING ROOM 12'4" × 14'10"
- KITCHEN /DINETTE 14' × 19'
- FAMILY ROOM 14' × 14'
- LIVING ROOM 14' × 16'4"
- MUD AREA
- 2 STORY FOYER
- BATH 3
- LAUNDRY
- GARAGE 22' × 22'4"
- STUDY 13' × 11'6"

Plan GL-2359-3

Loaded with Livability Features

- Inside an attractive exterior, you will find in this home a marvelous floor plan designed to provide the utmost in livability.

- The living and dining areas flow together to create a wonderful space for large gatherings.

- The family room/nook/kitchen combination provides ample space for a wide variety of activities for the busy family.

- Upstairs, the sumptuous master suite includes a deluxe bath and a large wardrobe closet.

- Two secondary bedrooms share a compartmentalized corner bath, and a large bonus room off the garage offers potential for many uses.

MAIN FLOOR

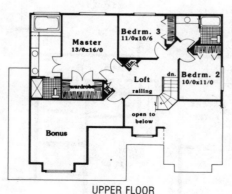

UPPER FLOOR

Plan R-2111

Bedrooms: 3	Baths: 2½
Space:	
Upper floor	945 sq. ft.
Main floor	1,115 sq. ft.
Bonus area	285 sq. ft.
Total Living Area	**2,345 sq. ft.**
Garage	851 sq. ft.
Exterior Wall Framing	2x4

Foundation options:
Crawlspace
(Foundation & framing conversion diagram available—see order form.)

Blueprint Price Code	C

Plan R-2111

Indoor and Outdoor Excitement

- A front wraparound, covered porch and open deck with spa and seating at the rear provides alternative outdoor living.
- The foyer is open to the upper level and has a clerestory Palladian window to let natural light in.
- At the center of the floor plan is a spacious Great Room with fireplace, cathedral ceiling and clerestory with arched window; the second-floor balcony overlooks the room.
- The large island kitchen handily serves the formal bayed dining room, bayed breakfast area with skylights and the Great Room.
- A fabulous master bedroom has bayed deck overlook with skylights and a private bath with garden tub and separate shower.

Plan DG-256

Bedrooms: 3-4	Baths: 3
Space:	
Upper floor	565 sq. ft.
Main floor	1,756 sq. ft.
Total Living Area	**2,321 sq. ft.**
Exterior Wall Framing	2x4

Foundation options:
Crawlspace
(Foundation & framing conversion diagram available—see order form.)

Blueprint Price Code	C

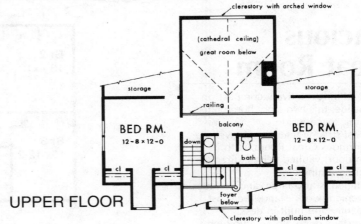

UPPER FLOOR

MAIN FLOOR

Plan DG-256

Spacious Great Room

- While looking relatively compact on the outside, this two-story home offers big living space inside.
- The most striking feature may well be the enormous Great Room, with its sunken floor, vaulted ceiling, fireplace and raised dining area.
- The kitchen is also large, and includes a convenient work island, breakfast area, pantry and built-in desk.
- A downstairs den with an adjoining bath is versatile enough to be used as an office or in-law suite.
- Upstairs, a deluxe master suite features a private bath, vaulted ceiling and huge walk-in closet.
- Two other bedrooms share a second bath and boast nice-sized closets. The upstairs balcony overlooks the Great Room below.

Plan B-87151

Bedrooms: 3-4	Baths: 3
Space:	
Upper floor	1,036 sq. ft.
Main floor	1,270 sq. ft.
Total Living Area	**2,306 sq. ft.**
Basement	1,270 sq. ft.
Garage	505 sq. ft.
Exterior Wall Framing	2x4

Foundation options:

Standard Basement
(Foundation & framing conversion diagram available—see order form.)

Blueprint Price Code	C

UPPER FLOOR

- Br 2 13-4x12
- Br 3 10x 12-2
- Master Suite 13-4x16 vaulted
- open to below

MAIN FLOOR

- Den/Br 4 10-8x12-4
- Great Room 26-4x17-8 vaulted
- Dining
- Kit/Brkfst 13-4x19-4
- Garage 21-4 23-8
- Deck
- 44'-8"
- 48'-8"

TO ORDER THIS BLUEPRINT, CALL TOLL-FREE 1-800-547-5570

Plan B-87151

SECOND FLOOR

First floor:	1,535 sq. ft.
Second floor:	765 sq. ft.
Total living area:	2,300 sq. ft.
(Not counting basement or garage)	

PLAN C-8535
WITH BASEMENT

Traditional Touches Dress Up a Country Cottage

Multipaned windows, shutters and a covered porch embellish the traditional exterior of this country cottage. The floor plan incorporates a central Great Room. A raised-hearth stone fireplace forms part of a wall separating the Great Room from the kitchen.

The large country kitchen features an island and abundant counter space. The breakfast room includes a bay window. A large dining room faces the front.

First-level master bedroom has its own super bath with separate shower, garden tub, twin vanities and walk in closets. Two large bedrooms, separate dressing areas and compartment tub occupy the second level.

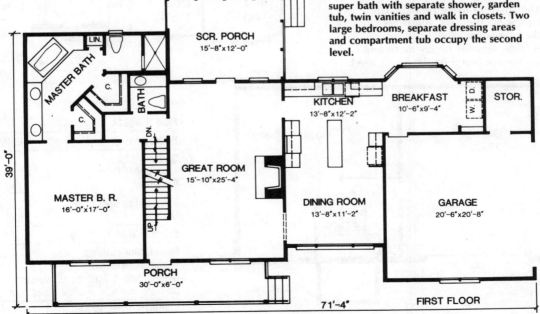

Blueprint Price Code C

Plan C-8535

TO ORDER THIS BLUEPRINT, CALL TOLL-FREE 1-800-547-5570
(prices and details on pp. 12-15.)

Three Bedroom Split Entry

- This lovely split entry combines contemporary and traditional styling in an affordable floor arrangement.
- The main/upper level houses the sleeping rooms, two baths, convenient laundry facilities, and the main living areas.
- A formal dining room is divided from the foyer by an open handrail; the room can also overlook the front yard through a large, boxed window wall.
- The adjacent living room boasts a handsome fireplace and sliders to the rear patio.
- A large versatile bonus space and garage are found on the lower level.

50'-0"

Patio

Master Br
12x17

Living Rm
14x14

Brkfst
11x7-6

Br 2
12x11-6

Br 3
11x12

Dining
12-2x12-8

DN UP

34'-4"

MAIN FLOOR

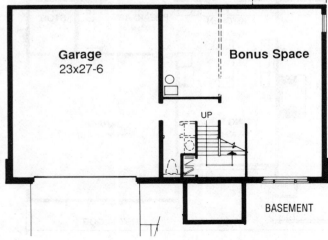

Garage
23x27-6

Bonus Space

UP

BASEMENT

Plan B-90014

Bedrooms: 3	Baths: 2-3

Space:

Main/upper floor:	1,549 sq. ft.
Basement:	750 sq. ft.
Total living area:	2,299 sq. ft.
Garage:	633 sq. ft.
Exterior Wall Framing:	2x4

Foundation options:
Daylight basement.
(Foundation & framing conversion diagram available — see order form.)

Blueprint Price Code:	C

Plan B-90014

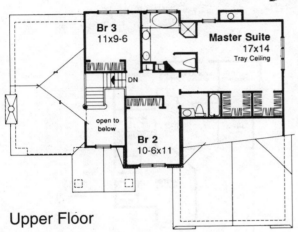

Upper Floor

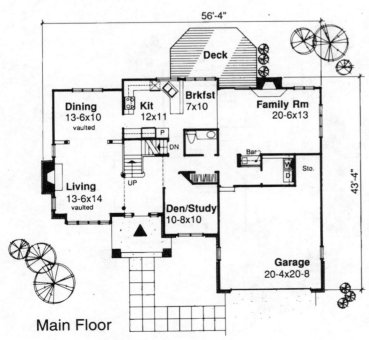

Main Floor

Decorative Columns, Outside & In

- Decorative columns adorn the front outside entrance and the inside living and dining room entryways of this updated traditional.
- The living room also features a boxed front window, fireplace and vaulted ceiling.
- An open kitchen and sunny breakfast area join the large family room with fireplace and wet bar to form a stretch of dining and relaxing pleasure; both areas overlook a rear deck.
- A beautiful master suite with tray ceiling, his 'n her walk-in closets, and a private bath with windowed garden tub and two secondary bedrooms share the upper level.

Plan B-90009	
Bedrooms: 3	**Baths:** 2 ½
Space:	
Upper floor	918 sq. ft.
Main floor	1,349 sq. ft.
Total Living Area	**2,267 sq. ft.**
Basement	1,349 sq. ft.
Garage	420 sq. ft.
Exterior Wall Framing	2x4
Foundation options:	
Standard Basement	
(Foundation & framing conversion diagram available—see order form.)	
Blueprint Price Code	C

Eye-Catching Hillside Design

Main floor:	1,010 sq. ft.
Upper floor:	958 sq. ft.
Lower level:	290 sq. ft.
Total living area:	2,258 sq. ft.
(Not counting garage)	

PLAN P-6604-4D

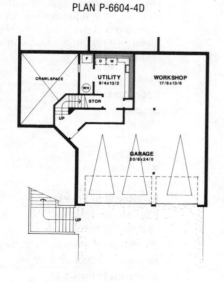

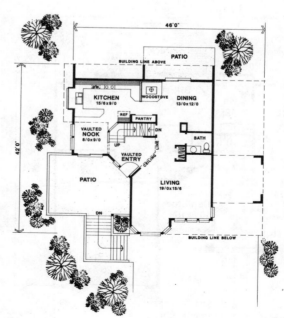

Blueprint Price Code C

Plan P-6604-4D

Exciting Outside, Bright Inside

- Contemporary lines with traditional touches make this an attractive and stylish plan for any neighborhood.
- The entry area is brightened by a large clerestory window, and an open stairway dramatizes the soaring ceiling.
- The living and dining rooms both include vaulted ceilings, and make a great combined space for entertaining.
- The kitchen is highlighted by a corner sink under large windows, and also includes a work island and a pantry.
- In combination with the nook and kitchen, the family room makes a beautiful and bright space for family activities.
- A downstairs den is available for duty as an office or a fourth bedroom.
- The second-floor master suite is also large and bright, and includes a luxurious bath and two closets.
- Two other bedrooms share another full bath, and the hallway overlooks the entry and living room below.

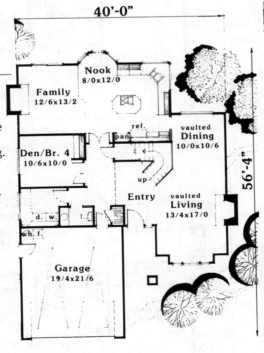

MAIN FLOOR

UPPER FLOOR

Plan R-2082

Bedrooms: 3-4	Baths: 2½
Space:	
Upper floor	920 sq. ft.
Main floor	1,286 sq. ft.
Total Living Area	**2,206 sq. ft.**
Garage	415 sq. ft.
Exterior Wall Framing	2x4

Foundation options:
Crawlspace
(Foundation & framing conversion diagram available—see order form.)

Blueprint Price Code   C

Plan R-2082

Colonial with a Contemporary Touch

- Open, flowing rooms highlighted by a two-story round-top window combine to give this colonial design a contemporary, today touch.
- To the left of the elegant, two-story foyer lies the living room, which flows into the rear-facing family room with fireplace.
- The centrally located kitchen serves both the formal dining room and the dinette, with a view of the family room beyond.
- All four bedrooms are located upstairs. The master suite includes a walk-in closet and private bath with double vanities, separate shower and whirlpool tub under skylights.

Plan AHP-9020

Bedrooms: 4	Baths: 2 ½
Space:	
Upper floor	1,021 sq. ft.
Main floor	1,125 sq. ft.
Total Living Area	**2,146 sq. ft.**
Basement	1,032 sq. ft.
Garage	480 sq. ft.
Exterior Wall Framing	2x6

Foundation options:
Standard Basement
Slab
(Foundation & framing conversion diagram available—see order form.)

Blueprint Price Code	C

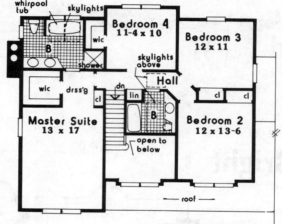

UPPER FLOOR

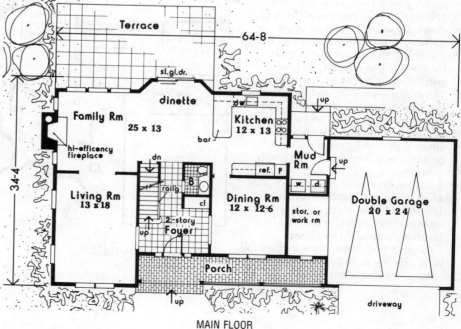

MAIN FLOOR

Plan AHP-9020

Upstairs Suite Creates Adult Retreat

● This multi-level design is ideal for a gently sloping site with a view to the rear.

● Upstairs master suite is a sumptuous "adult retreat" complete with magnificent bath, vaulted ceiling, walk-in closet, private deck and balcony loft.

● Living room includes wood stove area and large windows to the rear. Wood bin can be loaded from outside.

● Main floor also features roomy kitchen and large utility area.

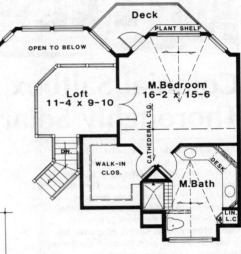

Deck

OPEN TO BELOW

PLANT SHELF

Loft
11-4 x 9-10

M.Bedroom
16-2 x 15-6

CATHEDRAL CLG.

WALK-IN CLOS.

DESK

M.Bath

LIN. L.C

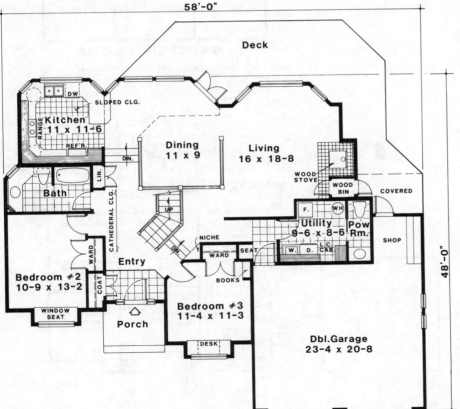

58'-0"

Deck

SLOPED CLG.

Kitchen
11 x 11-6

RANGE

DW

REF'R.

DN.

Dining
11 x 9

Living
16 x 18-8

WOOD STOVE

WOOD BIN

COVERED

CATHEDRAL CLG.

Bath

LIN.

UP

NICHE

SEAT

F.

WH

Utility
9-6 x 8-6

Pow. Rm.

SHOP

WARD

WARD

BOOKS

W.

D.

LC CAB.

Entry

Bedroom #2
10-9 x 13-2

COAT

Bedroom #3
11-4 x 11-3

WINDOW SEAT

Porch

DESK

Dbl. Garage
23-4 x 20-8

48'-0"

Plan NW-544-S	
Bedrooms: 3	Baths: 2½
Space:	
Upper floor:	638 sq. ft.
Main floor:	1,500 sq. ft.
Total living area:	2,138 sq. ft.
Garage:	545 sq. ft.
Exterior Wall Framing:	2x6
Foundation options: Crawlspace only. (Foundation & framing conversion diagram available — see order form.)	
Blueprint Price Code:	C

Plan NW-544-S

FRONT VIEW

REAR VIEW

Colonial Saltbox, Thoroughly Solar

Up-to-date inside while outwardly embracing the traditions of Colonial architecture, this passive solar salt box is thoroughly energy-conscious. The sheltered entry and air lock vestibule prevent blustery north winds from entering the house every time the door is opened. Many other energy saving elements are designed into the plan to make the house comfortable summer and winter.

From the central foyer, one has a full view of the back yard and can reach any part of the house with a minimum of steps. The focal point of the entire plan is the glorious sun room, set in the heart of the activity area and shared by the upper level.

The second floor offers three bedrooms. The master bedroom includes a walk-in closet and a private bath with a whirlpool tub. The library at the ground level can be a fourth bedroom.

Total living area, excluding the sun room, is 1,392 sq. ft. on the first floor and 735 sq. ft. on the second.

First floor:	1,392 sq. ft.
Second floor:	735 sq. ft.
Total living area:	2,127 sq. ft.
Garage	400 sq. ft.
Basement (Optional):	640 sq. ft.

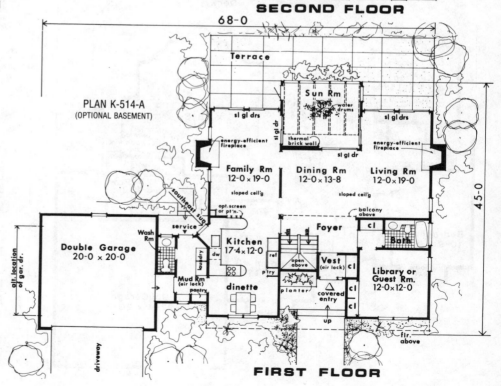

SECTION PASSIVE SOLAR AT WORK

SECOND FLOOR

Bedrm 2 12-0 x 12-0
Bedrm 3 10-0 x 11-4
Master Bedrm 12-0 x 14-0

PLAN K-514-A (OPTIONAL BASEMENT)

68-0

45-0

FIRST FLOOR

Terrace
Sun Rm
Family Rm 12-0 x 19-0
Dining Rm 12-0 x 13-8
Living Rm 12-0 x 19-0
Double Garage 20-0 x 20-0
Kitchen 17-4 x 12-0
Foyer
Vest (air lock)
Library or Guest Rm. 12-0 x 12-0
Mud Rm (air lock)
dinette

Blueprint Price Code C

Plan K-514-A

FRONT VIEW

Wrap It Up, I'll Take It

- A wrap-around covered porch at the front and sides of the house and an open deck at the back with storage provide plenty of outside living area.
- Arched rear windows and a sun room add exciting visual elements to the exterior while updating this country plan.
- The spacious Great Room has a fireplace, cathedral ceiling and clerestory with arched windows. The second level balcony overlooks the Great Room.
- The kitchen is centrally located between the dining area and Great Room for maximum flexibility in layout and has a food preparation island for convenience.
- The generous master bedroom with fireplace has direct access to the sun room and covered wrap-around porch. A large walk-in closet and double bowl vanity add to the master suite's appeal.
- The sun room has a hot tub with access to back deck, Great Room, and master bedroom to allow dispersal of solar heat during winter months.
- The second level has two bedrooms, storage and a full bath.

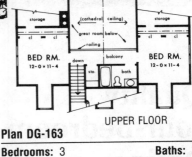

UPPER FLOOR

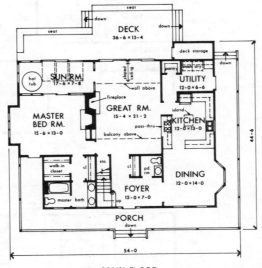

MAIN FLOOR

Plan DG-163

Bedrooms: 3	Baths: 2½

Space:

Upper floor:	537 sq. ft.
Main floor:	1,562 sq. ft.
Total living area:	**2,099 sq. ft.**
Exterior Wall Framing:	2x4

Foundation options:
Crawlspace.
(Foundation & framing conversion diagram available — see order form.)

Blueprint Price Code:	C

REAR VIEW

**TO ORDER THIS BLUEPRINT,
CALL TOLL-FREE 1-800-547-5570**
(prices and details on pp. 12-15.)

Plan DG-163

63

Quality Four-Bedroom Design

- Here's another fine example of a traditional plan that has faithfully stood the test of time.
- While not huge, the interior provides plenty of space for a busy family.
- The large family room includes a fireplace and adjoins the casual dinette area.
- A big kitchen includes a handy work island and is open to the dinette area.
- The living and dining rooms flow together when big space is needed for formal entertaining or large family gatherings.
- Upstairs, you'll find four roomy bedrooms and two full baths, one of which is private to the master bedroom.
- Also note the balcony overlooking the foyer below.

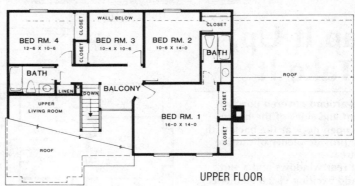

UPPER FLOOR

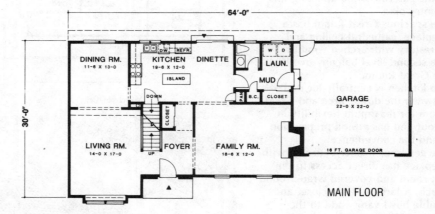

MAIN FLOOR

Plan A-2109-DS

Bedrooms: 4	Baths: 2½

Space:

Upper floor:	942 sq. ft.
Main floor:	1,148 sq. ft.
Total living area:	2,090 sq. ft.
Basement:	1,148 sq. ft.
Garage:	484 sq. ft.

Exterior Wall Framing: 2x4

Foundation options:
Standard basement only.
(Foundation & framing conversion diagram available — see order form.)

Blueprint Price Code: C

Plan A-2109-DS

Unique, Family Living

- This smart-looking, narrow, transitional design displays an exterior accented by half-windows, pillars and brick trim.
- A lovely vaulted parlor or study off the entry is entered through double doors and can also function as a guest room.
- Adjoining the parlor is the formal dining room with coffered ceiling and sliders that access the rear covered patio.
- The merging peninsula kitchen features a unique angled eating bar

and vaulted nook illuminated by skylights.
- Open to the kitchen is the spacious family room with dramatic corner fireplace and sliding glass doors to view the patio to the rear.
- Upstairs, the vaulted master suite has an elegant double-door entrance and a private bath with dressing area, skylit spa, and huge walk-in closet.
- The vaulted secondary bedrooms each have independent access to the bath between them, featuring separate vanities.

UPPER FLOOR

LOCATION OF STAIRS IN BASEMENT VERSION.

MAIN FLOOR

Plans P-7733-4A & P-7733-4D

Bedrooms: 3-4	Baths: 3

Space:

Upper floor:	960 sq. ft.
Main floor:	1,107 sq. ft.
Total living area:	**2,067 sq. ft.**
Daylight basement:	1,107 sq. ft.
Garage:	441 sq. ft.

Exterior Wall Framing:	2x6

Foundation options:

Daylight basement.	(P-7733-4D)
Crawlspace.	(P-7733-4A)

(Foundation & framing conversion diagram available — see order form.)

Blueprint Price Code:	C

Plans P-7733-4A & -4D

**TO ORDER THIS BLUEPRINT,
CALL TOLL-FREE 1-800-547-5570**
(prices and details on pp. 12-15.)

Fine Two-Story Family Home

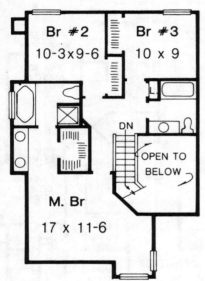

Br #2
10-3x9-6

Br #3
10 x 9

DN

OPEN TO BELOW

M. Br
17 x 11-6

- The exterior, with cedar siding and hip rooflines as well as a three-car garage, makes this a fine two-story home.
- A cozy family room features a wood stove and a French door that opens to a covered deck.
- For entertaining guests, the formal dining and living room features a vaulted ceiling and another private covered deck.
- The master suite, with a luxury bath and walk-in closet, is located on the second floor.
- Two more bedrooms share a hall bath on the second floor.

Plan NW-535-A

Bedrooms: 3-4	Baths: 3
Space:	
Upper floor:	755 sq. ft.
Main floor:	1,305 sq. ft.
Total living area:	2,060 sq. ft.
Exterior Wall Framing:	2x6

Foundation options:
Crawlspace.
(Foundation & framing conversion diagram available — see order form.)

Blueprint Price Code:	C

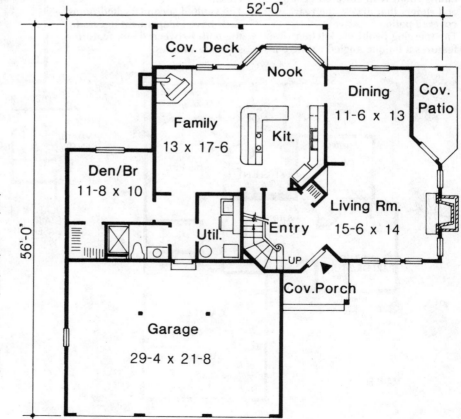

52'-0"

Cov. Deck

Nook

Dining
11-6 x 13

Cov. Patio

Family
13 x 17-6

Kit.

Den/Br
11-8 x 10

Living Rm.
15-6 x 14

56'-0"

Util.

Entry

UP

Cov. Porch

Garage
29-4 x 21-8

Plan NW-535-A

Inviting Porch Welcomes Guests

The inspiration for this charming turn-of-the-century house is found in Natchez, Mississippi. The inviting porch extends a gracious invitation to friends and neighbors.

Once inside, a very impressive foyer leads to the living room or the great room. A formal dining room, located conveniently between the kitchen and the living room, lends itself to easy entertaining.

The master bedroom has a bath with a separate shower stall, as well as an oversized tub. A large walk-in closet completes the amenities of this spacious room. The other bedrooms share a compartmentalized bath.

This plan is especially well-suited for a narrow lot.

First floor:	1,066 sq. ft.
Second floor:	913 sq. ft.
Total living area:	1,979 sq. ft.

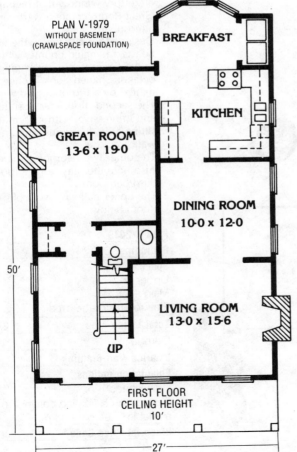

PLAN V-1979
WITHOUT BASEMENT
(CRAWLSPACE FOUNDATION)

BREAKFAST

KITCHEN

GREAT ROOM
13-6 x 19-0

DINING ROOM
10-0 x 12-0

LIVING ROOM
13-0 x 15-6

UP

50'

27'

FIRST FLOOR
CEILING HEIGHT
10'

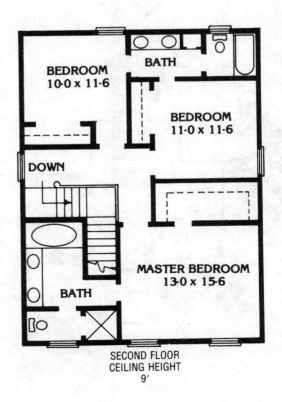

BEDROOM
10-0 x 11-6

BATH

BEDROOM
11-0 x 11-6

DOWN

MASTER BEDROOM
13-0 x 15-6

BATH

SECOND FLOOR
CEILING HEIGHT
9'

Blueprint Price Code B

Plan V-1979

Designed for Casual Living

- With its cheerful nook/kitchen/Great Room combination, this plan is great for families who rarely do any formal entertaining. In this plan, construction dollars are not expended for a living room which many families seldom use.
- The nook and kitchen face the front of the house, with a large Great Room and dining area to the rear.
- The soaring vaulted ceiling and clerestory window that highlight the Great Room create a warm and open atmosphere.
- Designed for efficiency, the kitchen boasts an angled counter which opens to the Great Room and dining area. An octagon-shaped nook is cheerfully lighted by a trio of angled windows.
- The second-floor master suite is large and impressive, with its semi-octagonal sitting area, luxurious bath and large walk-in closet.
- The other two bedrooms share a bath. Also note the play/storage room off the third bedroom.
- The upper hallway overlooks the Great Room below.

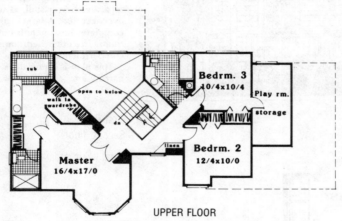

UPPER FLOOR

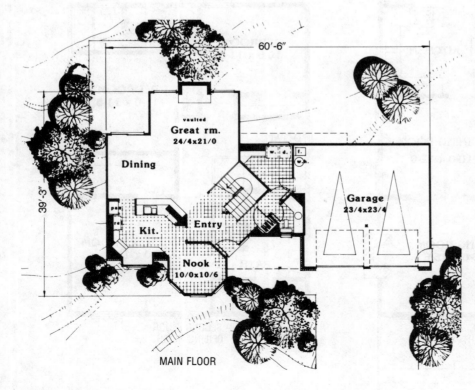

MAIN FLOOR

Plan R-2010

Bedrooms: 3	Baths: 2½
Space:	
Upper floor	942 sq. ft.
Main floor	996 sq. ft.
Play room/storage area	120 sq. ft.
Total Living Area	**2,058 sq. ft.**
Garage	544 sq. ft.
Exterior Wall Framing	2x4
Foundation options:	

Crawlspace
(Foundation & framing conversion diagram available—see order form.)

Blueprint Price Code	C

Plan R-2010

Farm House for Today

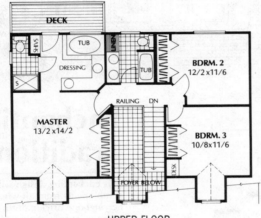

DECK

SHWR | TUB | LINEN
DRESSING | TUB
S

MASTER
13/2 x 14/2

RAILING DN

BDRM. 2
12/2 x 11/6

BDRM. 3
10/8 x 11/6

DESK

FOYER BELOW

UPPER FLOOR

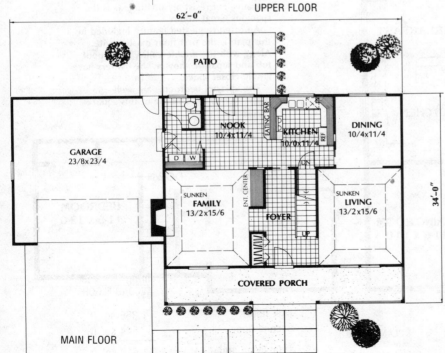

62'–0"

PATIO

GARAGE
23/8 x 23/4

NOOK
10/4 x 11/4

EATING BAR

KITCHEN
10/0 x 11/4

REF

DINING
10/4 x 11/4

D | W

SUNKEN
FAMILY
13/2 x 15/6

ENT. CENTER

FOYER

DN

SUNKEN
LIVING
13/2 x 15/6

UP

34'–0"

COVERED PORCH

MAIN FLOOR

- An inviting veranda and charming dormer windows lend traditional warmth to this attractive design.
- An up-to-date interior includes ample space for entertaining as well as for family life.
- An elegant foyer is flanked on one side by a formal, sunken living room and a sunken family room with fireplace on the other.
- A dining room joins the living room to increase the space available for parties.
- A roomy and efficient kitchen/nook/utility area combination with a half bath forms a spacious area for casual family life and domestic chores.
- Upstairs, a grand master suite includes a compartmentalized bath with separate tub and shower and a large closet.
- A second full bath serves the two secondary bedrooms.

Plan U-87-203

Bedrooms: 3	Baths: 2½
Space:	
Upper floor:	857 sq. ft.
Main floor:	1,064 sq. ft.
Total living area:	**1,921 sq. ft.**
Basement:	1,064 sq. ft.
Garage:	552 sq. ft.
Exterior Wall Framing:	2x4 & 2x6

Foundation options:
Standard basement.
Crawlspace.
Slab.
(Foundation & framing conversion diagram available — see order form.)

Blueprint Price Code:	B

Plan U-87-203

Enchanting Traditional

This enchanting design will generate compliments from all who visit. The herringbone brick pattern above the entrance is irresistibly inviting, as is the spacious Great Room.

An often requested feature included in this plan is the first floor master suite. Along with the double vanity, whirlpool tub and separate shower, the owners have ample closet space.

The upstairs bedrooms are well proportioned for a house of this square footage.

FIRST FLOOR

BATH

LAUNDRY

BREAKFAST

MASTER BEDROOM
13-6 x 14-6

KITCHEN

GREAT ROOM
13-6 x 18-6

DINING ROOM
11-6 x 14-0

UP

34'

47'

9'-0" CEILINGS THROUGHOUT FIRST FLOOR

8'-0" CEILINGS THROUGHOUT SECOND FLOOR

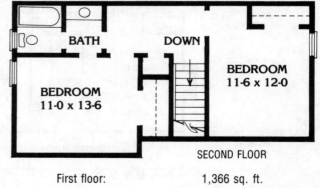

BATH   DOWN

BEDROOM
11-0 x 13-6

BEDROOM
11-6 x 12-0

SECOND FLOOR

First floor:	1,366 sq. ft.
Second floor:	544 sq. ft.
Total living area:	1,910 sq. ft.

PLAN V-1910
WITHOUT BASEMENT
(CRAWLSPACE FOUNDATION)

**TO ORDER THIS BLUEPRINT,
CALL TOLL-FREE 1-800-547-5570**

Blueprint Price Code B

Plan V-1910

CH-210-B

Alternate Exteriors

- Timeless exterior detailing and a functional, cost-effective interior are found in this traditional home.
- The kitchen, bayed breakfast room and vaulted family room with skylights and fireplace flow together to form the heart of the home.
- Lots of light filters into the front-facing formal living room.
- Upstairs, the master suite boasts a vaulted ceiling, large walk-in closet and private luxury bath.
- For the flavor of a full, covered front porch, Plan CH-210-B should be your choice.

BEDROOM 2
10'0" X 11'4"

BEDROOM 3
10'0" X 11'4"

MASTER BEDROOM
13'0" X 17'8"

DN

VAULT CLG.

EDGE OF OPTIONAL BRICK VENEER

UPPER FLOOR

44'-0"

BREAKFAST
9'1" X 7'4"

KITCHEN
10'0" X 12'8"

DINING ROOM
10'6" X 13'0"

VAULT CLG.

FAMILY ROOM
13'0" X 16'4"

EDGE OF OPTIONAL BRICK VENEER

DN

LIVING ROOM
13'0" X 15'0"

UP

FOYER

GARAGE
19'4" X 20'8"

38'-0"

MAIN FLOOR

Plan CH-210-A & -B

Bedrooms: 3	Baths: 2½
Space:	
Upper floor	823 sq. ft.
Main floor	1,079 sq. ft.
Total Living Area	**1,902 sq. ft.**
Basement	978 sq. ft.
Garage	400 sq. ft.
Exterior Wall Framing	2x4

Foundation options:
Standard Basement
Daylight Basement
(Foundation & framing conversion diagram available—see order form.)

Blueprint Price Code	**B**

CH-210-A

Plan CH-210-A, -B

TO ORDER THIS BLUEPRINT, CALL TOLL-FREE 1-800-547-5570
(prices and details on pp. 12-15.)

Country Expression

- The charm of this country farmhouse is expressed by its many windows and covered wraparound porch.
- Light streams into the two-story foyer through a clerestory dormer with palladian window.
- The dining room and breakfast room flank the kitchen oriented to the rear of the home, both offering sliders to the rear deck.
- For privacy and accessibility the master suite is located on the first floor; it has a stunning garden bath, separate shower and his 'n her vanities.
- A bonus room above the garage may be finished or added later.

Plan DG-235

Bedrooms: 3	Baths: 2½

Space:

Upper floor	542 sq. ft.
Main floor	1,356 sq. ft.
Bonus room	339 sq. ft.
Total Living Area	**2,237 sq. ft.**
Basement	1,408 sq. ft.
Garage	441 sq. ft.
Exterior Wall Framing	**2x4**

Foundation options:

Crawlspace
(Foundation & framing conversion diagram available—see order form.)

Blueprint Price Code	**C**

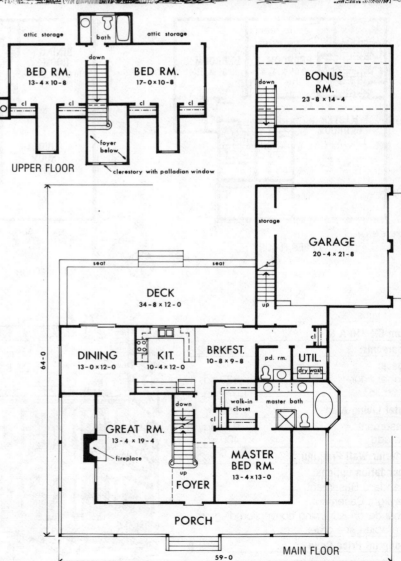

Plan DG-235

Updated Colonial Saltbox

- The long slope of the rear roof gives this traditional home its saltbox look, while the interior incorporates the best of the old and new.
- A large parlor off the front entry includes an impressive fireplace and provides space for formal entertaining.
- The family room/dining/kitchen space flow together to create a great place for family living and informal gatherings.
- The efficient kitchen includes a work island/bar and a pantry.
- A downstairs master suite features a private bath and large walk-in closet.
- The upstairs contains two more bedrooms with a sitting area between them. Two bonus rooms can be finished at any time to provide additional bedrooms, play space, a study or an exercise area.

Plan E-1822

Bedrooms: 3-5	Baths: 2

Space:

Upper floor	580 sq. ft.
Main floor	1,302 sq. ft.
Bonus area	250 sq. ft.
Total Living Area	**2,132 sq. ft.**
Basement (approx)	1,250 sq. ft.
Garage	616 sq. ft.
Storage, shop	108 sq. ft.
Porches	54 sq. ft.
Exterior Wall Framing	**2x6**

Foundation options:

Standard Basement
Crawlspace
Slab
(Foundation & framing conversion diagram available—see order form.)

Blueprint Price Code	**C**

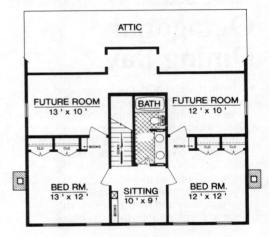

UPPER FLOOR

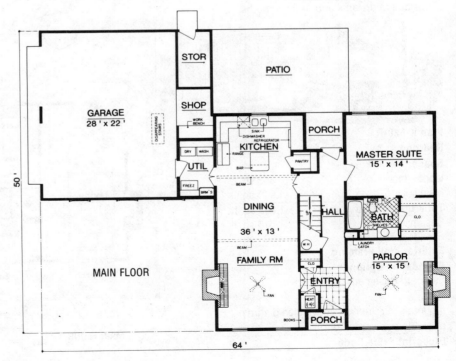

Plan E-1822

TO ORDER THIS BLUEPRINT,
CALL TOLL-FREE 1-800-547-5570
(prices and details on pp. 12-15.)

Octagonal Dining Bay

- Classic traditional styling is recreated with a covered front porch and triple dormers with half-round windows.
- Once inside, the interior feels open, airy and bright.
- The living room with fireplace leads into the formal dining room with octagonal bay windows.
- The island kitchen overlooks the breakfast bay and family room with second fireplace and sliders to the rear deck.
- A skylit hallway connects the four upstairs bedrooms and two full baths.

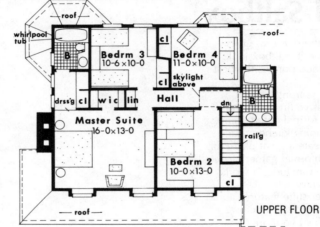

Plan K-680-R	
Bedrooms: 4	**Baths:** 2½
Space:	
Upper floor	853 sq. ft.
Main floor	1,015 sq. ft.
Total Living Area	**1,868 sq. ft.**
Basement	1,015 sq. ft.
Garage & Mud Room	504 sq. ft.
Exterior Wall Framing	2x4
Foundation options:	
Standard Basement	
Slab	
(Foundation & framing conversion diagram available—see order form.)	
Blueprint Price Code	**B**

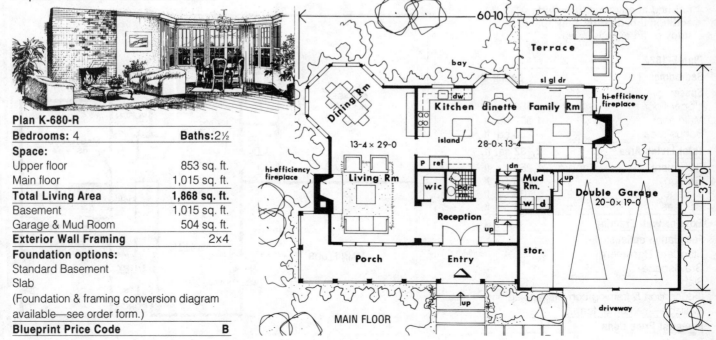

UPPER FLOOR

MAIN FLOOR

Plan K-680-R

Country Styling for Up-to-Date Living

- Nearly surrounded by a covered wood porch, this traditional 1,860 square-foot farm-styled home is modernized for today's active, up-to-date family.
- Inside, the efficient floor plan promotes easy mobility with a minimum of cross-traffic.
- The spacious living and dining area is warmed by a fireplace with a stone hearth; the U-shaped country kitchen is centrally located between these areas and the nook and family room with wood stove on the other side.
- Sliding glass doors lead out to both the rear patio and the deck that adjoins the dining and living rooms.
- The large master bedroom with corner window, dressing area and private bath and two other bedrooms with a second shared bath are found on the upper level.

Plans P-7677-2A & -2D	
Bedrooms: 3	**Baths:** 2 ½
Space:	
Upper floor	825 sq. ft.
Main floor	1,035 sq. ft.
Total Living Area	**1,860 sq. ft.**
Basement	1,014 sq. ft.
Garage	466 sq. ft.
Exterior Wall Framing	2x6
Foundation options:	Plan #
Daylight Basement	P-7677-2D
Crawlspace	P-7677-2A
(Foundation & framing conversion diagram available—see order form.)	
Blueprint Price Code	**B**

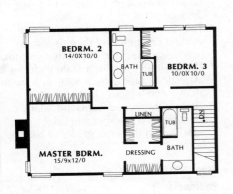

PLAN P-7677-2D
WITH DAYLIGHT BASEMENT

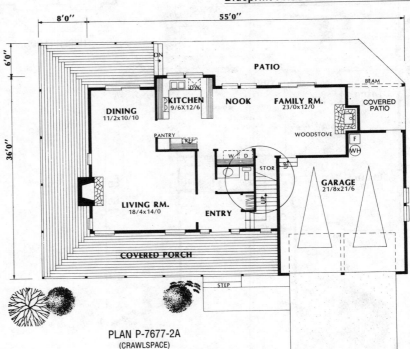

PLAN P-7677-2A
(CRAWLSPACE)

Plans P-7677-2A & -2D

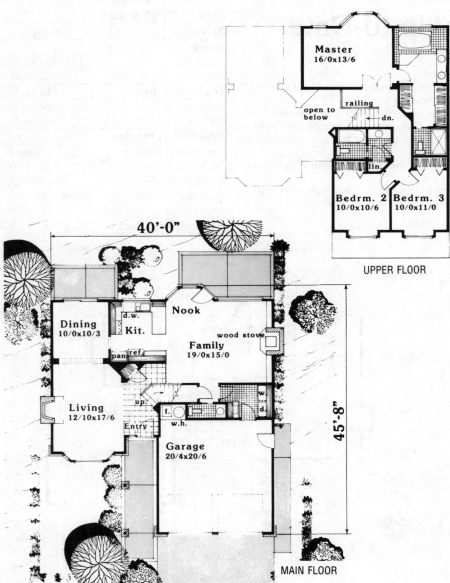

Master
16/0x13/6

open to below

railing

dn.

lin.

Bedrm. 2
10/0x10/6

Bedrm. 3
10/0x11/0

UPPER FLOOR

40'-0"

Dining
10/0x10/3

d.w.

Kit.

Nook

pan ref.

wood stove

Family
19/0x15/0

Living
12/10x17/6

up.

f.

w.

d.

Entry

w.h.

Garage
20/4x20/6

45'-8"

MAIN FLOOR

Traditional Design Overtones

- Contemporary styling with traditional overtones is the hallmark of this design, with its gables and multi-paned windows.
- A well designed traffic pattern inside provides easy access to all areas of the house without sacrificing a lot of space.
- The large family room includes space for a cozy wood stove, and a bright breakfast nook protrudes onto a rear deck or patio.
- The dining and living rooms feature vaulted ceilings, and there is also a handsome fireplace in the living room.
- The upper-level master suite includes a majestic master bath as well as a sunny alcove and a large closet.
- The two other bedrooms are nearly identical and both feature bright windows in the front gables of the home.

Plan R-2100

Bedrooms: 3	Baths: 2½
Space:	
Upper floor	840 sq. ft.
Main floor	994 sq. ft.
Total Living Area	**1,834 sq. ft.**
Garage	416 sq. ft.
Exterior Wall Framing	2x4
Foundation options:	
Crawlspace	
(Foundation & framing conversion diagram available—see order form.)	
Blueprint Price Code	B

Cozy Country Cottage

- This two-story cozy country cottage is perfect for the growing family with the availability of an unfinished basement and bonus room above the garage.
- The two-story entrance foyer has a palladian window in the clerestory dormer above to let the natural light flood in.
- The Great Room has a fireplace and columned division from the formal dining room.
- The master suite is on the first level for privacy and accessibility. The master bath boasts a whirlpool tub with skylight above, shower and double bowl vanity. The second level consists of two bedrooms, a full bath and plenty of storage.
- A spacious bonus room can be finished off above the garage for a host of activities.

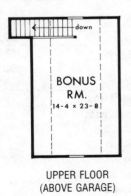

BONUS RM.
14-4 x 23-8

UPPER FLOOR
(ABOVE GARAGE)

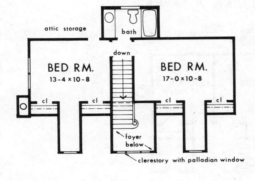

attic storage

bath

BED RM.
13-4 x 10-8

down

BED RM.
17-0 x 10-8

cl cl cl cl

foyer below

clerestory with palladian window

UPPER FLOOR

seat

DECK
31-8 x 12-0

DINING
12-0 x 12-0

KIT.
9-0 x 11-8

BRKFST.
9-8 x 9-8

UTILITY
10-4 x 6-4

pd. rm.

up

storage

dry wash   cl

50-4

GREAT RM.
13-4 x 19-4

fireplace

down

walk-in closet

master bath

GARAGE
21-8 x 20-4

cl

up

MASTER BED RM.
13-4 x 13-0

palladian window above

PORCH
33-8 x 6-0

66-4

MAIN FLOOR

Plan DG-224	
Bedrooms: 3	**Baths:** 2½

Space:

Upper floor:	542 sq. ft.
Main floor:	1,289 sq. ft.

Total living area:	1,831 sq. ft.
Basement:	1,289 sq. ft.
Garage:	441 sq. ft.
Storage area:	approx. 50 sq. ft.

Exterior Wall Framing:	2x4

Ceiling Height:

Main floor:	9'

Foundation options:
Standard basement.
Crawlspace.
(Foundation & framing conversion diagram available — see order form.)

Blueprint Price Code:	B

Country Comfort

- The traditional exterior of this two-story contrasts comfortably with its modern, open and airy interior.
- For family activities and entertaining, the living room and dining room combine, both with vaulted ceilings.
- The large, eat-in kitchen offers a combination breakfast bar and work island; adjoined is a sunken family room with fireplace and double doors to an optional outdoor alternative.
- A lovely front study could also serve as a fourth bedroom.
- A beautiful front window wall and vaulted ceiling accent the upstairs master bedroom, also with generous luxury bath.

Plan CH-220-A

Bedrooms: 3-4		Baths: 2 ½
Space:		
Upper floor		700 sq. ft.
Main floor		1,082 sq. ft.
Total Living Area		**1,782 sq. ft.**
Basement		980 sq. ft.
Garage		451 sq. ft.
Exterior Wall Framing		2x4
Foundation options:		
Standard Basement		
Daylight Basement		
(Foundation & framing conversion diagram available—see order form.)		
Blueprint Price Code		B

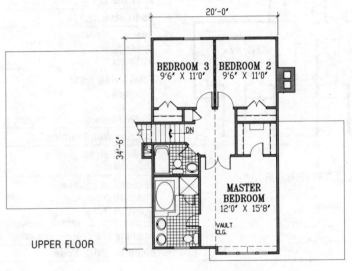

UPPER FLOOR

- 20'-0"
- 34'-6"
- BEDROOM 3 9'6" X 11'0"
- BEDROOM 2 9'6" X 11'0"
- DN
- MASTER BEDROOM 12'0" X 15'8"
- VAULT CLG.

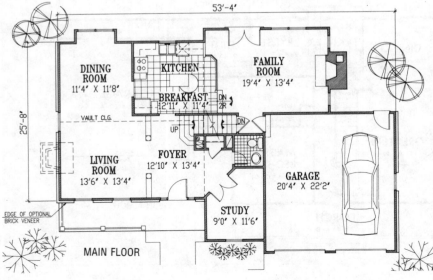

MAIN FLOOR

- 53'-4"
- 25'-8"
- DINING ROOM 11'4" X 11'8"
- KITCHEN
- FAMILY ROOM 19'4" X 13'4"
- BREAKFAST 12'11" X 11'4"
- DN 2R
- VAULT CLG.
- UP
- DN
- LIVING ROOM 13'6" X 13'4"
- FOYER 12'10" X 13'4"
- GARAGE 20'4" X 22'2"
- STUDY 9'0" X 11'6"
- EDGE OF OPTIONAL BRICK VENEER

Plan CH-220-A

Compact Design Flair

- This compact home features unique design flair in an efficient flow of space.
- The large, central family room boasts a masonry fireplace and wood box that doubles as an entertainment center.
- An angled counter bar separates the roomy kitchen from the family room and adjoining breakfast room.
- Formal living and dining rooms with vaulted ceilings and an optional fireplace complete the main level.
- Upstairs, the vaulted master suite features a dressing area and luxury bath; two additional bedrooms are also included.

Plan CH-611-A	
Bedrooms: 3	**Baths:** 2 ½
Space:	
Upper floor	771 sq. ft.
Main floor	1,008 sq. ft.
Total Living Area	**1,779 sq. ft.**
Basement	901 sq. ft.
Garage	390 sq. ft.
Exterior Wall Framing	2x4
Foundation options:	
Standard Basement	
Daylight Basement	
(Foundation & framing conversion diagram available—see order form.)	
Blueprint Price Code	B

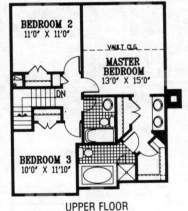

BEDROOM 2
11'0" X 11'0"

VAULT CLG.

MASTER BEDROOM
13'0" X 15'0"

DN

BEDROOM 3
10'0" X 11'10"

UPPER FLOOR

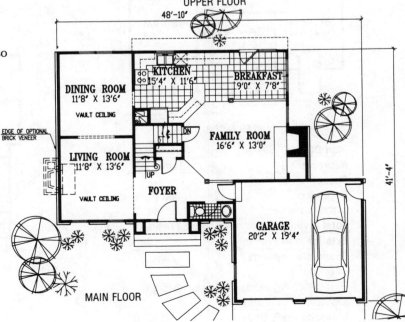

48'-10'

KITCHEN
15'4" X 11'6"

BREAKFAST
9'0" X 7'8"

DINING ROOM
11'8" X 13'6"

VAULT CEILING

EDGE OF OPTIONAL BRICK VENEER

FAMILY ROOM
16'6" X 13'0"

DN

LIVING ROOM
11'8" X 13'6"

UP

VAULT CEILING

FOYER

41'-4'

GARAGE
20'2" X 19'4"

MAIN FLOOR

Plan CH-611-A

For the Economically Minded

- There is little wasted space in this economical family home.
- Exciting exterior visual elements include a covered wraparound porch, a front Palladian window and rear arched windows.
- A spacious Great Room offers a cathedral ceiling, fireplace and sliders to the rear deck.
- Conveniently located between the bayed dining room and breakfast nook is the kitchen, with handy pass-thru to the Great Room.
- The master suite has extra closet space, large luxury bath with separate shower, and private access to the rear deck.

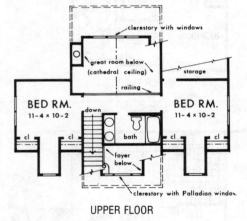

UPPER FLOOR

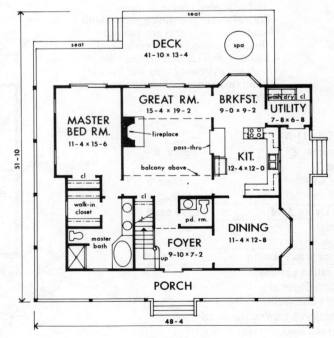

MAIN FLOOR

Plan DG-236	
Bedrooms: 3	**Baths:** 2 ½
Space:	
Upper floor	453 sq. ft.
Main floor	1,325 sq. ft.
Total Living Area	**1,778 sq. ft.**
Exterior Wall Framing	2×4
Foundation options:	
Crawlspace	
(Foundation & framing conversion diagram available—see order form.)	
Blueprint Price Code	B

Plan DG-236

PLANS H-3711-1 & H-3711-1A
(WITH GARAGE)

**NOTE: The above photographed home may have been modified by the homeowner. Please refer to floor plan and/or drawn elevation shown for actual blueprint details.

All-American Country Home

- Romantic, old-fashioned and spacious living areas combine to create this modern home.
- Off the entryway is the generous living room with fireplace and French doors which open onto the traditional rear porch.
- Country kitchen features an island table for informal occasions, while the adjoining family room is ideal for family gatherings.
- Practically placed, a laundry/mud room lies off the garage for immediate disposal of soiled garments.
- This plan is available with garage (H-3711-1) or without garage (H-3711-2) and with or without basement.

PLANS H-3711-2 & H-3711-2A
(WITHOUT GARAGE)

Plans H-3711-1/1A & -2/2A

Bedrooms: 4	Baths: 2½

Space:

Upper floor:	1,176 sq. ft.
Main floor:	1,288 sq. ft.

Total living area:	2,464 sq. ft.
Basement:	approx. 1,288 sq. ft.
Garage:	505 sq. ft.

Exterior Wall Framing:	2x6

Foundation options:
Standard basement (Plans H-3711-1 & -2).
Crawlspace (Plans H-3711-1A & -2A).
(Foundation & framing conversion diagram available — see order form.)

Blueprint Price Code:	C

UPPER FLOOR

WALK-IN CLOSET 7'-6" x 7'-6"

BATH

BATH

BEDROOM 13'-3" x 11'-0"

LINEN 6'-0"

STOR.

UP TO ATTIC

CLOSET 6'-9"   CLOSET 4'-9"

up   down

BEDROOM 13'-0" x 19'-0"

CLOSET 4'-9"

BEDROOM 15'-0" x 10'-0"

BEDROOM 10'-0" x 13'-3"

MAIN FLOOR

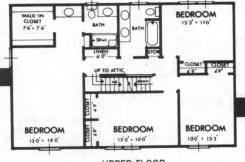

74'-0"

FRENCH DRS.

DINING 11'-9" x 13'-3"

DW

LAUNDRY 13'-0" x 7'-6"

STORAGE 15'-6" x 13'-6"

PANTRY

ISLAND

COUNTRY KITCHEN 15'-0" x 27'-0"

REF.

D   W

WH

down

GARAGE 23'-6" x 21'-6"

44'-0"

LIVING ROOM 13'-0" x 27'-0"

up   down

ENTRY

CLOS. 3'-0"

LAV.

FAMILY ROOM

8' WIDE COVERED PORCH

Panoramic Porch

- A gracious, ornate rounded front porch and a two-story turreted bay lend a Victorian charm to this home.
- A two-story foyer with round-top transom windows and plant ledge above greets guests at the entry.
- The living room enjoys a panoramic view overlooking the front porch and yard.
- The formal dining room and den each feature a bay window for added style.
- The kitchen/breakfast room incorporates an angled island cooktop, from which the sunken family room with corner fireplace can be enjoyed.
- The three bedrooms and two full baths upstairs are highlighted by a stunning master suite. The master bath offers a quaint octagonal sitting area within the turret bay.

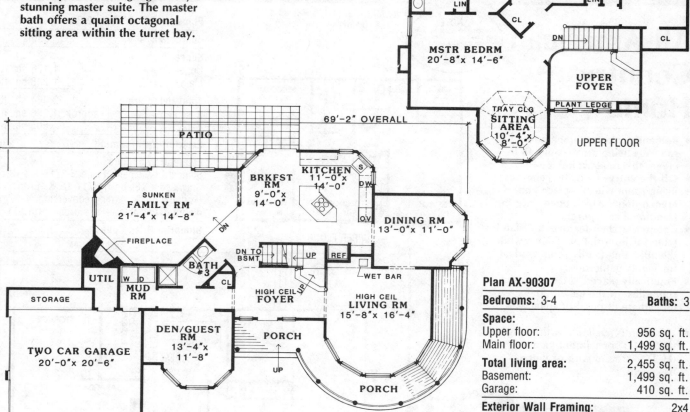

UPPER FLOOR

MAIN FLOOR

Plan AX-90307	
Bedrooms: 3-4	**Baths:** 3
Space:	
Upper floor:	956 sq. ft.
Main floor:	1,499 sq. ft.
Total living area:	2,455 sq. ft.
Basement:	1,499 sq. ft.
Garage:	410 sq. ft.
Exterior Wall Framing:	2x4

Foundation options:
Standard basement.
Slab.
(Foundation & framing conversion diagram available — see order form.)

Blueprint Price Code:	C

TO ORDER THIS BLUEPRINT,
CALL TOLL-FREE 1-800-547-5570

Plan AX-90307

Design Exudes Warmth and Comfort

- This plan represents a return to traditional styling with the open concept interior so much in demand today.
- Vaulted entry and living room with adjacent dining room make up the formal design of this plan.
- Spacious hall leads the large informal entertaining area composed of the kitchen, nook and family rooms.

- The second floor offers a large master suite and two additional bedrooms with a future bonus space that can be left unfinished until needed.
- Exterior roof lines are all gabled for ease of construction and lower framing costs. Brick veneer garage face echoes the brick columns supporting the covered entry.

Plan S-8389	
Bedrooms: 3-4	**Baths:** 2½

Space:	
Upper floor:	932 sq. ft.
Main floor:	1,290 sq. ft.
Bonus area:	228 sq. ft.

Total living area:	2,450 sq. ft.
Basement:	Approx. 1,290 sq. ft.
Garage:	429 sq. ft.

Exterior Wall Framing:	2x6

Foundation options:
Crawlspace.
Standard basement.
(Foundation & framing conversion diagram available — see order form.)

Blueprint Price Code:	C

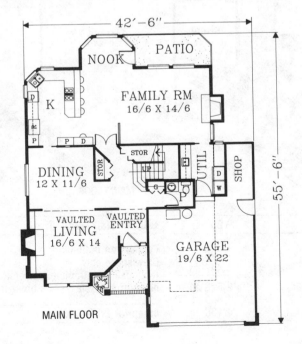

MAIN FLOOR

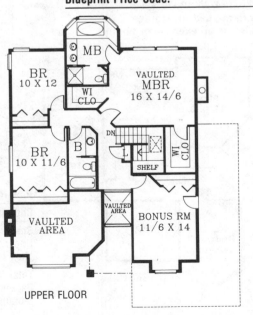

UPPER FLOOR

Plan S-8389

Photo by Mark Englund/HomeStyles

Classic Lines, Elegant Flair

- The rich brick arches and classic lines of this home lend an elegant air which will never be outdated.
- Inside, graceful archways lead from the vaulted entry to the living and dining rooms, which both feature heightened ceilings.
- The kitchen offers abundant counter space, an expansive window over the kitchen sink, large island, desk and pantry.
- The kitchen also is open to the nook and family room, which combine to make a great space for family living.
- The master suite is a pure delight, with a luxurious whirlpool tub and his-and-hers walk-in closets.
- The room marked for storage could also be an exercise or hobby room.

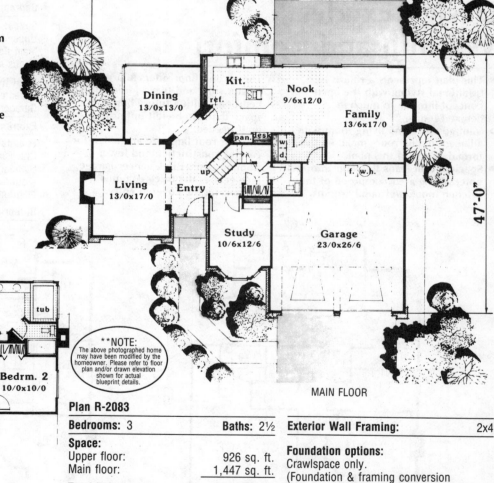

**NOTE:
The above photographed home may have been modified by the homeowner. Please refer to floor plan and/or drawn elevation shown for actual blueprint details.

MAIN FLOOR

UPPER FLOOR

Plan R-2083

Bedrooms: 3	Baths: 2½	Exterior Wall Framing:	2x4

Space:

Upper floor:	926 sq. ft.
Main floor:	1,447 sq. ft.
Total living area:	**2,373 sq. ft.**
Garage:	609 sq. ft.
Storage:	138 sq. ft.

Foundation options:
Crawlspace only.
(Foundation & framing conversion diagram available — see order form.)

Blueprint Price Code: C

TO ORDER THIS BLUEPRINT, CALL TOLL-FREE 1-800-547-5570

(prices and details on pp. 12-15.)

Plan R-2083

Striking Countrypolitan Home

- An eye-catching exterior design encloses a modern interior to provide a great family plan for any setting.
- A pleasant covered porch leads into an entry which includes a half-bath and access to the stairs, dining room or hallway leading to the rest of the house.
- The large living room includes an impressive fireplace and a vaulted ceiling.
- The super country kitchen includes a work island and pantry, and is flanked by a large informal eating area, a formal dining room and a roomy utility area.
- The master bedroom suite is fit for a king and queen, with a deluxe bath and an entire wall of closets.

- Upstairs, three more bedrooms share another full bath and all have large closets.

UPPER FLOOR

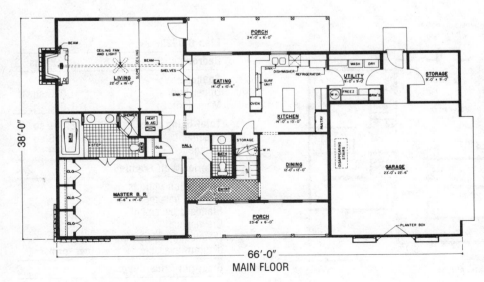

38'-0"

66'-0"
MAIN FLOOR

Plan E-2303	
Bedrooms: 4	**Baths:** 2½
Space:	
Upper floor	814 sq. ft.
Main floor	1,553 sq. ft.
Total Living Area	**2,367 sq. ft.**
Basement	1,553 sq. ft.
Garage	517 sq. ft.
Storage	81 sq. ft.
Porches	285 sq. ft.
Exterior Wall Framing	2x6

Foundation options:
Standard Basement
Crawlspace
Slab
(Foundation & framing conversion diagram available—see order form.)

Blueprint Price Code	C

Plan E-2303

Gracious Traditional

- Traditional style ranch is perfect for a corner building lot. Long windows and dormers add distinctive elegance.
- Floor plan has popular "split-bedroom" design. Master bedroom is secluded away from other bedrooms.
- Large Great Room has vaulted ceiling and stairs leading up to a loft.

- Upstairs loft is perfect for recreation area, and also has a full bath.
- Master bedroom bath has large corner tub and his-n-her vanities. Large walk-in closet provides plenty of storage.
- Two other bedrooms have large walk-in closets, desks, and share a full bath.
- Kitchen and private breakfast nook are located conveniently near the utility/garage area.

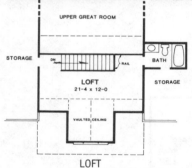

LOFT

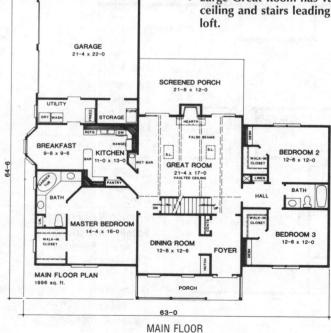

MAIN FLOOR

Plan C-8920

Bedrooms: 3	Baths: 3

Space:	
Upper floor:	305 sq. ft.
Main floor:	1,996 sq. ft.

Total living area:	**2,301 sq. ft.**
Basement:	1,996 sq. ft.
Garage:	469 sq. ft.

Exterior Wall Framing:	2x4

Foundation options:
Daylight basement.
Standard basement.
Crawlspace.
(Foundation & framing conversion diagram available — see order form.)

Blueprint Price Code:	C

Plan C-8920

Photo by Mark Englund

Fantastic Floor Plan!

- This is the famous house shown on the PBS "Hometime" television series.
- Impressive floor plan includes a deluxe master suite with a private courtyard, magnificent bath and large closet.
- The large island kitchen/nook combination includes a corner pantry and easy access to a rear deck.
- The spacious family room includes a fireplace and vaulted ceiling.
- The two upstairs bedrooms share a bath with double sinks.
- Note the convenient laundry room in the garage entry area.

Plan B-88015

Bedrooms: 3	Baths: 2½
Space:	
Upper floor:	534 sq. ft.
Main floor:	1,689 sq. ft.
Total living area:	**2,223 sq. ft.**
Basement:	approx. 1,689 sq. ft.
Garage:	455 sq. ft.
Exterior Wall Framing:	2x4

Foundation options:
Standard basement only.
(Foundation & framing conversion diagram available — see order form.)

Blueprint Price Code: C

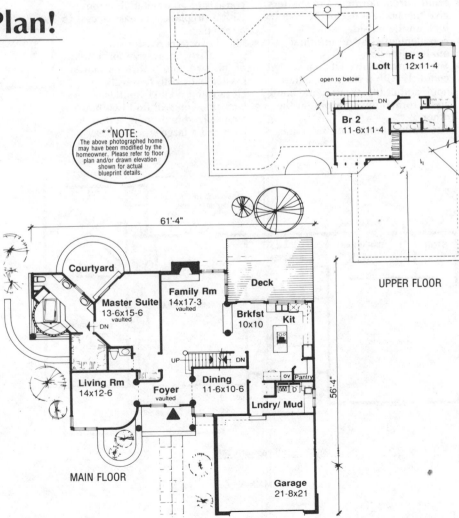

NOTE:
The above photographed home may have been modified by the homeowner. Please refer to floor plan and/or drawn elevation shown for actual blueprint details.

UPPER FLOOR

Br 3 12x11-4
Loft
open to below
DN
Br 2 11-6x11-4

MAIN FLOOR

61'-4"
56'-4"

Courtyard
Master Suite 13-6x15-6 vaulted
DN
Family Rm 14x17-3 vaulted
Deck
Brkfst 10x10
Kit
Living Rm 14x12-6
UP
DN
Dining 11-6x10-6
ov Pantry
W D
Foyer vaulted
Lndry/ Mud
Garage 21-8x21

Country Kitchen and Deluxe Master Bath

- Front porch, dormers and shutters give this home a decidedly country look on the outside, which is complemented by an informal modern interior.
- The roomy country kitchen connects with a sunny breakfast nook and utility area on one hand and a formal dining room on the other.
- The central portion of the home consists of a large family room with a fireplace and easy access to a rear deck.
- The downstairs master suite is particularly impressive for a home of this size, and features a majestic master bath with two walk-in closets and double vanities.
- Upstairs, you will find two more ample-sized bedrooms, a double bath and a large storage area.

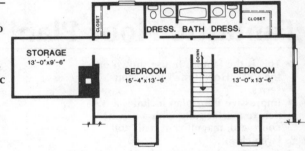

UPPER FLOOR

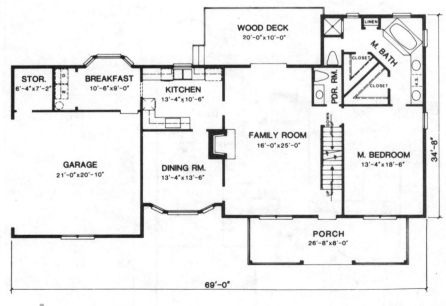

MAIN FLOOR

Plan C-8645

Bedrooms: 3	Baths: 2½
Space:	
Upper floor:	704 sq.ft.
Main floor:	1,477 sq.ft.
Total living area:	2,181 sq.ft.
Basement:	Approx. 1,400 sq.ft.
Garage:	438 sq.ft.
Storage:	123 sq.ft.
Exterior Wall Framing:	2x4

Foundation options:
Standard basement.
Crawlspace.
Slab.
(Foundation & framing conversion diagram available — see order form.)

Blueprint Price Code:	C

Plan C-8645

Gracious Living at Its Best

- A time-tested design, this plan says gracious living from its front porch columns all the way to the balcony bedroom at the upper rear.
- An efficient entry leads to a large living room or to the stairway.
- A cozy porch is nestled in the L-shape formed by the living room and adjoining formal dining room.
- A spacious, angled kitchen is adjoined by a sunny atrium and handy utility area leading to the garage.
- An informal eating area is also well-lighted with windows on three of its eight sides.
- A deluxe master suite includes a splendid private bath with two walk-in closets.
- Upstairs, you have the flexibility of two bedrooms, or one bedroom plus an upper library, studio, office or private sitting area with a balcony overlook to the dining room below.

Photo by Mark Englund/HomeStyles

NOTE:
The above photographed home may have been modified by the homeowner. Please refer to floor plan and/or drawn elevation shown for actual blueprint details.

MAIN FLOOR

UPPER FLOOR

Plan E-2002	
Bedrooms: 2-3	**Baths: 2½**
Space:	
Upper floor	512 sq. ft.
Main floor	1,546 sq. ft.
Total Living Area	**2,058 sq. ft.**
Garage	462 sq. ft.
Storage	54 sq. ft.
Porches	272 sq. ft.
Exterior Wall Framing	**2x6**

Foundation options:
Standard Basement
Crawlspace
Slab
(Foundation & framing conversion diagram available—see order form.)

Blueprint Price Code	**C**

Plan E-2002

TO ORDER THIS BLUEPRINT,
CALL TOLL-FREE 1-800-547-5570
(prices and details on pp. 12-15.)

The Woodstock

- This charming country-inspired home is economical to build and requires only a small lot.
- The powder room and guest closet are conveniently located near the foyer, as well as a large combination living/dining room with walk-in bay window.
- A low partition visually separates the kitchen and adjacent family room, which features angled fireplace, cathedral ceiling with skylight, and sliding glass doors open to the rear yard.
- The second floor features an optional loft or fourth bedroom.

Plan AX-8923-A

Bedrooms: 3-4	Baths: 2½
Space:	
Upper floor:	853 sq. ft.
Main floor:	1,082 sq. ft.
Total living area:	**1,935 sq. ft.**
Basement:	approx. 1,082 sq. ft.
Garage:	420 sq. ft.
Exterior Wall Framing:	2x4

Foundation options:
Standard basement.
Slab.
(Foundation & framing conversion diagram available — see order form.)

Blueprint Price Code:	B

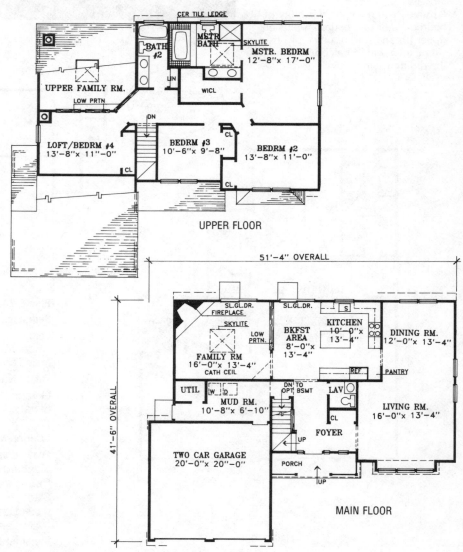

UPPER FLOOR

MAIN FLOOR

Plan AX-8923-A

Photo by Mark Englund/HomeStyles

Exciting, Economical Design

Exciting but economical, this 1,895 sq. ft., three-bedroom house is arranged carefully for maximum use and enjoyment on two floors, and is only 42 feet wide to minimize lot size requirements. The multi-paned bay windows of the living room and an upstairs bedroom add contrast to the hip rooflines and lead you to the sheltered front entry porch.

The open, vaulted foyer is brightened by a skylight as it sorts traffic to the downstairs living areas or to the upper bedroom level. A few steps to the right puts you in the vaulted living room and the adjoining dining area. Sliding doors in the dining area and the nook, and a pass-through window in the U-shaped kitchen, make the patio a perfect place for outdoor activities and meals.

A large fireplace warms the spacious family room, which has a corner wet bar for efficient entertaining. A utility room leading to the garage and a powder room complete the 1,020 sq. ft. main floor.

An open stairway in the foyer leads to the 875 sq. ft. upper level. The master bedroom has a large walk-in wardrobe, twin vanity, shower and bathroom. The front bedroom has a seat in the bay window and the third bedroom has a built-in seat overlooking the vaulted living room. A full bath with twin vanity serves these bedrooms.

The daylight basement version of the plan adds 925 sq. ft. of living space.

Main floor:	1,020 sq. ft.
Upper floor:	875 sq. ft.
Total living area:	1,895 sq. ft.

(Not counting basement or garage)

PLAN P-7681-3D
BASEMENT LEVEL: 925 sq. ft.

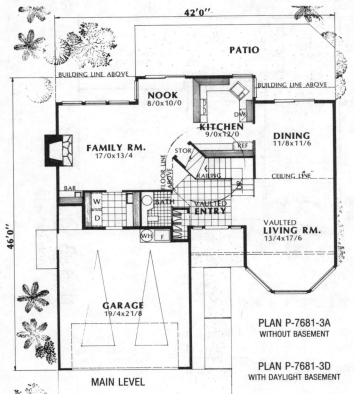

PLAN P-7681-3A
WITHOUT BASEMENT

PLAN P-7681-3D
WITH DAYLIGHT BASEMENT

MAIN LEVEL

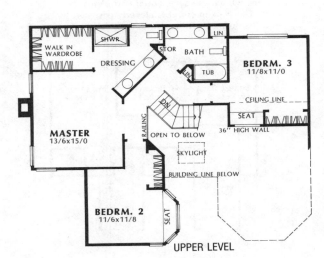

UPPER LEVEL

Blueprint Price Code B

Plans P-7681-3A & 3D

Distinctive Charm

Shuttered dormers and traditional detailing add distinctive charm to this three-bedroom home.

The kitchen is illuminated by a large window over the sink and a convenient pantry. A desk is located in the adjoining nook, providing an excellent area for paying bills and organizing household accounts.

Double doors open into a fantastic master bedroom. For those who can never get enough closet space, you'll find plenty here. The walk-in closet is cleverly designed into the dormer with a pleasant window seat.

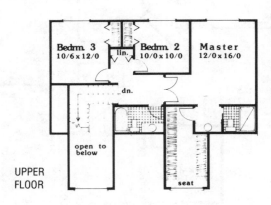

UPPER FLOOR

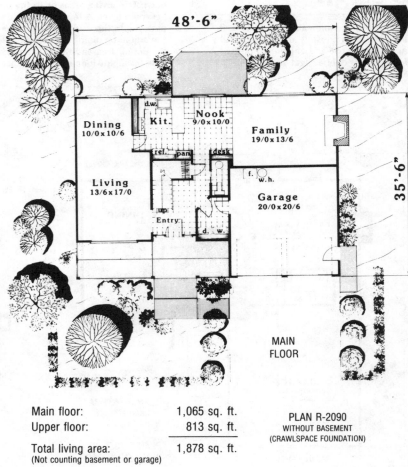

MAIN FLOOR

PLAN R-2090
WITHOUT BASEMENT
(CRAWLSPACE FOUNDATION)

Main floor:	1,065 sq. ft.
Upper floor:	813 sq. ft.
Total living area:	1,878 sq. ft.

(Not counting basement or garage)

Blueprint Price Code B
Plan R-2090

Compact and Luxurious

- The best from the past and the present is bundled up in this compact design, reminiscent of a New England saltbox.
- Cozy kitchen has center island with breakfast counter and built-in range/oven; corner sink saves on counter space.
- Formal dining room, separated from the living room by a railing, affords a view to the sunken living room and the fireplace and deck beyond.
- Living room has vaulted ceiling and built-in shelves for entertainment center.
- Second-floor master suite features a hydro-spa, shower, and walk-in closet.

Plan H-1453-1A

Bedrooms: 3	Baths: 2

Space:	
Upper floor:	386 sq. ft.
Main floor:	1,385 sq. ft.

Total living area:	1,771 sq. ft.

Exterior Wall Framing:	2x6

Foundation options:
Crawlspace only.
(Foundation & framing conversion diagram available — see order form.)

Blueprint Price Code:	B

UPPER FLOOR

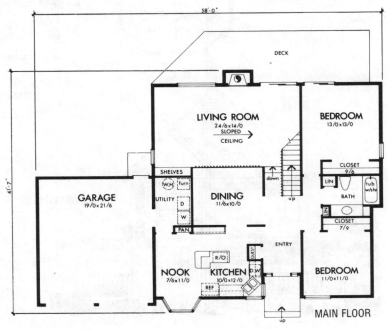

MAIN FLOOR

Plan H-1453-1A

ELEVATION A

Compact Victorian

- This compact Victorian design incorporates four bedrooms and three full baths into a home that's only 30 feet wide.
- The upstairs master suite includes a deluxe bath and a bayed sitting area.
- The roomy parlor includes a fireplace, and the formal dining room has a beautiful bay window.
- The downstairs bedroom, with its adjoining full bath, makes a great office or guest bedroom.
- Please specify attached garage if desired.

ELEVATION B

Plan C-8347

Plan C-8347	
Bedrooms: 3-4	**Baths:** 3
Space:	
Upper floor	783 sq. ft.
Main floor	954 sq. ft.
Total Living Area	**1,737 sq. ft.**
Exterior Wall Framing	2x4
Foundation options:	
Crawlspace	
Slab	
(Foundation & framing conversion diagram available—see order form.)	
Blueprint Price Code	**B**

TO ORDER THIS BLUEPRINT, CALL TOLL-FREE 1-800-547-5570

Stately Classic Design

- This stately design exhibits a timeless class that is impressive in any community.
- The interior features a large living/dining combination that provides a huge space for entertaining.
- The efficient kitchen includes a breakfast bar and adjoins a handy utility room.
- The main-floor master suite is truly majestic for a home of this size, and features a luxurious bath and large walk-in closet.
- The upstairs includes another full bath and two bedrooms, one of which includes a balcony overlooking the living room below.

Plan E-1627

Bedrooms: 3	Baths: 2

Space:

Upper floor	503 sq. ft.
Main floor	1,180 sq. ft.
Total Living Area	**1,683 sq. ft.**
Carport	440 sq. ft.
Storage	64 sq. ft.
Porches	267 sq. ft.
Exterior Wall Framing	2x6

Foundation options:

Crawlspace

Slab

(Foundation & framing conversion diagram available—see order form.)

Blueprint Price Code	**B**

UPPER FLOOR

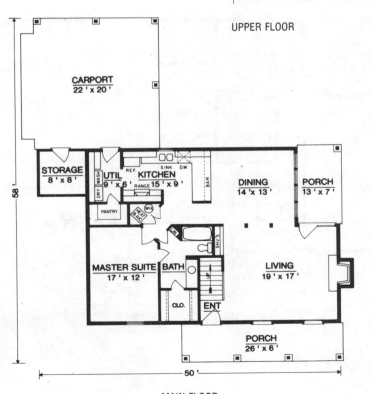

MAIN FLOOR

Plan E-1627

Photo courtesy of Breland & Farmer Designers, Inc.

Three-Bedroom Home Features Screened-In Porch

- This classic story-and-a-half design encompasses a thoroughly modern interior on a compact foundation area.
- Living and dining rooms flow together, yet are divided by a screened porch which provides more space in nice weather.
- Deluxe master bedroom is larger

than you might expect in a home this size, and includes a big walk-in closet and a dressing area.
- The large kitchen includes abundant counter space, and adjoins a roomy utility area.
- The upstairs includes two nice-sized bedrooms and a convenient bath.

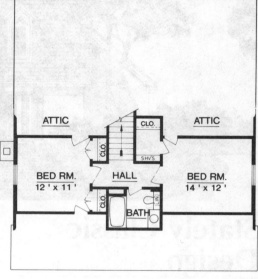

UPPER FLOOR

Plan E-1626

Bedrooms: 3	Baths: 2

Space:

Upper floor:	464 sq. ft.
Main floor:	1,136 sq. ft.

Total living area:	1,600 sq. ft.
Porches:	393 sq. ft.
Garage:	462 sq. ft.
Storage:	11 sq. ft.

Exterior Wall Framing:	2x6

Foundation options:
Crawlspace.
Slab.
(Foundation & framing conversion diagram available — see order form.)

Blueprint Price Code:	B

MAIN FLOOR

NOTE:
The above photographed home may have been modified by the homeowner. Please refer to floor plan and/or drawn elevation shown for actual blueprint details.

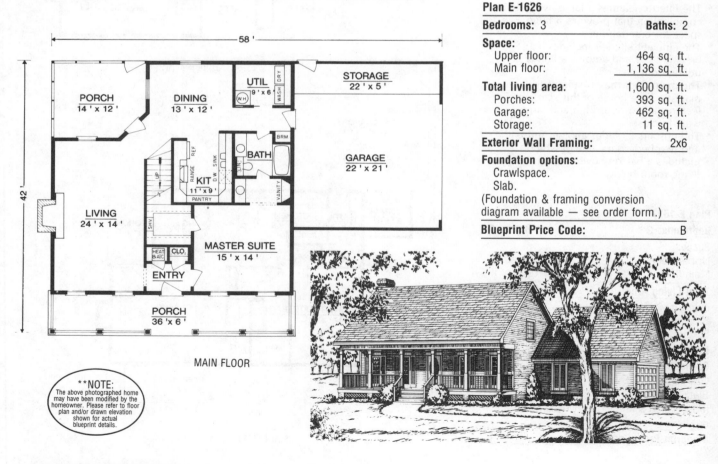

Plan E-1626

Modern Country Cottage for Small Lot

This drive-under garage design is great for smaller lots. But even though the home is relatively compact, it's still loaded with modern features. The deluxe master bedroom has a large bath with garden tub and shower. The country kitchen/dining room combination has access to a deck out back. The large living room with fireplace is accessible from the two story foyer.

The upper floor has two large bedrooms and a full bath, and the large basement has room for two cars and expandable living areas.

This plan is available with basement foundation only.

Main floor:	1,100 sq. ft.
Second floor:	664 sq. ft.
Total living area: (Not counting basement or garage)	1,764 sq. ft.
Basement:	1,100 sq. ft.

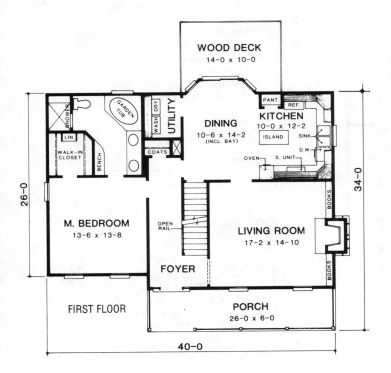

PLAN C-8870
WITH BASEMENT

Blueprint Price Code B

Plan C-8870

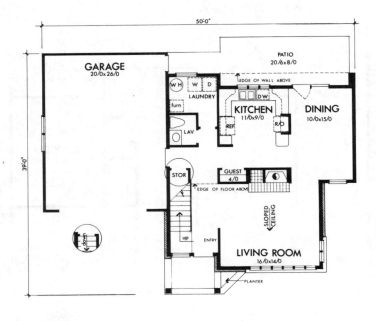

Compact Design with Energy-Saving Features

- This stylish family home is wrapped in an attractive exterior of wood siding and brick veneer accents
- Covered entry leads into commodious living room with heat-circulating fireplace and sloped ceilings.
- Dining room opens to a patio via French doors and lies opposite an efficient U-shaped kitchen.
- Ample closet space, master bedroom, and two additional bedrooms comprise the second level.

Plans H-3741-1 & -1A

Bedrooms: 3	Baths: 2½
Space:	
Upper floor:	900 sq. ft.
Main floor:	853 sq. ft.
Total living area:	1,753 sq. ft.
Basement:	approx. 853 sq. ft.
Garage:	520 sq. ft.
Exterior Wall Framing:	2x6

Foundation options:
Standard basement (Plan H-3741-1).
Crawlspace (Plan H-3741-1A).
(Foundation & framing conversion diagram available — see order form.)

Blueprint Price Code:	B

Plans H-3741-1 & -1A

Contemporary, Yet Country

- A covered front entry, a projected living room window and varied rooflines give interesting shadow lines to this contemporary country home.
- The open entry offers a view straight back to the fireplace and flanking windows of the family room. An optional wet bar located at the center of the floor plan can service any room.
- The modern kitchen and sunny breakfast area share an open arrangement with the family room, separated only by an open railing. A deck off the breakfast room is perfect for outdoor dining.
- The upper floor boasts a large master bedroom with dual closets and a personal bath. A laundry closet is conveniently close.
- Two additional bedrooms share a second bath.

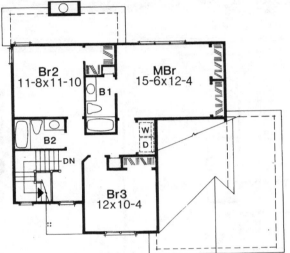

UPPER FLOOR

Plan UDG-91007

Bedrooms: 3	Baths: 2½
Living Area:	
Upper floor	817 sq. ft.
Main floor	932 sq. ft.
Total Living Area:	**1,749 sq. ft.**
Standard basement	932 sq. ft.
Garage	447 sq. ft.
Exterior Wall Framing:	2x4
Foundation Options:	
Standard basement	
(Typical foundation & framing conversion diagram available—see order form.)	
BLUEPRINT PRICE CODE:	**B**

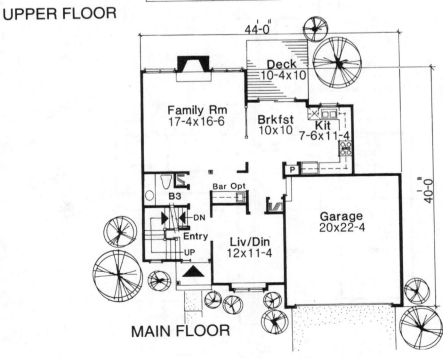

MAIN FLOOR

Plan UDG-91007

First floor: 1,152 sq. ft.
Second floor: 559 sq. ft.

Total living area: 1,711 sq. ft.
Carport: 380 Sq. Ft.
Storage: 85 sq. ft.

Total: 2,284 sq. ft.

Specify basement, crawlspace or slab foundation.

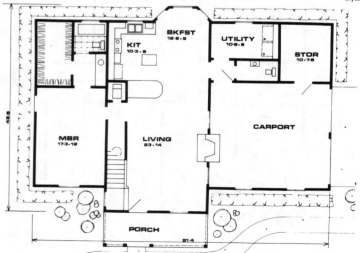

Farmhouse For The Growing Family

There's more to this house than its charming front porch, steeply pitched roof and dormer windows. Tucked away in the attic is potential living space designed to meet the needs of a growing family. The 8-ft. ceilings throughout the second story give this 1,700 sq. ft. farmhouse the potential to be a four- or even five-bedroom house.

A door at the top of the stairs provides access to attic space that could be turned into an extra bedroom. Another door between the two walk-in closets leads to more attic space. Some families have converted the larger bedroom — with the triple dormer windows and window seat — into a playroom, adding bedrooms on both sides of the house.

The first floor has 9-ft. ceilings, making the 1,152 sq. ft. on this level seem much larger. The feeling of spaciousness is further enchanced by the openness of the floor plan, with the living room, or Great Room, facing the kitchen/breakfast area. A snack bar separates the two rooms.

The back door leads from the carport to the utility room, which is convenient to the kitchen and half-bath. The rear entrance also lets the utility room double as a mudroom.

A special feature is the roomy master bedroom, with a large walk-in closet and a private bathroom.

Blueprint Price Code B
Plan J-86133

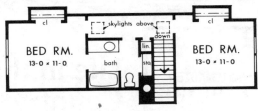

UPPER FLOOR

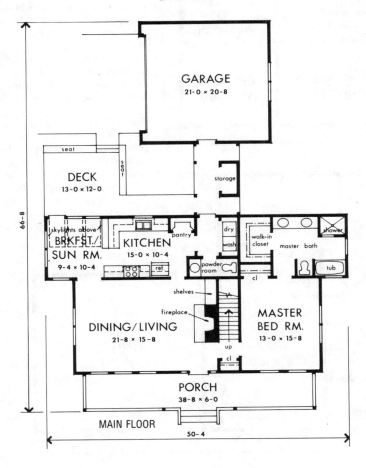

MAIN FLOOR

Delightful Living Assured

- Delightful country-style living in this symmetrically proportioned compact home is assured.
- The large, covered front porch provides a comfortable place for outdoor relaxation in addition to the large dining/living room with fireplace and abundant windows.
- The kitchen incorporates a skylit breakfast/sun room with access to the rear deck, which adds to the indoor/outdoor livability.
- The main-floor master suite includes a walk-in closet and open-feeling master bath with double vanity and separate tub and shower.
- There are two more bedrooms upstairs which share a full bath, accessible by a skylit hallway.

Plan DG-157

Bedrooms: 3	Baths: 2½

Space:	
Upper floor:	493 sq. ft.
Main floor:	1,215 sq. ft.

Total living area:	1,708 sq. ft.
Garage:	434 sq. ft.

Exterior Wall Framing:	2x4

Foundation options:
Crawlspace.
(Foundation & framing conversion diagram available — see order form.)

Blueprint Price Code:	B

Plan DG-157

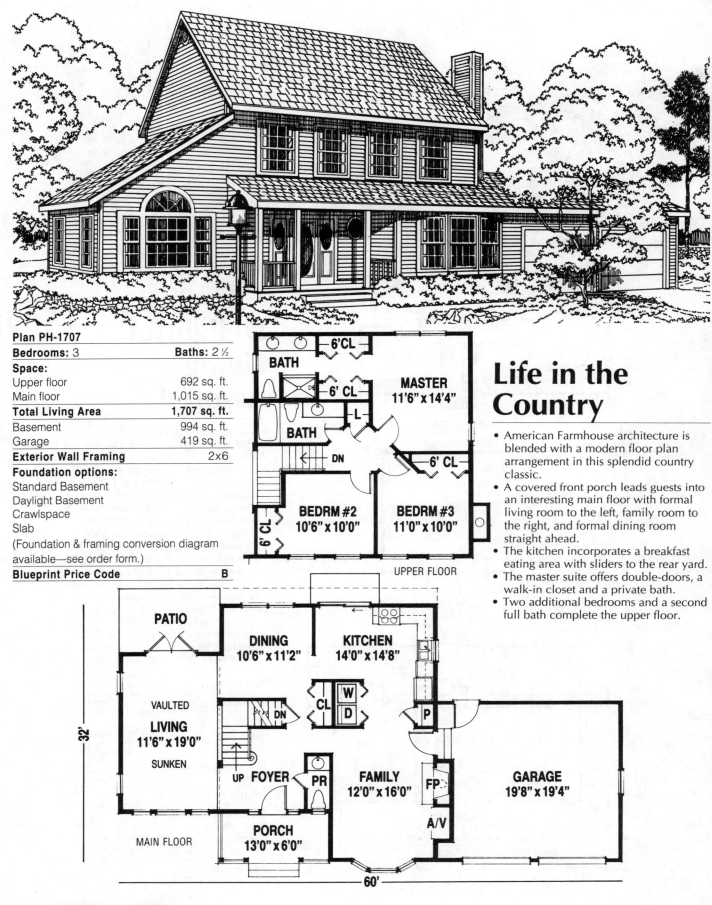

Plan PH-1707

Bedrooms: 3	Baths: 2 ½

Space:

Upper floor	692 sq. ft.
Main floor	1,015 sq. ft.
Total Living Area	**1,707 sq. ft.**
Basement	994 sq. ft.
Garage	419 sq. ft.
Exterior Wall Framing	**2x6**

Foundation options:

Standard Basement
Daylight Basement
Crawlspace
Slab
(Foundation & framing conversion diagram available—see order form.)

Blueprint Price Code	**B**

UPPER FLOOR

6'CL

BATH

6' CL

MASTER
11'6" x 14'4"

BATH

L

DN

6' CL

6' CL

BEDRM #2
10'6" x 10'0"

BEDRM #3
11'0" x 10'0"

Life in the Country

- American Farmhouse architecture is blended with a modern floor plan arrangement in this splendid country classic.
- A covered front porch leads guests into an interesting main floor with formal living room to the left, family room to the right, and formal dining room straight ahead.
- The kitchen incorporates a breakfast eating area with sliders to the rear yard.
- The master suite offers double-doors, a walk-in closet and a private bath.
- Two additional bedrooms and a second full bath complete the upper floor.

MAIN FLOOR

PATIO

DINING
10'6" x 11'2"

KITCHEN
14'0" x 14'8"

VAULTED

LIVING
11'6" x 19'0"

SUNKEN

DN

CL

W
D

P

UP FOYER

PR

FAMILY
12'0" x 16'0"

FP

GARAGE
19'8" x 19'4"

A/V

PORCH
13'0" x 6'0"

32'

60'

Plan PH-1707

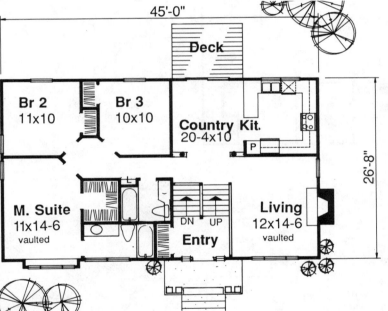

45'-0"

Deck

Br 2
11x10

Br 3
10x10

Country Kit.
20-4x10

P

26'-8"

M. Suite
11x14-6
vaulted

Living
12x14-6
vaulted

DN   UP

Entry

MAIN FLOOR

Plan B-90012

Bedrooms: 3	Baths: 2-3

Space:

Main/upper level:	1,203 sq. ft.
Basement:	460 sq. ft.
Total living area:	**1,663 sq. ft.**
Garage:	509 sq. ft.

Exterior Wall Framing:	2x4

Foundation options:
Daylight basement.
(Foundation & framing conversion
diagram available — see order form.)

Blueprint Price Code:	B

Split Entry with Country Kitchen

- The split entry of this updated traditional opens up to a large vaulted living room with fireplace and a lovely country kitchen with sliders to a deck.
- Down the hall you'll find the vaulted master suite with large walk-in closet and private bath.
- Two additional bedrooms and a second bath are also included.
- The lower level is unfinished and left up to the owner to choose its function; room for a third bath and laundry facilities is provided.

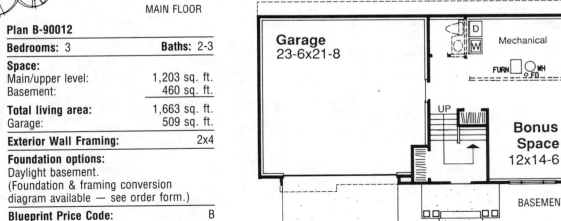

Garage
23-6x21-8

Mechanical

D
W

FURN   WH
FD

UP

Bonus
Space
12x14-6

BASEMENT

Plan B-90012

Countrypolitan Four-Bedroom

- Equally at home in a suburban or rural setting, this plan offers an impressive exterior and a quality interior.
- An efficient entry area includes a handy powder room and coat closet.
- The formal living and dining rooms are spacious and flow together to create a large space for family gatherings or parties.
- The family room adjoins the efficient kitchen and opens to a rear patio or deck.
- The master suite is upstairs, and includes a deluxe bath with a dressing area and large closet. A second walk-in closet is provided across the room.
- Three other bedrooms also have ample closet space and share a second full bath.
- A daylight basement version adds even more versatility to the plan.

Plans P-7575-2A & -2D

Bedrooms: 4	Baths: 2½
Space:	
Upper floor	830 sq. ft.
Main floor	795 sq. ft.
Total Living Area	**1,625 sq. ft.**
Basement	795 sq. ft.
Garage	455 sq. ft.
Exterior Wall Framing	2x4
Foundation options:	
Daylight Basement	P-7575-2D
Crawlspace	P-7575-2A
(Foundation & framing conversion diagram available—see order form.)	
Blueprint Price Code	**B**

UPPER FLOOR

PLAN P-7575-2D
WITH BASEMENT

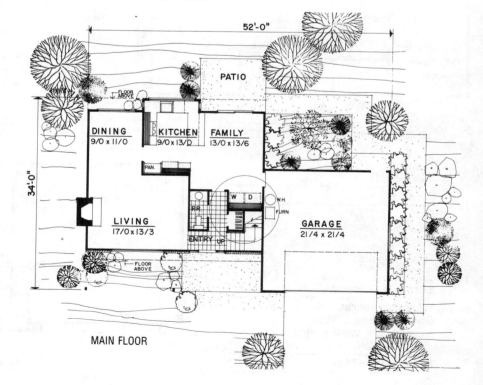

MAIN FLOOR

Plans P-7575-2A & -2D

Cozy Two-Story

- This compact two-story design offers plenty of living space on a small "footprint."
- The downstairs offers living and dining rooms that are both large for a home of this size, as well as a spacious and well-planned kitchen.
- The living room includes a wet bar and a fireplace, and also opens out onto a rear patio or deck.
- Also note the handy utility area and half-bath, both convenient to the kitchen.
- Upstairs, you'll find three bedrooms and a large bonus room over the garage.
- The master suite offers a private bath and two large walk-in closets. Two secondary bedrooms share another full bath.
- The bonus space offers potential for a playroom, study, exercise area or additional sleeping space.

Plan E-1624

Bedrooms: 3-4	Baths: 2½
Space:	
Upper floor	808 sq. ft.
Main floor	792 sq. ft.
Bonus area	264 sq. ft.
Total Living Area	**1,864 sq. ft.**
Basement	792 sq. ft.
Garage	506 sq. ft.
Storage & shop	110 sq. ft.
Exterior Wall Framing	**2x6**

Foundation options:

Standard Basement

Crawlspace

Slab

(Foundation & framing conversion diagram available—see order form.)

Blueprint Price Code	**B**

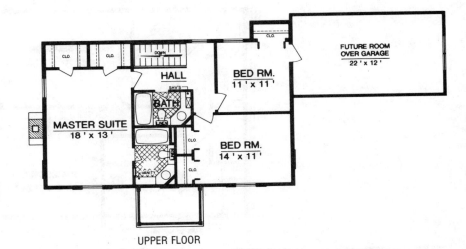

UPPER FLOOR

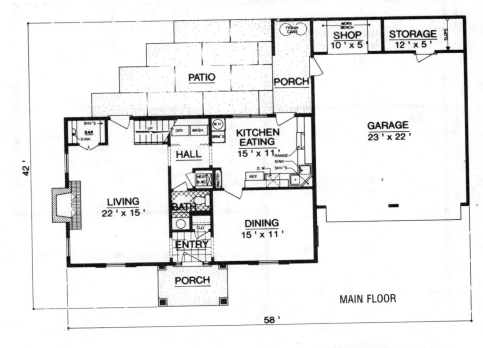

MAIN FLOOR

TO ORDER THIS BLUEPRINT,
CALL TOLL-FREE 1-800-547-5570
(prices and details on pp. 12-15.)

Plan E-1624

A Family Gem

- Flexibility and affordability make this traditional design a great family choice.
- The large family room, dinette and kitchen combine along the rear of the home to form a unique dining or entertaining solution.
- The dining and living rooms join to the right of the foyer for a more formal alternative.
- The upper-level master bedroom offers a walk-in closet and private access to the bathroom, also shared with the two secondary bedrooms.

Plan GL-1597

Bedrooms: 3	Baths: 1 ½
Space:	
Upper floor	672 sq. ft.
Main floor	925 sq. ft.
Total Living Area	**1,597 sq. ft.**
Basement	925 sq. ft.
Garage	413 sq. ft.
Exterior Wall Framing	2x6
Foundation options:	
Standard Basement	
(Foundation & framing conversion diagram available—see order form.)	
Blueprint Price Code	B

UPPER FLOOR

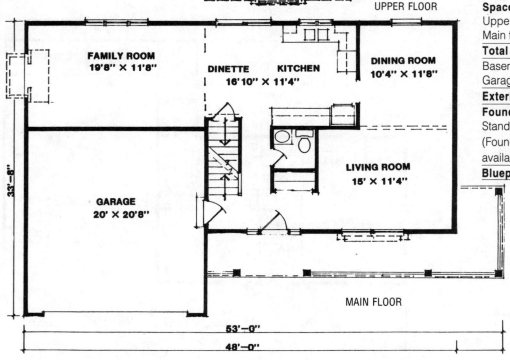

MAIN FLOOR

TO ORDER THIS BLUEPRINT, CALL TOLL-FREE 1-800-547-5570

Plan GL-1597

Spacious Country Kitchen

Main floor:	834 sq. ft.
Upper floor:	722 sq. ft.
Total living area:	1,556 sq. ft.
(Not counting basement or garage)	

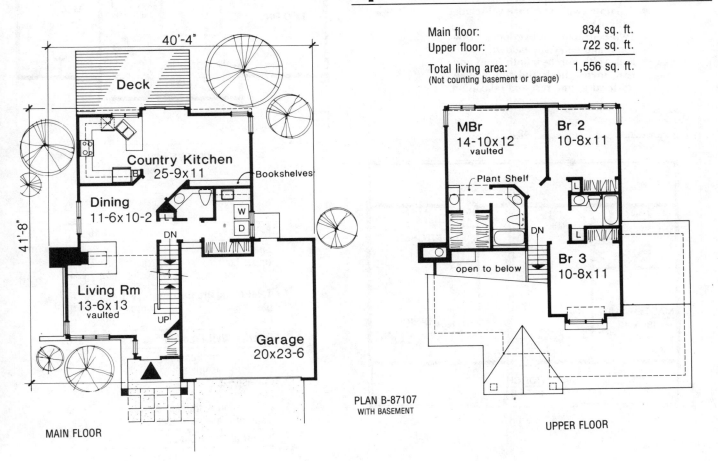

MAIN FLOOR

40'-4"

41'-8"

Deck

Country Kitchen
25-9x11

Bookshelves

Dining
11-6x10-2

W
D

DN

Living Rm
13-6x13
vaulted

UP

Garage
20x23-6

PLAN B-87107
WITH BASEMENT

MBr
14-10x12
vaulted

Br 2
10-8x11

Plant Shelf

DN

open to below

Br 3
10-8x11

UPPER FLOOR

Blueprint Price Code B

Plan B-87107

**TO ORDER THIS BLUEPRINT,
CALL TOLL-FREE 1-800-547-5570**
(prices and details on pp. 12-15.)

Compact, Cozy, Inviting

- Liberal-sized living room is centrally located and features corner fireplace and sloped ceilings.
- Separate two-car garage is included with plan.
- Two-bedroom loft overlooks living room and entryway below.
- Full-width porches, both front and rear, invite guests and family alike for leisure time rest and relaxation.

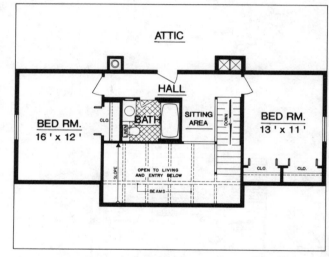

UPPER FLOOR

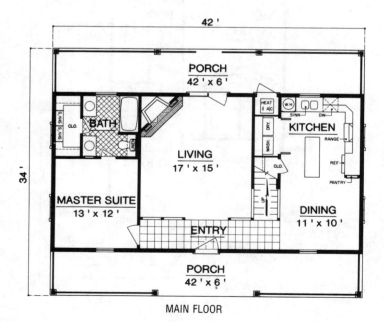

MAIN FLOOR

Plan E-1421

Bedrooms: 3	Baths: 2

Space:

Upper floor:	561 sq. ft.
Main floor:	924 sq. ft.

Total living area:	**1,485 sq. ft.**
Basement:	approx. 924 sq. ft.
Porches:	504 sq. ft.

Exterior Wall Framing:	2x6

Foundation options:
Standard basement.
Crawlspace.
Slab.
(Foundation & framing conversion diagram available — see order form.)

Blueprint Price Code: A

Plan E-1421

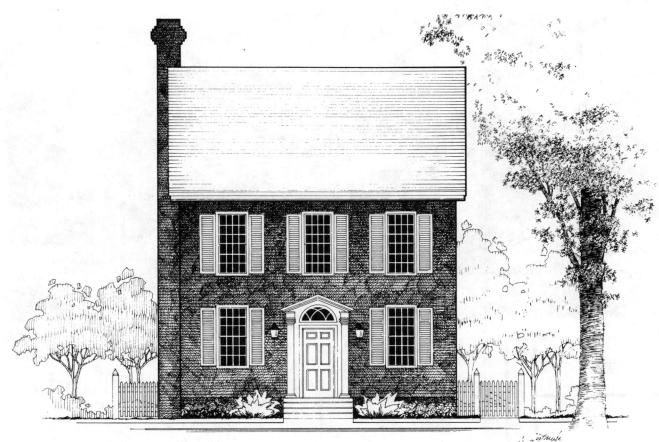

Stately Charm for Small Lot

Small but stately, this charming dwelling with its classic and perfectly proportioned lines is ideal for a diminutive lot in an urban setting. Economical to construct, this enchanting design will generate compliments from all who see it. The generously sized living room appears even larger than it is, due to the open-stringed stairway which rises from it. The formal dining room, framed by a large cased opening, is filled with light from its long windows.

The master bedroom suite supplies the owners with a particularly inviting bath. A well-placed skylight will flood the dressing area with light. If desired, the owners could postpone the completion of the second floor until the expansion of their family requires additional space.

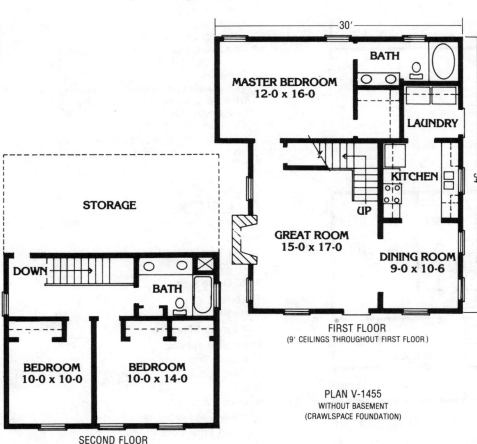

FIRST FLOOR
(9' CEILINGS THROUGHOUT FIRST FLOOR)

SECOND FLOOR
(8' CEILINGS ON SECOND FLOOR)

PLAN V-1455
WITHOUT BASEMENT
(CRAWLSPACE FOUNDATION)

First floor:	936 sq. ft.
Second floor:	519 sq. ft.
Total living area:	1,455 sq. ft.

Blueprint Price Code A

Plan V-1455

***TO ORDER THIS BLUEPRINT,
CALL TOLL-FREE 1-800-547-5570***
(prices and details on pp. 12-15.) **109**

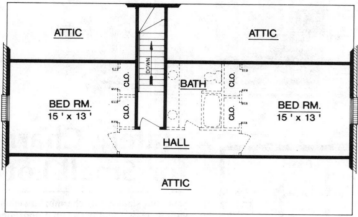

UPPER FLOOR

MAIN FLOOR

Stately Veranda

- This relatively compact home boasts a stately, full-width veranda and an efficient, functional floor plan.
- The front-facing kitchen opens to a dining area, which flows into the living room for an open, airy effect.
- The living room offers easy access to a rear deck, and features a cozy fireplace as well.
- The master suite includes a dressing room, a large walk-in closet and access to a private deck.
- The upper level, which can be left unfinished until needed, offers space for two more bedrooms and another full bath.

Plan E-1317

Bedrooms: 2-4	Baths: 1-2
Space:	
Upper floor	656 sq. ft.
Main floor	1,384 sq. ft.
Total Living Area	**2,040 sq. ft.**
Basement	1,440 sq. ft.
Storage	56 sq. ft.
Exterior Wall Framing	2x6

Foundation options:
Standard Basement
Crawlspace
Slab
(Foundation & framing conversion diagram available—see order form.)

Blueprint Price Code	C

Plan E-1317

Compact Three-Bedroom Home

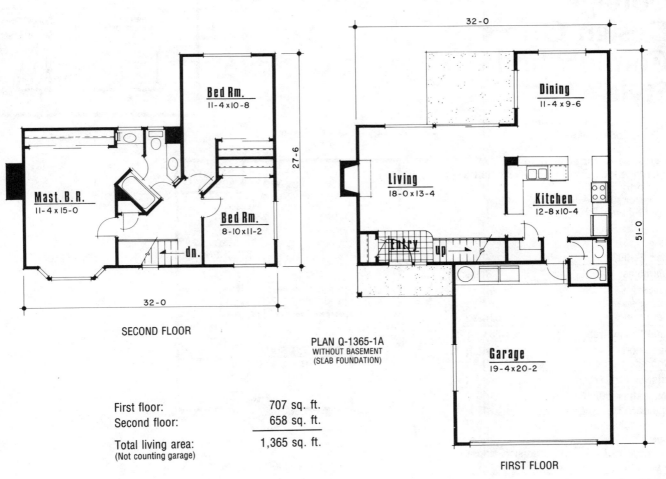

SECOND FLOOR

- Bed Rm. 11-4 x 10-8
- Mast. B.R. 11-4 x 15-0
- Bed Rm. 8-10 x 11-2
- dn.
- 27-6
- 32-0

PLAN Q-1365-1A
WITHOUT BASEMENT
(SLAB FOUNDATION)

First floor: 707 sq. ft.
Second floor: 658 sq. ft.

Total living area: 1,365 sq. ft.
(Not counting garage)

- 32-0
- Dining 11-4 x 9-6
- Living 18-0 x 13-4
- Kitchen 12-8 x 10-4
- Entry
- up
- Garage 19-4 x 20-2
- 51-0

FIRST FLOOR

Blueprint Price Code A

Plan Q-1365-1A

TO ORDER THIS BLUEPRINT,
CALL TOLL-FREE 1-800-547-5570
(prices and details on pp. 12-15.) 111

Cottage Design Offers Comfort and Style

- Upper balcony bedroom overlooks living room below.
- Combined living/dining area makes great space for entertaining.
- Unique kitchen arrangement includes laundry area.
- Master suite features bay window sitting area.

Plan E-1002

Bedrooms: 1-2	Baths: 2
Space:	
Upper floor	267 sq. ft.
Main floor	814 sq. ft.
Total Living Area	**1,081 sq. ft.**
Basement	814 sq. ft.
Unheated area	59 sq. ft.
Exterior Wall Framing	2x4

Foundation options:
Standard Basement
Crawlspace
Slab
(Foundation & framing conversion diagram available—see order form.)

Blueprint Price Code	A

UPPER FLOOR

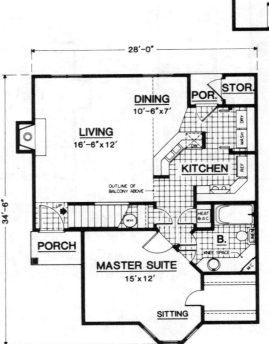

MAIN FLOOR

Plan E-1002

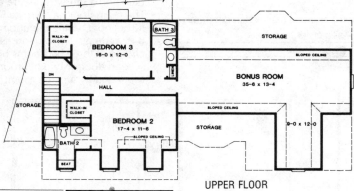

UPPER FLOOR

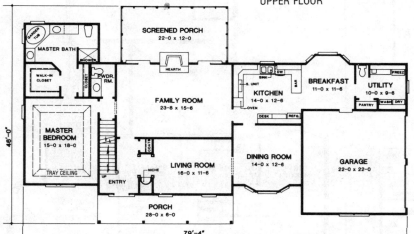

MAIN FLOOR

Deluxe Main-Floor Master Suite

- Traditional-style exterior with modern floor plan. Dormers and stone add curb appeal to this home.
- Formal entry with staircase leads to formal living or large family room.
- Large kitchen is conveniently located between formal dining room and secluded breakfast nook with bay window.
- Private master suite has tray ceiling and walk-in closet. Master bath has corner tub, shower, and dual vanities.
- Large screened porch off family room is perfect for outdoor living.
- Large utility room with pantry and toilet are conveniently located off the garage.
- Second floor features two large bedrooms with walk-in closets and two full baths.
- Optional bonus room (624 sq. ft.) can be finished as a large game room, bedroom, office, etc.

Plan C-8915

Bedrooms: 3	Baths: 3½

Space:

Upper floor:	832 sq. ft.
Main floor:	1,927 sq. ft.
Bonus area:	624 sq. ft.
Total living area:	**3,383 sq. ft.**
Basement:	1,674 sq. ft.
Garage:	484 sq. ft.

Exterior Wall Framing:	2x4

Ceiling Heights:

First floor:	9'
Second floor:	8'

Foundation options:
Daylight basement.
Crawlspace.
(Foundation & framing conversion diagram available — see order form.)

Blueprint Price Code:	E

Plan C-8915

Fill Your Life with Sunshine

- This home is as warm and inviting on the inside as it is on the outside. Two fireplaces, lots of sunny living spaces and a superb master suite are among its many attributes.
- The master suite claims one of the fireplaces, plus offers a luxurious bath and twin walk-in closets. French doors lead both to the rear garden and to the relaxing front porch.
- The living room hosts the remaining fireplace and also has French doors opening to the front porch. The adjoining dining room includes an elegant bow window.
- The kitchen and the breakfast room overlook an inviting sun room. A half-bath and a utility room are close by.
- The main floor has 9-ft. ceilings throughout, while the upper floor has 8-ft. ceilings. The blueprints include a choice of three bedrooms on the second floor or two bedrooms separated by a game room.

Plan J-91068

Bedrooms: 3-4	**Baths:** 2½

Space:

Upper floor	893 sq. ft.
Main floor	1,947 sq. ft.
Total Living Area	**2,840 sq. ft.**
Basement	1,947 sq. ft.
Garage	441 sq. ft.
Exterior Wall Framing	**2x4**

Foundation options:

Standard Basement
Crawlspace
Slab
(Foundation & framing conversion diagram available—see order form.)

Blueprint Price Code　　　　　**D**

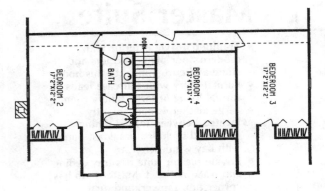

UPPER FLOOR
WITH THREE BEDROOMS

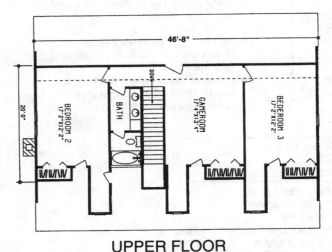

UPPER FLOOR
WITH TWO BEDROOMS AND GAME ROOM

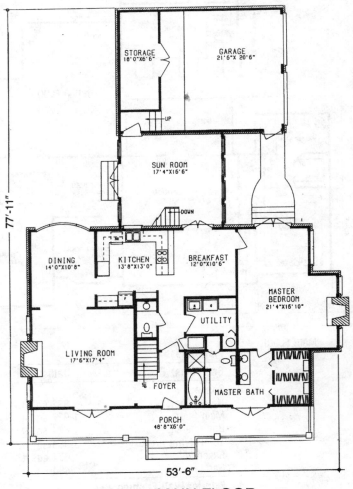

MAIN FLOOR

TO ORDER THIS BLUEPRINT,
CALL TOLL-FREE 1-800-547-5570

Plan J-91068

Modern Country Charm

- A double-deck veranda combines with modern touches to create an eye-catching design.
- A central two-story foyer with wrap-around balcony provides access to the upper-level veranda.
- Formal living and dining rooms are positioned at the front of the home for gracious entertaining.
- The casual family area in the rear features a large kitchen/nook combination.

- A spacious family room includes a cozy fireplace.
- A deluxe master bedroom suite upstairs includes a luxurious private bath and a large walk-in closet.
- Three other bedrooms and a bath complete the second floor, with the front bedroom boasting a vaulted ceiling and a striking Palladian window arrangement.

Plan N-1219	
Bedrooms: 4	**Baths:** 2½
Living Area:	
Upper floor	1,369 sq. ft.
Main floor	1,428 sq. ft.
Total Living Area:	**2,797 sq. ft.**
Standard basement	1,428 sq. ft.
Garage	491 sq. ft.
Exterior Wall Framing:	2x4
Foundation Options:	
Standard basement (Typical foundation & framing conversion diagram available—see order form.)	
BLUEPRINT PRICE CODE:	D

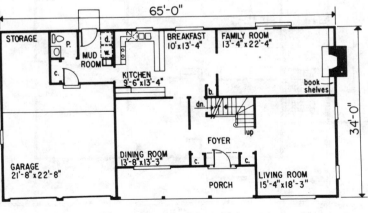

MAIN FLOOR

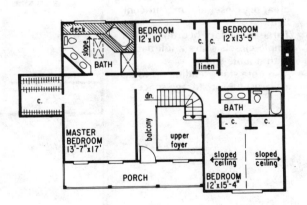

UPPER FLOOR

Plan N-1219

(prices and details on pp. 12-15.)

Classic Country-Style Home

- Almost completely surrounded by an expansive wrap-around porch that measures almost 1,200 sq. ft., this classic plan exudes warmth and grace.
- The foyer is liberal in size and leads guests to a formal dining room at left or the large living room at right.
- A large country kitchen includes a sunny, bay-windowed breakfast nook.
- The main floor also includes a utility area and full bath.
- Upstairs, the master suite is impressive, with its large sleeping area, big closet and magnificent bath.
- Three secondary bedrooms with ample closets share a full bath with double sinks.
- Also note stairs leading up to an attic, useful for storage space.

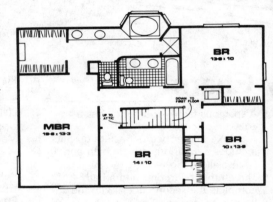

UPPER FLOOR

Plan J-86134

Bedrooms: 4	Baths: 3

Space:

Upper floor:	1,195 sq. ft.
Main floor:	1,370 sq. ft.

Total living area:	2,565 sq. ft.
Basement:	1,370 sq. ft.
Garage:	576 sq. ft.
Storage:	144 sq. ft.
Porch:	1,181 sq. ft.

Exterior Wall Framing:	2x4

Foundation options:
Standard basement.
Crawlspace.
Slab.
(Foundation & framing conversion diagram available — see order form.)

Blueprint Price Code:	D

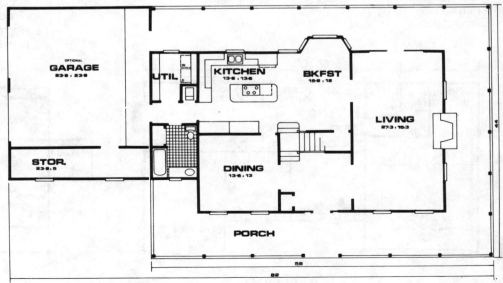

MAIN FLOOR

Plan J-86134

Two-Story Bay Window

- A two-story bay window and Victorian design elements give a special character to this family-oriented home.
- A large living room and a dining room are great for formal entertaining, while a spacious family room offers opportunities for a more casual style.
- A bright breakfast nook adjoins an efficient U-shaped kitchen.
- Upstairs, a large, bay-windowed master bedroom includes a private bath and two closets.
- Three secondary bedrooms all have large closets and share another full bath.

Plan N-1213

Bedrooms: 4	Baths: 2½
Living Area:	
Upper floor	1,221 sq. ft.
Main floor	1,333 sq. ft.
Total Living Area:	**2,554 sq. ft.**
Standard basement	1,333 sq. ft.
Garage	455 sq. ft.
Exterior Wall Framing:	2x4

Foundation Options:
Standard basement
Crawlspace
Slab
(Typical foundation & framing conversion diagram available—see order form.)

BLUEPRINT PRICE CODE:	D

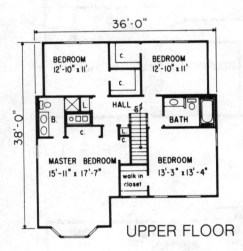

UPPER FLOOR

WITHOUT BASEMENT

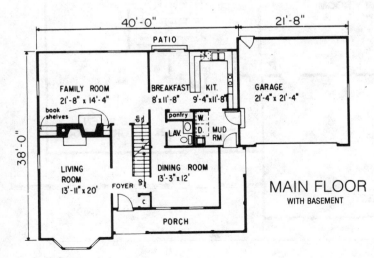

MAIN FLOOR
WITH BASEMENT

Plan N-1213

Style and Function

- Equally at home in suburban or pastoral settings, this traditional design exudes both style and function.
- The friendly front porch, shuttered windows and wood siding accented with stone veneer give the home stylish presence.
- Inside, a spacious foyer opens to a sunken Great Room. Straight ahead, double doors lead to the large family living spaces at the rear of the home.
- The sunken family room offers a vaulted ceiling, a fireplace and French doors that open to a patio or deck. The bayed breakfast area is open to the kitchen, which in turn extends into the formal dining room.
- The upper level includes a laundry room and a multi-purpose bonus room, in addition to three bedrooms and two baths. The master suite offers a spacious sleeping area and a private bath that includes a walk-in closet, dual-sink vanity, garden tub and separate shower.

Plan APS-2116

Bedrooms: 3-4	Baths: 2 ½
Space:	
Upper floor	925 sq. ft.
Main floor	1,225 sq. ft.
Optional Bonus Room	276 sq. ft.
Total Living Area	**2,426 sq. ft.**
Garage	441 sq. ft.
Exterior Wall Framing	2x4

Foundation options:
Crawlspace
Slab
(Foundation & framing conversion diagram available—see order form.)

Blueprint Price Code	C

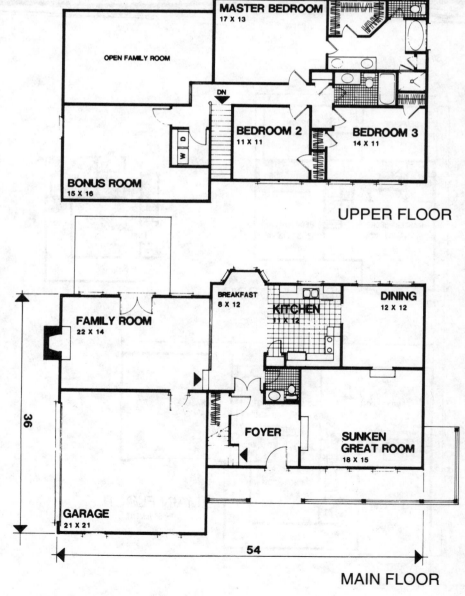

UPPER FLOOR

MAIN FLOOR

Plan APS-2116

***TO ORDER THIS BLUEPRINT,
CALL TOLL-FREE 1-800-547-5570***

Impressive, Surprising Victorian

- This impressive Victorian is full of surprises — from its spectacular gazebo-style porch at the left to its second-floor laundry room.
- The spacious main floor includes an impressive foyer, a huge activity room, formal living and dining rooms, a large kitchen and a sunny breakfast area.
- An angled stairway leads to the second floor, which includes three bedrooms, two baths and a laundry area, not to mention a balcony overlooking the foyer below.
- The master suite is majestic, with a huge sleeping room, a sitting area, two walk-in closets and a deluxe master bath.

Plan N-1298

Bedrooms: 3	Baths: 2½
Living Area:	
Upper floor	1,089 sq. ft.
Main floor	1,281 sq. ft.
Total Living Area:	**2,370 sq. ft.**
Standard basement	1,281 sq. ft.
Garage (optional)	462 sq. ft.
Exterior Wall Framing:	2x4

Foundation Options:

Standard basement
(Typical foundation & framing conversion diagram available—see order form.)

BLUEPRINT PRICE CODE:	C

UPPER FLOOR

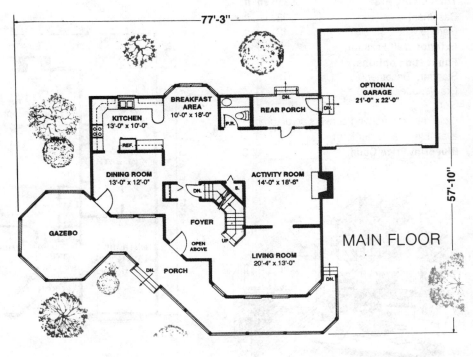

MAIN FLOOR

Plan N-1298

Flamboyant Floor Plan

- A host of architectural styles went into the making of this interesting design, from country and Victorian to contemporary. A mixture of gable and hip roofs, a bayed front porch and several differently shaped windows give the exterior plenty of impact.
- A dramatic open floor plan combines to make the home stylishly up to date. High ceilings throughout much of the main level add to the flamboyant floor plan.
- The fantastic family room features a soaring ceiling, a fireplace and an abundance of windows. The adjoining breakfast room has a cathedral ceiling and is open to the kitchen. The attached sun porch is enclosed in glass, with skylights in the sloped ceiling. Formal dining is reserved for the unusual dining room at the front of the home.
- The first-floor master suite boasts a cathedral ceiling, lots of closet space and an irresistible garden tub.
- Three bedrooms and a full bath make up the second level. Each of the bedrooms has a walk-in closet.

Plan AX-1318

Bedrooms: 4	Baths: 2 ½
Space:	
Upper floor	697 sq. ft.
Main floor	1,642 sq. ft.
Total Living Area	**2,339 sq. ft.**
Basement	1,384 sq. ft.
Garage	431 sq. ft.
Exterior Wall Framing	**2x4**

Foundation options:
Standard Basement
Crawlspace
Slab
(Foundation & framing conversion diagram available—see order form.)

Blueprint Price Code	C

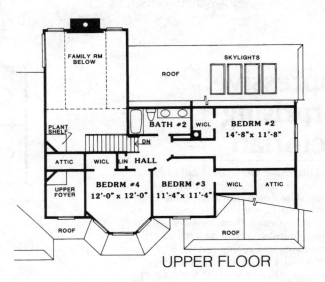

UPPER FLOOR

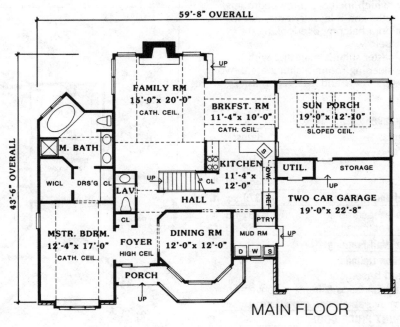

MAIN FLOOR

Plan AX-1318

Updated Traditional

- The traditional front of this home offers a mixture of brick and siding for a warm, inviting look.
- The efficient floor plan is introduced by a spectacular foyer with a vaulted ceiling and an open stairway that leads to an overhead balcony.
- The spacious family living areas are grouped at the rear of the home. The centrally located kitchen is embraced by two dining areas.
- The formal dining room flows into the living room for elegant entertaining. The dinette, separated from the kitchen by a snack bar and a pantry closet, adjoins the family room for informal occasions.
- The family room is destined to be a favorite gathering place, with its enticing fireplace, high ceiling and window wall overlooking the backyard.
- Main-floor laundry facilities and a half-bath are easily reached from both the garage entrance and the main hall.
- The second-story balcony provides a stunning view of the foyer below. The oversized master bedroom is complemented by a private bath with whirlpool tub and a walk-in closet.
- The three smaller bedrooms share a second full bath.

UPPER FLOOR

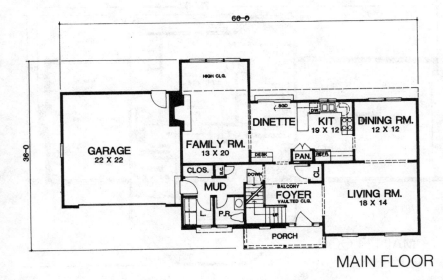

MAIN FLOOR

Plan A-2147-DS	
Bedrooms: 4	**Baths:** 2 ½
Space:	
Upper floor	1,104 sq. ft.
Main floor	1,196 sq. ft.
Total Living Area	**2,300 sq. ft.**
Basement	1,196 sq. ft.
Garage	484 sq. ft.
Exterior Wall Framing	2x6
Foundation options:	
Standard Basement	
(Foundation & framing conversion diagram available—see order form.)	
Blueprint Price Code	C

Plan A-2147-DS

Stately Victorian

- An inviting wraparound porch beckons visitors and family alike to "come in and sit a spell."
- Inside, a gorgeous formal dining room is the focal point, and a large living room includes sloped ceilings and a fireplace.
- A spacious family room adjoins a sunny breakfast nook and a roomy kitchen.
- Upstairs, the palatial master bedroom suite includes a luxurious bath and a large walk-in closet.
- Three secondary bedrooms share another full bath. Also note the laundry area in the upstairs hallway.

Plan N-1308

Bedrooms: 4	Baths: 2½
Living Area:	
Upper floor	1,049 sq. ft.
Main floor	1,231 sq. ft.
Total Living Area:	**2,280 sq. ft.**
Standard basement	1,231 sq. ft.
Garage	504 sq. ft.
Exterior Wall Framing:	2x4

Foundation Options:
Standard basement
(Typical foundation & framing conversion diagram available—see order form.)

BLUEPRINT PRICE CODE: C

UPPER FLOOR

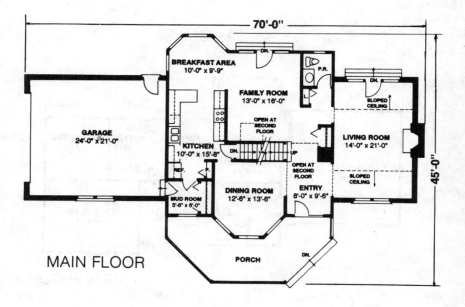

MAIN FLOOR

Plan N-1308

Traditional Cape Cod

- A covered front porch and a pair of dormers add old-fashioned charm to this traditional Cape Cod design.
- The two-story-high foyer opens up to a large vaulted living room through an arched opening. The living room is accented by a transom window and a fireplace.
- The open kitchen, nook and family room arrangement at the rear of the home features a convenient cooktop island, a cozy breakfast alcove, a wood stove and an adjoining deck.
- The master bedroom on the upper level has a private den, a bath with dual vanities and a large walk-in closet.
- Two additional bedrooms, a skylighted main bath and a handy laundry room are also included on the upper floor.
- Room for a future bedroom, bath and recreation room is found on the lower walkout level.

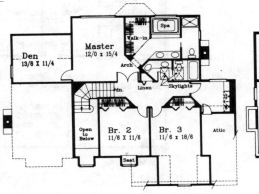

UPPER FLOOR

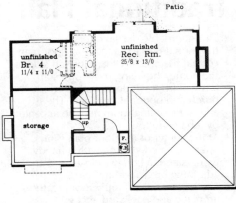

DAYLIGHT BASEMENT

Plan CDG-2034

Bedrooms: 3-4	Baths: 2½-3½
Living Area:	
Upper floor	1,060 sq. ft.
Main floor	1,123 sq. ft.
Total Living Area:	**2,183 sq. ft.**
Daylight basement	1,029 sq. ft.
Garage	568 sq. ft.
Exterior Wall Framing:	2x4

Foundation Options:
Daylight basement
Slab
(Typical foundation & framing conversion diagram available—see order form.)

BLUEPRINT PRICE CODE: C

MAIN FLOOR

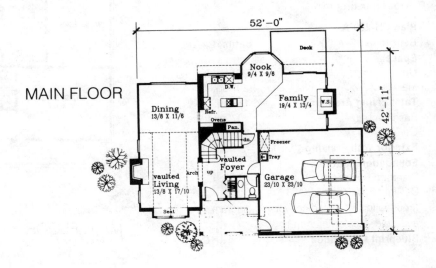

Plan CDG-2034

Modern Features with Traditional Flair

- This affordable design offers a traditional flair to its modern floor plan.
- Formal living areas share the left side of the home; the living room offers an array of front windows that overlook the porch and optional fireplace. The adjoining dining room may be accented by a bay window.
- At the center of the floor plan is an open, updated kitchen with a handy work island, a laundry closet and an adjoining breakfast bay.
- The large vaulted family room features a fireplace and backyard access.
- The sleeping area on the upper level includes a vaulted master bedroom with private garden bath, generous closet space and an optional sitting room entered through double doors. The sitting room may also be used as a fourth bedroom.

Plan CH-230-A

Bedrooms: 3-4	Baths: 2½
Space:	
Upper floor	971 sq. ft.
Main floor	1,207 sq. ft.
Total Living Area	**2,178 sq. ft.**
Basement	1,207 sq. ft.
Garage	400 sq. ft.
Exterior Wall Framing	2x4
Foundation options:	
Standard Basement	
Daylight Basement	

(Foundation & framing conversion diagram available—see order form.)

Blueprint Price Code	C

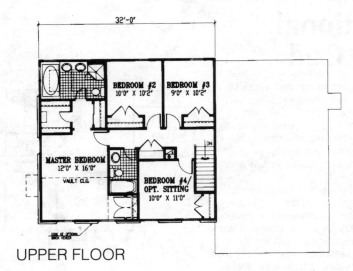

UPPER FLOOR

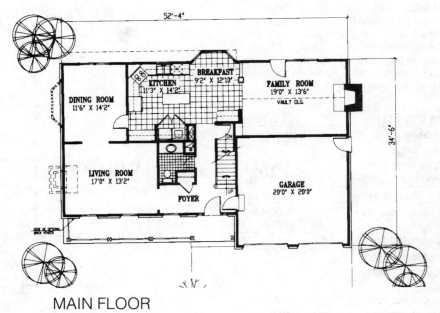

MAIN FLOOR

Plan CH-230-A

Classy Country-Style Home

- Modest in size but big on living space, this home has lots of class.
- The classic country exterior is refined by the archway leading to the front porch and the elegant entry door topped by an arched window.
- The vaulted foyer opens to the formal dining room, framed by stylish columns. Straight ahead are the living room, breakfast nook and kitchen, which are fashioned using the open Great Room concept.
- The living room focuses on a central fireplace with a French door on one side and a window on the other. The breakfast nook overlooks the rear patio and is open to both the living room and the kitchen. The walk-through kitchen also provides easy access to the formal dining room.
- The main-floor master suite includes two walk-in closets, a double vanity, a luxurious garden tub and a separate shower.
- The upper level features two spacious bedrooms that share a hall bath. The optional bonus room above the garage is reached by back stairs located off the laundry area on the main level.

Plan APS-1712

Bedrooms: 3-4	Baths: 2 ½
Space:	
Upper floor	532 sq. ft.
Main floor	1,215 sq. ft.
Optional Bonus Room	398 sq. ft.
Total Living Area	**2,145 sq. ft.**
Garage	440 sq. ft.
Exterior Wall Framing	2x4
Foundation options:	
Crawlspace	
Slab	
(Foundation & framing conversion diagram available—see order form.)	
Blueprint Price Code	C

UPPER FLOOR

BEDROOM 2
14 X 12

BEDROOM 3
12 X 12

BONUS ROOM
22 X 17

OPEN TO FOYER

MAIN FLOOR

PATIO

LIVING
15 X 16

BREAKFAST

W D

STORAGE

KITCHEN

GARAGE
22 X 20

MASTER BEDROOM
14 X 14

DINING
14 X 10

58

35

Plan APS-1712

TO ORDER THIS BLUEPRINT,
CALL TOLL-FREE 1-800-547-5570
(prices and details on pp. 12-15.) **125**

Cozy Country Victorian

- This plan exudes a warm, cozy look that is attractive to family and passers-by alike.
- The spacious, house-spanning porch invites visitors into a central foyer that distributes traffic efficiently to the living room, dining room or recreation room.
- The large kitchen is adjoined on the left by a large, bright breakfast area, which offers easy access to a screened porch.
- Upstairs, a magnificent master bedroom boasts a deluxe master bath and a large walk-in closet.
- Two secondary bedrooms share a second full bath, and a large storage space is also located on the second floor.

Plan N-1305

Bedrooms: 3	Baths: 2½
Living Area:	
Upper floor	847 sq. ft.
Main floor	1,162 sq. ft.
Total Living Area:	**2,009 sq. ft.**
Standard basement	1,162 sq. ft.
Exterior Wall Framing:	2x4

Foundation Options:

Standard basement
(Typical foundation & framing conversion diagram available—see order form.)

BLUEPRINT PRICE CODE: C

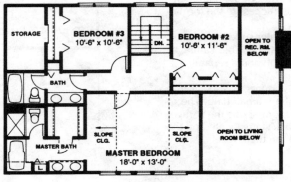

UPPER FLOOR

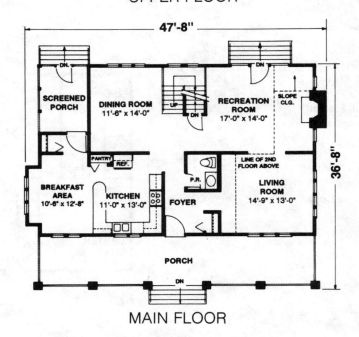

MAIN FLOOR

Plan N-1305

Affordable Victorian

- With its modest size and simple construction, this plan offers affordable space in a classic design.
- A cozy veranda leads into a central hallway, with a roomy activity area, a dining room and a family room on the left.
- To the right is an efficient kitchen with a large pantry, plus a half-bath and an inviting back porch.
- The upstairs consists of two bedrooms and a large, compartmentalized bath. Also note the private balcony off the bay-windowed master bedroom.

Plan N-1295	
Bedrooms: 2	**Baths:** 1½
Living Area:	
Upper floor	570 sq. ft.
Main floor	1,092 sq. ft.
Total Living Area:	**1,662 sq. ft.**
Standard basement	1,092 sq. ft.
Exterior Wall Framing:	2x4
Foundation Options:	
Standard basement	
(Typical foundation & framing conversion diagram available—see order form.)	
BLUEPRINT PRICE CODE:	**B**

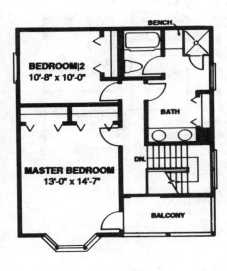

MAIN FLOOR

26'-0"

44'-0"

FAMILY ROOM
13'-0" x 11'-6"

DN.

BACK PORCH

P.R.

DINING ROOM
13'-0" x 10'-0"

REF.

KITCHEN
8'-3" x 10'-0"

PANTRY

ACTIVITY AREA
13'-0" x 17'-1"

DN.
UP

VERANDA

DN.

UPPER FLOOR

BENCH

BEDROOM 2
10'-8" x 10'-0"

BATH

MASTER BEDROOM
13'-0" x 14'-7"

DN.

BALCONY

Plan N-1295

A Ranch with Distinction

- A covered front porch supported by pillars gives a formal appearance to this distinguished one-story.
- Flanking the foyer is a study or fourth bedroom and formal living and dining rooms.
- The big family room at the rear shares views of a covered porch with the adjoining breakfast room; the family room also has a sloped ceiling centered over a warming fireplace.
- A modern, island kitchen sits between the morning room and the dining room for convenient service to both. A half-bath and laundry room are nearby.
- A 10-foot-high gambrel ceiling and rear window wall highlight the generous-sized master bedroom. Its private bath features his 'n her vanities, walk-in closets and a garden tub.

Plan DD-2606

Bedrooms: 3-4	Baths: 2½
Space:	
Main floor	2,606 sq. ft.
Total Living Area	**2,606 sq. ft.**
Basement	2,606 sq. ft.
Garage	393 sq. ft.
Exterior Wall Framing	2x4

Foundation options:
Standard Basement
Crawlspace
Slab
(Foundation & framing conversion diagram available—see order form.)

Blueprint Price Code	D

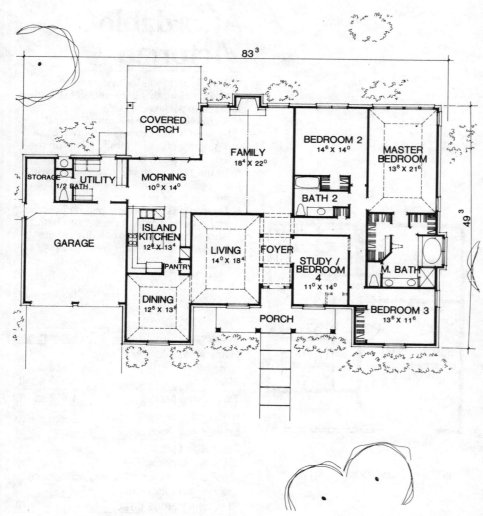

COVERED PORCH

FAMILY
18⁴ X 22⁰

BEDROOM 2
14⁶ X 14⁰

MASTER BEDROOM
13⁸ X 21⁶

STORAGE

UTILITY
1/2 BATH

MORNING
10⁰ X 14⁰

BATH 2

ISLAND KITCHEN
12⁸ X 13⁴

GARAGE

PANTRY

LIVING
14⁰ X 18⁴

FOYER

M. BATH

STUDY / BEDROOM 4
11⁰ X 14⁰

DINING
12⁸ X 13⁶

PORCH

BEDROOM 3
13⁶ X 11⁶

83³

49³

Plan DD-2606

Great Garden Home

- This four-bedroom ranch home is especially great for outdoor lovers. The angled design offers more flexiblity in orienting the home to its site, allowing you to take best advantage of the view. The interior spaces feature lots of glass, bringing the outdoors in,.
- All of the home's living areas revolve around the eye-catching family room. Floor-to-ceiling windows virtually surround the octagonal room, with a spectacular two-way fireplace separating the family room from the living room. Exposed beams in the cathedral ceiling give the room even more impact, and sliding glass doors open to the large rear patio.
- The kitchen and dinette also face the patio. The kitchen has corner windows while the entire rear wall of the dinette is glass. A laundry room and half-bath are stationed near the back door.
- The sleeping wing includes four bedrooms and two full baths. The master bedroom is huge, with a walk-in closet and a private bath.

PATIO

sl. gl. dr.

FAMILY RM
(cathedral ceiling)
26'-8" x 23'-0"

service

dw

DINETTE
13'-0" x 7'-10"

s.

range top

KITCH
13'-0" x 9'-6"

LAV.

ref. — ov.

exposed beams

2-way fireplace

TWO CAR GARAGE
20'-0" x 20'-0"

dn

MUD RM

laundry

DINING RM
13'-6" x 12'-0"

FOYER

STORAGE
bicycles etc.

trellis above

LIVING RM
19'-0" x 13'-0"

BATH

powder rm.

BATH

BED RM
11'-0"x10'-0"

HALL

lin.

walk-in closet

MASTER BED RM
18'-0" x 13'-0"

BED RM
12'-0"x10'-0"

BED RM
12'-4"x11'-2"

77'-0"

97'-10"

Plan HFL-1280-LY

Bedrooms: 3-4	**Baths:** 2 ½

Space:

Main floor	2,495 sq. ft.
Total Living Area	**2,495 sq. ft.**
Partial Basement	954 sq. ft.
Garage	400 sq. ft.
Exterior Wall Framing	**2x4**

Foundation options:

Partial Basement

Crawlspace

Slab

(Foundation & framing conversion diagram available—see order form.)

Blueprint Price Code	**C**

Plan HFL-1280-LY

Delightful Details

- The living and informal dining areas are oriented to the rear of this traditional ranch.
- Sliders in both the family room and the breakfast room access a rear patio. The family room also showcases a two-way fireplace shared with the adjoining sunken living room. Both rooms offer functional built-in shelving.
- The big foyer opens to a sunken formal dining room. The dining room's entry is flanked with decorative railings. The open kitchen handily services both the dining room and the breakfast room.
- A large walk-in closet and a generous private bath border the master bedroom for added privacy. The two secondary bedrooms are located opposite the main hallway.

Plan AX-9707

Bedrooms: 3	Baths: 2 ½

Space:

Main floor	2,451 sq. ft.
Total Living Area	**2,451 sq. ft.**
Garage	440 sq. ft.
Exterior Wall Framing	2x4

Foundation options:

Slab

(Foundation & framing conversion diagram available—see order form.)

Blueprint Price Code	C

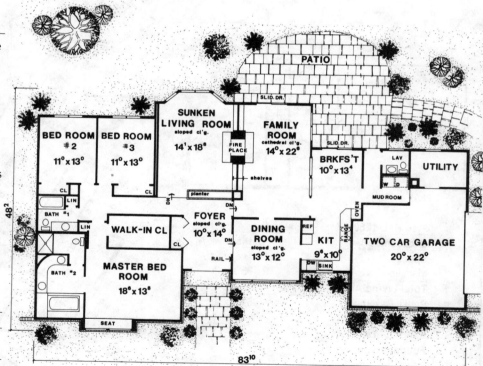

Plan AX-9707

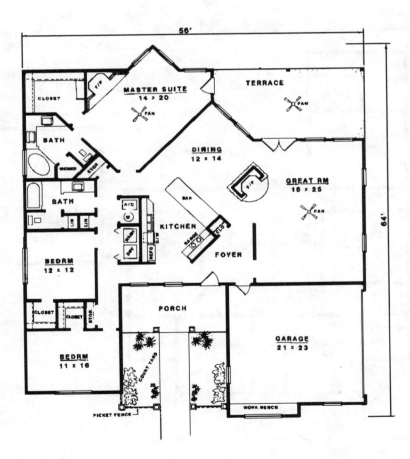

Attractive Angles

- Unique angles and open circulation is the theme for this traditional Early American styled home.
- Centered around a stone fireplace are the foyer, Great Room, dining room and angled kitchen with counter bar, all with a rear view to the terrace and backyard.
- The unique angles carry through to the exciting master suite, which offers its own cozy fireplace, panoramic rear view and private access to the terrace; the colorful master bath offers a garden tub, twin vanities and separate shower.
- A nice hall bath, convenient laundry facilities and two more bedrooms complete the floor plan.

Plan VL-2121

Bedrooms: 3	Baths: 2
Space:	
Main floor	2,121 sq. ft.
Total Living Area	**2,121 sq. ft.**
Garage	483 sq. ft.
Exterior Wall Framing	2x4
Foundation options:	
Crawlspace	
Slab	
(Foundation & framing conversion diagram available—see order form.)	
Blueprint Price Code	C

Plan VL-2121

Oriented for a View to the Rear

- While this plan offers an attractive and cozy-looking front view, it is especially designed for settings with a view to the rear.
- The rooms used most frequently are located in the rear, and offer easy access to a large deck or porch.
- The spacious Great Room includes a large fireplace and windows to the rear.
- A convenient kitchen area features a laundry room on one end and a breakfast nook on the other. A large walk-in pantry connects the kitchen to the garage.
- A deluxe master suite includes a bath with separate tub and shower, plus a walk-in closet.

Plan V-2088	
Bedrooms: 3	**Baths:** 2
Space:	
Main floor	2,088 sq. ft.
Total Living Area	**2,088 sq. ft.**
Garage	540 sq. ft.
Exterior Wall Framing	2x6
Foundation options:	
Crawlspace	
(Foundation & framing conversion diagram available—see order form.)	
Blueprint Price Code	C

TO ORDER THIS BLUEPRINT,
CALL TOLL-FREE 1-800-547-5570

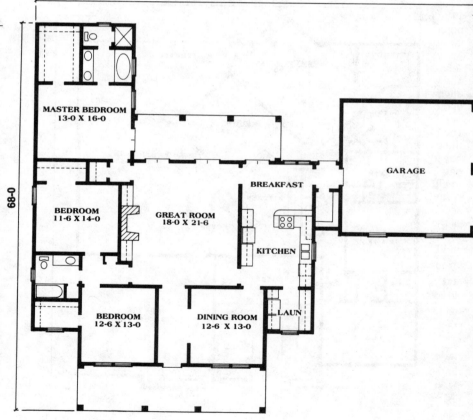

MAIN FLOOR

75-0

68-0

MASTER BEDROOM
13-0 X 16-0

BEDROOM
11-6 X 14-0

GREAT ROOM
18-0 X 21-6

BREAKFAST

KITCHEN

GARAGE

BEDROOM
12-6 X 13-0

DINING ROOM
12-6 X 13-0

LAUN

Plan V-2088

Lavish Ranch

- A spectacular central living room with 11' ceiling, corner fireplace and rear porch lies at the center of this luxurious farmhouse.
- An angled eating bar is the only separation from the adjoining kitchen and bayed nook; a formal dining alternative is located on the opposite end of the kitchen, overlooking the front porch.
- The lavish master suite is separated from the other bedrooms; it boasts a private, bayed sitting area, panoramic rear view, and a bath with dual vanities and walk-in closet.
- A study, two additional bedrooms and a second full bath are located to the right of the foyer.

Plan VL-2085

Bedrooms: 3	Baths: 2 ½
Space:	
Main floor	2,085 sq. ft.
Total Living Area	**2,085 sq. ft.**
Garage	460 sq. ft.
Ceiling height:	9 ft.
Exterior Wall Framing	2x4

Foundation options:

Crawlspace

Slab

(Foundation & framing conversion diagram available—see order form.)

Blueprint Price Code	C

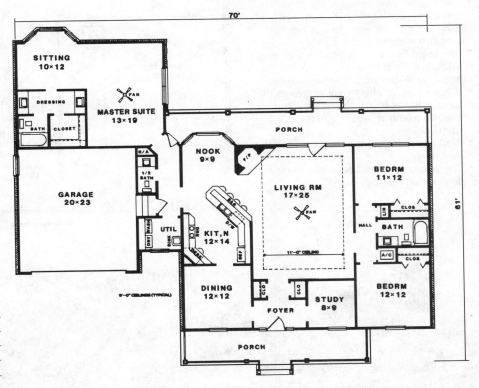

Plan VL-2085

FRONT VIEW

A Modern Charmer

- This attractive plan combines the charm of an Early American exterior with a modern interior floor plan.
- The master suite, isolated for privacy, boasts a magnificent bath with garden tub, separate shower, double vanities and two walk-in closets.
- The large living room adjoins the kitchen via a convenient snack bar, and also features a corner fireplace.
- A roomy foyer offers easy access to the formal dining room, the living room, or a study which is ideally situated for a home office.
- A sunny eating nook protrudes onto the rear porch.
- The two secondary bedrooms share a second full bath.

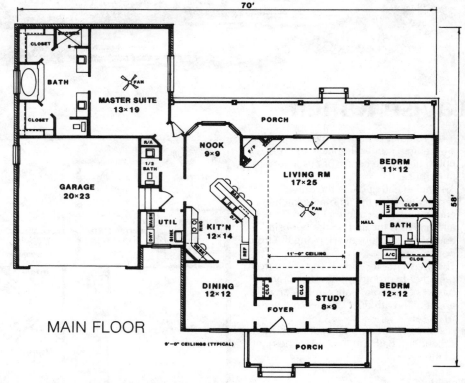

MAIN FLOOR

REAR VIEW

Plan VL-2069	
Bedrooms: 3	**Baths:** 2 ½
Space:	
Main floor	2,069 sq. ft.
Total Living Area	**2,069 sq. ft.**
Garage	460 sq. ft.
Exterior Wall Framing	2x4
Foundation options:	
Crawlspace	
Slab	
(Foundation & framing conversion diagram available—see order form.)	
Blueprint Price Code	C

Plan VL-2069

Durable and Rustic

- Durable and maintenance-free brick surrounds three sides of this rustic, ranch home; the front is finished with wood accented by stone.
- Inside, a large Great Room lies at the center of the floor plan; two of its walls act as buffers to the main hallway and bedrooms. The room offers a raised ceiling, huge corner fireplace and rear sliders to the covered porch.
- An octagonal breakfast nook is sandwiched between the fireplace and kitchen peninsula.
- A handy pantry, extra freezer and washer/dryer are conveniently located near the garage entrance.
- The private master suite has a bayed lounging area with porch access and a nice-sized bath with separate vanities, whirlpool tub and separate shower.

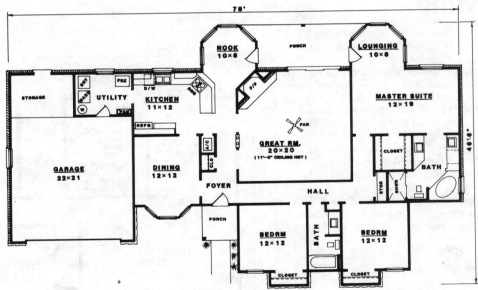

Plan VL-1997

Bedrooms: 3	Baths: 2

Space:

Main floor	1,997 sq. ft.
Total Living Area	**1,997 sq. ft.**
Garage	462 sq. ft.
Storage:	85 sq. ft.

Exterior Wall Framing   2x4

Foundation options:
Crawlspace
Slab
(Foundation & framing conversion diagram available—see order form.)

Blueprint Price Code   B

Plan VL-1997

Gracious Louisiana Styling

- This Louisiana-style home exhibits a distinct French heritage with its steeply pitched hip roof.
- Inside, an exceptionally large Great Room opens onto a formal dining room.
- The roomy kitchen includes a sunny breakfast nook as well as a snack bar. A laundry room and a pantry adjoin the kitchen.
- The master bedroom suite features a luxurious bath with a large shower and a garden tub, plus two large walk-in closets.
- Two secondary bedrooms share a compartmentalized bath with a double-bowl vanity.

Plan V-1952

Bedrooms: 3	Baths: 2

Space:	
Main floor	1,952 sq. ft.
Total Living Area	**1,952 sq. ft.**
Exterior Wall Framing	2x6

Foundation options:

Crawlspace
(Foundation & framing conversion diagram available—see order form.)

Blueprint Price Code	**B**

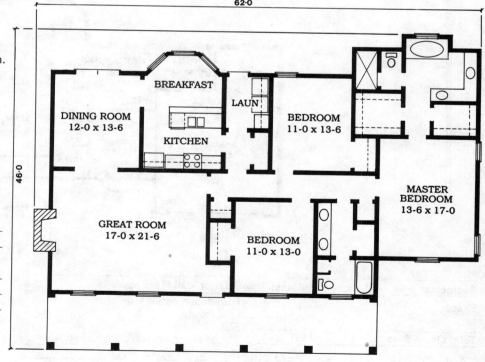

Plan V-1952

The Warmth and Charm of Stucco

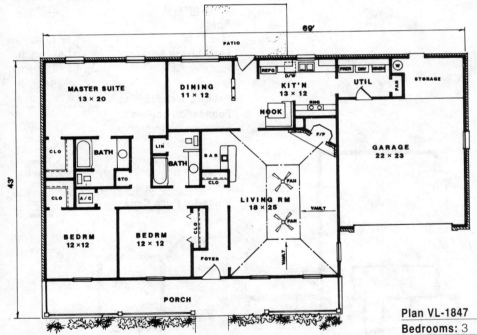

- The inviting front view features a full-width front porch and an attractive, low-maintenance stucco exterior.
- Inside, a spacious living room is made even larger by a vaulted ceiling. A large corner fireplace and a built-in wet bar are also featured.
- The roomy kitchen includes a built-in nook and adjoins a formal dining room.
- The master suite includes a private bath and a walk-in closet.
- Note the convenient utility room in the garage entry area, and the storage space in the two-car garage.

Plan VL-1847	
Bedrooms: 3	**Baths:** 2
Space:	
Main floor	1,847 sq. ft.
Total Living Area	**1,847 sq. ft.**
Garage	506 sq. ft.
Exterior Wall Framing	2x4
Foundation options:	
Crawlspace	
Slab	
(Foundation & framing conversion diagram available—see order form.)	
Blueprint Price Code	**B**

Plan VL-1847

Covered Porch Offers Three Entries

- Showy window treatments, columns and covered front and rear porches give this Southern-style home a welcoming exterior. Entry is possible through three separate front entrances.
- 12' ceilings in the living room, the dining area and the kitchen add volume to the economical 1,600+ square feet of living space.
- A corner fireplace and a rear view to the back porch are found in the living room. A counter bar separates the kitchen from the formal dining area and from the informal eating area on the opposite side.
- The private master suite offers a cathedral ceiling, a walk-in closet and a large luxury bath. Two additional bedrooms are located at the opposite end of the home and share a second bath.

Plan E-1602	
Bedrooms: 3	Baths: 2
Space:	
Main floor	1,672 sq. ft.
Total Living Area	**1,672 sq. ft.**
Basement	1,672 sq. ft.
Garage	484 sq. ft.
Exterior Wall Framing	2x6
Foundation options:	
Standard Basement	
Crawlspace	
Slab	
(Foundation & framing conversion diagram available—see order form.)	
Blueprint Price Code	B

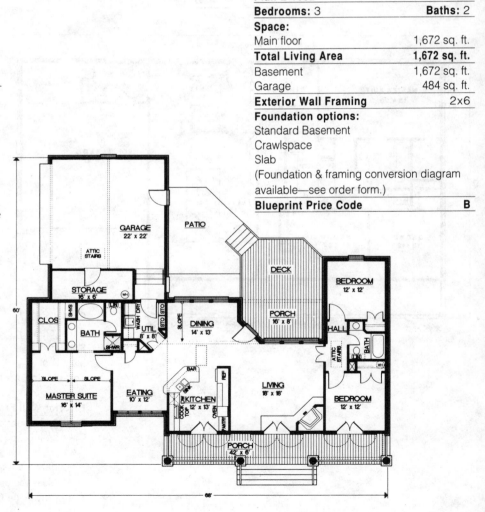

Plan E-1602

Ranch with Country Accent

- An attractive and appealing front porch lends a country accent to this comfortable ranch home.
- The entry leads to a large living room on the right or straight back to a huge family room, which serves as the focal point for this design.
- The adjoining U-shaped kitchen is flanked on the right by a utility area, which also serves as an entry from the garage or from the backyard.
- The master bedroom includes a private bath and a large walk-in closet, and two secondary bedrooms share another full bath.

Plan N-1101	
Bedrooms: 3	**Baths:** 2
Living Area:	
Main floor	1,643 sq. ft.
Total Living Area:	**1,643 sq. ft.**
Standard basement	1,643 sq. ft.
Garage	448 sq. ft.
Exterior Wall Framing:	2x4

Foundation Options:
Standard basement
Slab
(Typical foundation & framing conversion
diagram available—see order form.)

BLUEPRINT PRICE CODE: B

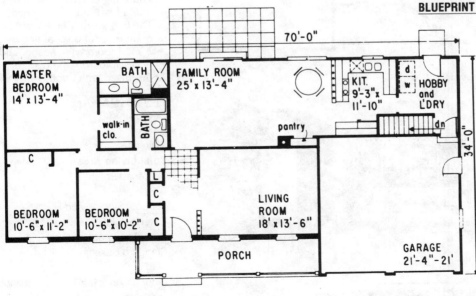

MAIN FLOOR

Plan N-1101

Single-Story with Sparkle

- A lovely front porch with decorative posts, a cameo front door, bay windows and dormers give this country-style home extra sparkle.
- The Great Room is at the center of the floor plan, where it merges with the dining room, kitchen and screened porch. The Great Room features a tray ceiling, a wall of windows facing the patio, a fireplace and a built-in wet bar.
- The eat-in kitchen has a half-wall that keeps it open to the Great Room and hallway. The dining room has a half-wall facing the foyer and a bay window overlooking the front porch.
- The delectable master suite is isolated from the other bedrooms and includes a charming bay window, a tray ceiling and a luxurious private bath.
- The two smaller bedrooms are off the main foyer and separated by a full bath.
- A mud room with washer and dryer is accessible from the two-car garage, disguised with another bay window.

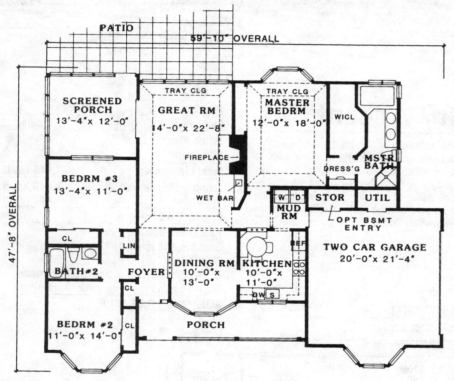

Plan AX-91312	
Bedrooms: 3	**Baths:** 2
Space:	
Main floor	1,595 sq. ft.
Total Living Area	**1,595 sq. ft.**
Screened Porch	178 sq. ft.
Basement	1,595 sq. ft.
Garage, Storage and Utility	508 sq. ft.
Exterior Wall Framing	2x4
Foundation options:	
Standard Basement	
Slab	
(Foundation & framing conversion diagram available—see order form.)	
Blueprint Price Code	B

View into Great Room from dining room

Plan AX-91312

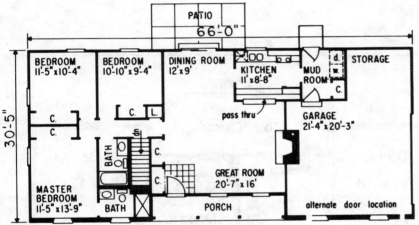

MAIN FLOOR
WITH BASEMENT

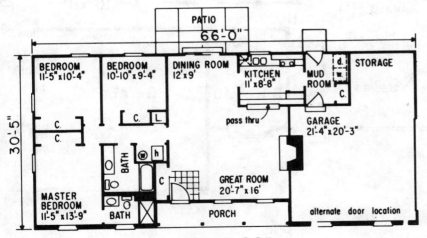

MAIN FLOOR
WITHOUT BASEMENT

Colonial Ranch

- A brick front and multi-paned windows add a Colonial touch to this simple and economical ranch.
- A large Great Room is the focal point of this floor plan, and a dining area at the rear offers easy access to a patio or deck.
- Note the convenient mud room and utility area off the kitchen, and the extra storage space in the garage.
- The master bedroom offers a private bath and a large closet, while two secondary bedrooms share a second full bath.

Plan N-1124

Bedrooms: 3	**Baths:** 2

Living Area:	
Main floor	1,345 sq. ft.
Total Living Area:	**1,345 sq. ft.**
Standard basement	1,345 sq. ft.
Garage	432 sq. ft.
Exterior Wall Framing:	2x4

Foundation Options:
Standard basement
Slab
(Typical foundation & framing conversion diagram available—see order form.)

BLUEPRINT PRICE CODE:	**A**

Plan N-1124

Simple and Balanced

- Balanced living and sleeping areas are found in this quaint, country ranch.
- Overlooking the front covered porch through a bay window are the living and dining rooms, with fireplace, snack counter and adjoining covered deck at the rear.
- The open kitchen has a view of both rooms, as well as the deck; convenient laundry facilities are just steps away.
- The master bedroom, secluded to the rear, has a walk-in closet, separate dressing area and private deck access.
- Two additional bedrooms share a second bath.

Plan NW-258	
Bedrooms: 3	**Baths:** 2
Space:	
Main floor	1,289 sq. ft.
Total Living Area	**1,289 sq. ft.**
Garage	430 sq. ft.
Exterior Wall Framing	**2x6**
Foundation options:	
Crawlspace	
(Foundation & framing conversion diagram available—see order form.)	
Blueprint Price Code	**A**

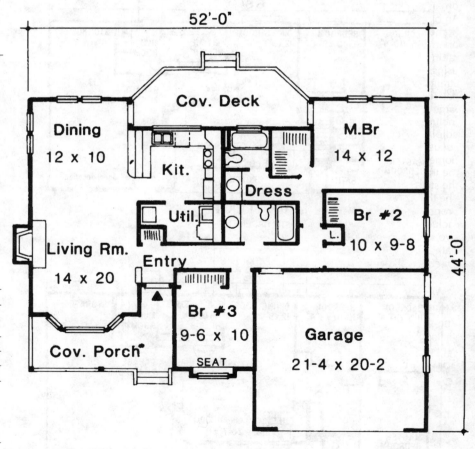

Plan NW-258

Charming One-Story

- This charming one-story home has much to offer, despite its modest size and economical bent.
- The lovely full-width porch has old-fashioned detailing, such as the round columns, decorative railings and ornamental moulding.
- An open floor plan maximizes the home's square footage. The front door opens to the living room, where a railing creates a hallway effect while using very little space.
- Straight ahead is the dining area, which has sliding glass doors opening to a large rear patio. The dining area includes a compact laundry closet and adjoins the kitchen with center island.
- Focusing on quality rather than size, the home also offers deluxe features such as the tray ceiling in the living room and the stepped ceiling in the dining room.
- The three bedrooms are well proportioned. The master bedroom includes a private bathroom, while the two smaller bedrooms share another full bath. Note that the fixtures are arranged to reduce plumbing runs.

Plan AX-91316

Bedrooms: 3	Baths: 2
Living Area:	
Main floor	1,097 sq. ft.
Total Living Area:	**1,097 sq. ft.**
Standard basement	1,097 sq. ft.
Garage	461 sq. ft.
Exterior Wall Framing:	2x4
Foundation Options:	
Standard basement	
Slab	
(Typical foundation & framing conversion diagram available—see order form.)	
BLUEPRINT PRICE CODE:	A

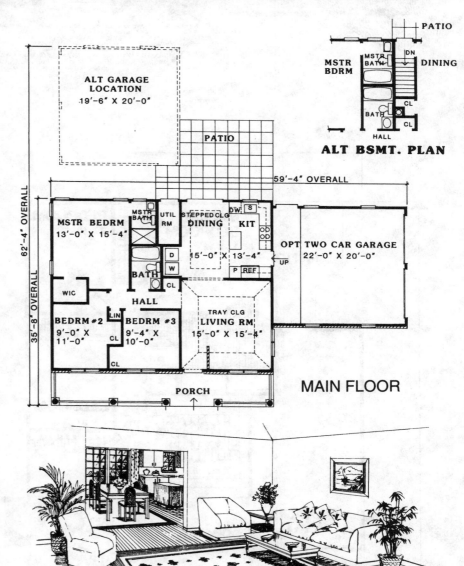

MAIN FLOOR

ALT BSMT. PLAN

VIEW INTO LIVING ROOM, DINING ROOM AND KITCHEN.

Plan AX-91316

Country-Style Coziness

- Designed as a starter or retirement home, this delightful plan has a charming exterior and an open, airy interior.
- The spacious front porch gives guests a warm welcome and provides added space for relaxing or entertaining. The modified hip roof, half-round louver vent and decorative porch railings are other distinguishing features of the facade.
- Inside, the open dining and living rooms are heightened by dramatic vaulted ceilings. The streamlined kitchen has a snack counter joining it to the dining room. All three rooms reap the benefits of the fireplace.
- A laundry closet is in the hall leading to the three bedrooms. The main bath is close by.
- The master bedroom suite offers its own bath, plus a private patio sequestered behind the garage.

Plan APS-1002

Bedrooms: 3	Baths: 2
Space:	
Main floor	1,050 sq. ft.
Total Living Area	**1,050 sq. ft.**
Garage	288 sq. ft.
Exterior Wall Framing	2x4
Foundation options:	
Slab	
(Foundation & framing conversion diagram available—see order form.)	
Blueprint Price Code	**A**

36

42

MASTER BEDROOM
11 X 12

BEDROOM
9 X 12

PATIO

W D

KITCHEN
9 X 11

BEDROOM
9 X 10

VAULT

GARAGE
12 X 24

DINING
9 X 10

VAULT

LIVING
14 X 14

Plan APS-1002

Space to Spare

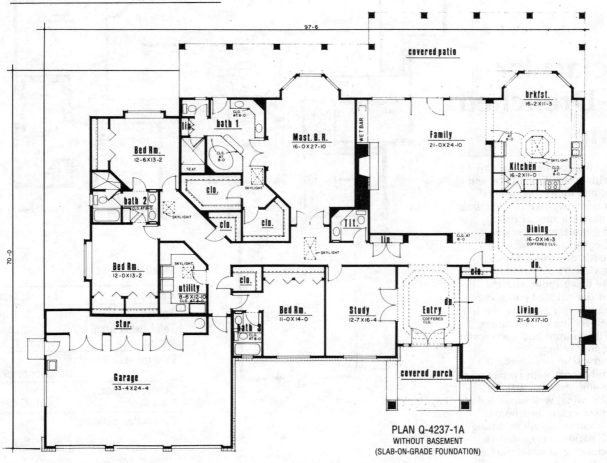

covered patio

brkfst.
16-2 X 11-3

CLG AT 8-0

bath 1

Mast. B.R.
16-0 X 27-10

WET BAR

Family
21-0 X 24-10

Kitchen
16-2 X 11-0

CLG AT 8-0

SKYLIGHT

Bed Rm.
12-6 X 13-2

CLG AT 8-0

SEAT

clo.

SKYLIGHT

clo.

clo.

bath 2
CLG AT 8-0

SKYLIGHT

T.t.

lin.

SKYLIGHT

Dining
16-0 X 14-3
COFFERED CLG.

CLG AT 8-0

clo.

dn.

Bed Rm.
12-0 X 13-2

SKYLIGHT

utility
8-6 X 12-10
CLG AT 8-0

clo.

Bed Rm.
11-0 X 14-0

Study
12-7 X 16-4

Entry
COFFERED CLG.

dn.

Living
21-6 X 17-10

stor.

bath 3
CLG AT 8-0

covered porch

Garage
33-4 X 24-4

PLAN Q-4237-1A
WITHOUT BASEMENT
(SLAB-ON-GRADE FOUNDATION)

Total living area: 4,237 sq. ft.
(Not counting garage)

Blueprint Price Code G

Plan Q-4237-1A

**TO ORDER THIS BLUEPRINT,
CALL TOLL-FREE 1-800-547-5570**
(prices and details on pp. 12-15.) **145**

Spectacular Sun-Drenched Home

- Sweeping hip rooflines, stucco siding with interesting quoins and banding, and interesting arched transom windows give this exciting sunbelt design a special flair.

- From an important 1½ story covered entry leading into the foyer, guests are greeted with a stunning view. A bay-window-wall opens the living room, straight ahead, to the covered patio, rear yard, and possible pool. To the left is an open-feeling formal dining room with columns and spectacular receding tray ceiling.

- The island kitchen overlooks the large family room with corner fireplace and breakfast bay.

- The master wing, well separated from the secondary bedrooms, features a coffered ceiling, sitting area with patio access, massive walk-in closet, and sun-drenched garden bath.

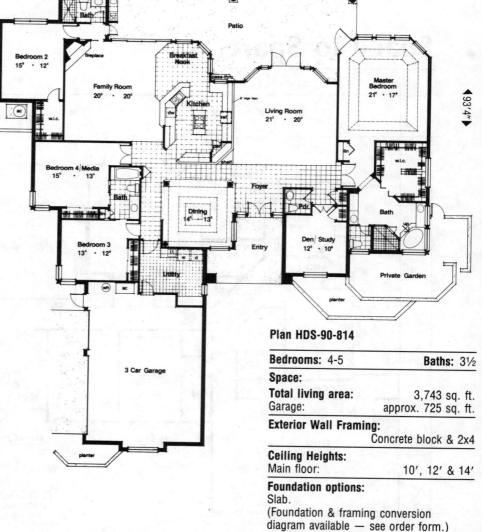

Plan HDS-90-814

Bedrooms: 4-5	Baths: 3½
Space:	
Total living area:	3,743 sq. ft.
Garage:	approx. 725 sq. ft.
Exterior Wall Framing:	
	Concrete block & 2x4
Ceiling Heights:	
Main floor:	10', 12' & 14'
Foundation options:	
Slab.	
(Foundation & framing conversion diagram available — see order form.)	
Blueprint Price Code:	F

TO ORDER THIS BLUEPRINT, CALL TOLL-FREE 1-800-547-5570

Plan HDS-90-814

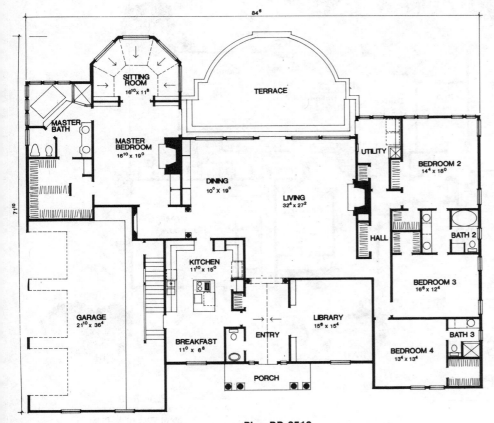

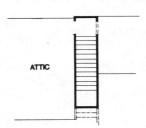

SITTING ROOM
16¹⁰ x 11⁸

TERRACE

MASTER BATH

MASTER BEDROOM
16¹⁰ x 19⁰

UTILITY

BEDROOM 2
14⁴ x 18⁰

DINING
10⁰ x 19⁰

LIVING
32⁴ x 27²

HALL

BATH 2

KITCHEN
11¹⁰ x 15⁰

BEDROOM 3
16⁸ x 12⁴

GARAGE
21¹⁰ x 36⁴

LIBRARY
15⁸ x 15⁴

BATH 3

BREAKFAST
11⁰ x 6⁸

ENTRY

BEDROOM 4
13⁴ x 13⁴

PORCH

ATTIC

84⁶

7¹⁰

For Luxurious Living

- A high, sweeping roofline with dormers, an important-looking arched entry with support columns, and half-round window details all give a formal, estate look to this one-story plan.
- A cathedral ceilinged entryway leads past the island kitchen/ breakfast and library room into the grand living room.
- With 10' ceilings, a fireplace, and glasswall views to the rear terrace, the combination living/formal dining room can accommodate large, formal gatherings or day-to-day family life equally well.
- The stunning master suite features a fireplace with built-ins, a cozy octagonal sitting room, lavish master bath and an enormous walk-in closet.
- The three secondary bedrooms offer abundant closet space and are served by two more baths.

Plan DD-3512

Bedrooms: 4	Baths: 3½

Space:

Total living area:	3,512 sq. ft.
Garage:	793 sq. ft.

Exterior Wall Framing:	2x6

Ceiling Heights:

Main floor:	9' - 10'

Foundation options:
Slab.
(Foundation & framing conversion diagram available — see order form.)

Blueprint Price Code:	E

TO ORDER THIS BLUEPRINT, CALL TOLL-FREE 1-800-547-5570
(prices and details on pp. 12-15.)

Plan DD-3512

103'-0"

59'-0"

Sitting

Master
15/0x18/6

Mstr.Bath

wardrobe

Br.3
11/0x13/0

Dining
12/0x15/6

Nook
10/0x10/0

Family
18/0x16/6

Kitchen
21/6x15/6

dw

Br.2
14/6x13/0

Bath

Entry

bar

w. d.

Util.
7/0x11/0

pant.

down

Living
20/6x17/0

Den/Br.4
12/0x16/0

seat

Garage
31/0x23/6

Luxurious Master Bedroom Suite

This is a one-level dream home with a three-car garage and 3,455 sq. ft. The gourmet kitchen comes equipped with an island, breakfast nook, and a separate pantry. The family room has a beautiful fireplace and even a bar!

Then, for the ultimate in comfort, check out the master suite. While strolling through, one will find a cozy sitting area. The spacious bathroom comes with all of the extras, including a spa and a very large walk-in wardrobe.

PLAN R-1071
WITHOUT BASEMENT
(CRAWLSPACE FOUNDATION)

Total living area: 3,455 sq. ft.
(Not counting garage)

Blueprint Price Code E
Plan R-1071

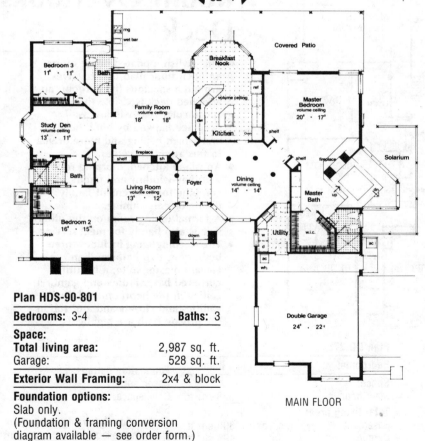

◄ 82'-4" ►

80'-4"

rng
wet bar

Bedroom 3
11⁴ · 11⁶

Bath

Breakfast
Nook

Covered Patio

ref

Family Room
volume ceiling
18⁰ · 18⁰

volume ceiling

Kitchen

Oven

shelf

Master
Bedroom
volume ceiling
20⁴ · 17⁰

Study Den
volume ceiling
13⁴ · 11⁶

lin

lin

Bath

fireplace

shelf   sh

shelf

fireplace

Solarium

ac

Living Room
volume ceiling
13³ · 12²

Foyer

Dining
volume ceiling
14' · 14'

up

dn

Master
Bath

Bedroom 2
16⁴ · 15⁵

down

w.i.c.

desk

Utility

d

ac

wh

ac

Double Garage
24⁴ · 22⁰

MAIN FLOOR

Plan HDS-90-801

Bedrooms: 3-4	Baths: 3

Space:

Total living area:	2,987 sq. ft.
Garage:	528 sq. ft.

Exterior Wall Framing:	2x4 & block

Foundation options:
Slab only.
(Foundation & framing conversion
diagram available — see order form.)

Blueprint Price Code:	D

Gracious Mediterranean Style

- This design speaks of elegance and luxury both inside and out.
- A cloud shade and arched windows add elegance to the entrance.
- The foyer opens up to the breathtaking openness of high vaulted ceilings and a gorgeous octagonal dining room.
- The generously sized family room expands visually as the eye follows the high interior vaults.
- The kitchen also features a vaulted ceiling, and adjoins a nook which lends an open-air appearance to the area.
- The spectacular suite boasts a raised-hearth fireplace that's open to both the bath and bedroom sides.
- Bedroom 2 is spacious, and shares a connecting bath with the den, which could serve as a guest bedroom.
- Bedroom 3 adjoins another bath, and includes a large closet.
- A large covered patio across the back of the home includes a built-in wet bar and outdoor grill.

Plan HDS-90-801

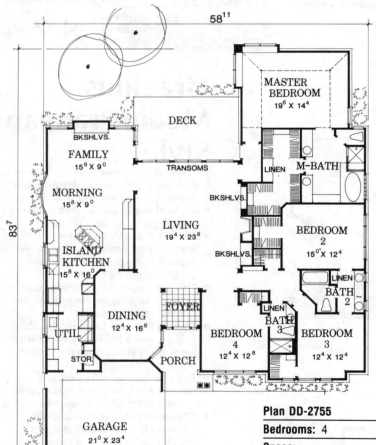

Dimensions on floor plan:
58^11 (top)
83^7 (left side)

MASTER BEDROOM 19^6 X 14^4
DECK
BKSHLVS.
FAMILY 15^8 X 9^0
TRANSOMS
LINEN M-BATH
MORNING 15^8 X 9^0
BKSHLVS.
LIVING 19^4 X 23^8
BKSHLVS.
BEDROOM 2 15^0 X 12^4
ISLAND KITCHEN 15^8 X 16^0
LINEN
BATH 2
DINING 12^4 X 16^8
FOYER
UTIL.
LINEN
BATH 3
STOR.
BEDROOM 4 12^4 X 12^8
BATH
BEDROOM 3 12^4 X 12^4
PORCH
GARAGE 21^0 X 23^4

Central Living Room Overlooks Deck

- This stylish, updated home offers an open floor plan that revolves around a spacious living room; an attached deck is visible through a spectacular rear window wall. A fireplace flanked by bookshelves and a high ceiling add more drama to this attention center.
- An island kitchen, morning room with bay window and family room combine for convenient family dining or entertaining.
- A formal dining room on the other side is also handy for meal serving.
- The sleeping wing includes three bedrooms, two baths and an elegant master suite; a beautiful cornered bay window and gambrel ceiling in the bedroom and dual vanities and closets and a 6' tub in the private bath are highlights.

Plan DD-2755

Bedrooms: 4		Baths: 3
Space:		
Main floor:		2,868 sq. ft.
Total living area:		2,868 sq. ft.
Basement:	(approx.)	2,800 sq. ft.
Garage:		496 sq. ft.
Exterior Wall Framing:		2x4

Foundation options:
Basement.
Crawlspace.
Slab.
(Foundation & framing conversion diagram available — see order form.)

Blueprint Price Code: D

TO ORDER THIS BLUEPRINT, CALL TOLL-FREE 1-800-547-5570
150 (prices and details on pp. 12-15.)

Plan DD-2755

Designed for Maximum Livability

- An elegant French Provincial design, this home represents an impressive facade to visitors, family and passers-by.
- Interior is designed for maximum flexibility for the busy family that entertains frequently.

- The optional fourth bedroom is located so it can easily serve as a library, den, office or music room.
- A living/sitting room with a 12' ceiling may serve as a formal living room or a master suite sitting room.
- The large, high-ceilinged family room blends into the sunny morning room and spacious kitchen.
- The master suite includes a huge, luxurious master bath with two large walk-in closets and two vanity sinks.
- A sunny atrium leads to a game room for family or party guests.

Plan E-2704

Bedrooms: 3-4	Baths: 2

Space:

Total living area:	2,791 sq. ft.
Garage:	682 sq. ft.
Porches, etc.:	543 sq. ft.

Exterior Wall Framing:	2x6

Foundation options:
Crawlspace.
Slab.
(Foundation & framing conversion diagram available — see order form.)

Blueprint Price Code:	D

Plan E-2704

Large Great Room in Traditional Design

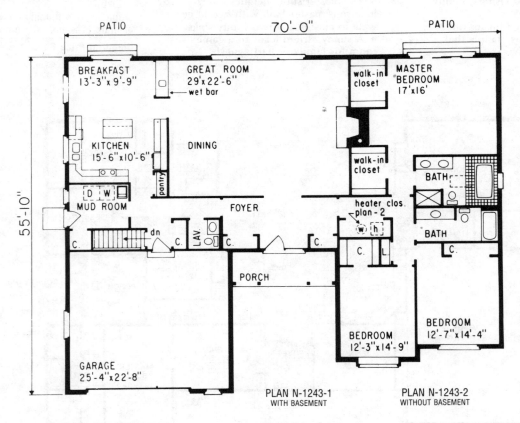

PATIO   70'-0"   PATIO

BREAKFAST
13'-3" x 9'-9"

GREAT ROOM
29' x 22'-6"
← wet bar

walk-in closet

MASTER BEDROOM
17' x 16'

55'-10"

KITCHEN
15'-6" x 10'-6"

DINING

walk-in closet

BATH

MUD ROOM

D W

pantry

FOYER

heater clos.
plan - 2

w h

BATH

dn

c.

LAV.

c.

C.

c.

C.

L.

C.

GARAGE
25'-4" x 22'-8"

PORCH

BEDROOM
12'-3" x 14'-9"

BEDROOM
12'-7" x 14'-4"

PLAN N-1243-1
WITH BASEMENT

PLAN N-1243-2
WITHOUT BASEMENT

Total living area: 2,705 sq. ft.

TO ORDER THIS BLUEPRINT,
CALL TOLL-FREE 1-800-547-5570

Blueprint Price Code D

Plans N-1243-1 & N-1243-2

Bold and Beautiful

- An angled garage adds a unique touch to the bold exterior of this brick-trimmed ranch.
- Inside, an open, vaulted foyer allows a view to the vaulted living room with brilliant front window wall, a den or study with elegant double doors and the kitchen and nook straight ahead.
- Double doors can close off the kitchen from the foyer if desired; but, you'll want to show off the modern island cooktop and huge bay window that surrounds the nook.
- A massive wood stove warms the adjoining vaulted family room that offers access to one of three rear patios.
- Double doors access both the master bedroom and private bath; a skylight and spa tub, vaulted ceiling and patio are exciting extras.

Plan CDG-1008

Bedrooms: 3-4	**Baths:** 2

Space:

Main floor	2,445 sq. ft.
Total Living Area	**2,445 sq. ft.**
Garage	763 sq. ft.
Exterior Wall Framing	2x4

Foundation options:

Crawlspace

(Foundation & framing conversion diagram available—see order form.)

Blueprint Price Code	C

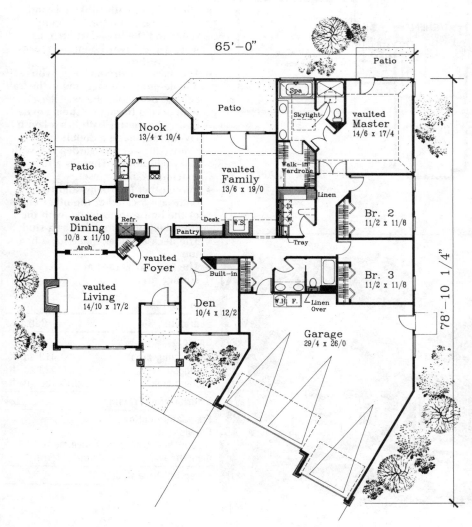

Plan CDG-1008

FRONT

Welcoming Front Exterior

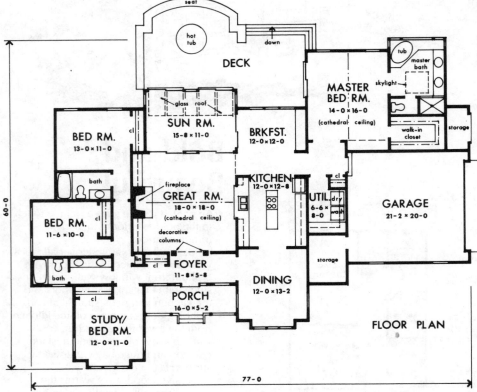

seat

hot tub

DECK

down

glass roof

SUN RM.
15-8 × 11-0

BRKFST.
12-0 × 12-0

MASTER BED RM.
14-0 × 16-0
(cathedral ceiling)

tub

master bath

skylight

walk-in closet

storage

BED RM.
13-0 × 11-0

cl

bath

fireplace

GREAT RM.
18-0 × 18-0
(cathedral ceiling)

KITCHEN
12-0 × 12-8

cl

UTIL.
6-6 ×
8-0

dry

wash

storage

GARAGE
21-2 × 20-0

BED RM.
11-6 × 10-0

cl

bath

decorative columns

lin

cl

FOYER
11-8 × 5-8

DINING
12-0 × 13-2

storage

cl

PORCH
16-0 × 5-2

FLOOR PLAN

STUDY/
BED RM.
12-0 × 11-0

60-0

77-0

- Multipaned windows, dormers, a covered porch and two projected windows at the dining room and study with shed roofs offer a welcoming front exterior.
- The Great Room, with cathedral ceiling, fireplace, built-in cabinets and book shelves, has direct access to the sunroom through two sliding glass doors. Columns between the foyer and Great Room create a dramatic entrance to the Great Room.
- The kitchen, with cooking island, services both the formal dining room and the breakfast area, as well as the Great Room, by means of a pass-thru.
- The master bedroom suite, with double-door entrance and cathedral ceiling, overlooks the rear deck, with access through a sliding glass door. The master bath has a lavish layout to include a double-bowl vanity, shower and garden tub with a skylight above. There is also a spacious walk-in closet.
- Three other bedrooms and two baths are located at the other end of the house for privacy, with the front bedroom doubling as a study.
- The deck includes space for a hot tub.
- The two-car garage also offers a storage area.

Plan DG-168	
Bedrooms: 3-4	**Baths:** 3
Space:	
Total living area:	2,413 sq. ft.
Garage:	420 sq. ft.
Storage area:	approx. 50 sq. ft.
Exterior Wall Framing:	2x4

Foundation options:
Crawlspace.
(Foundation & framing conversion diagram available — see order form.)

Blueprint Price Code:	C

REAR

TO ORDER THIS BLUEPRINT, CALL TOLL-FREE 1-800-547-5570

Plan DG-168

Elegant
L-Shaped
Ranch

This especially handsome ranch home attracts admiration with its exterior facade of brick and horizontal siding. The house layout is practical and straightforward. From the elegant central foyer, to the left is the sleeping area which is neatly separated from the living and eating quarters. The three bedrooms form a private wing with two full baths and lots of closet space. A central fireplace flanked with bookshelves enhances the beamed-ceiling family room which opens to the rear patio via glass sliding doors. The kitchen/breakfast area is well designed and is adjacent to the lavatory and utility room which opens to the two-car garage.

Total living area: 2,324 sq. ft.
(Not counting basement or garage)

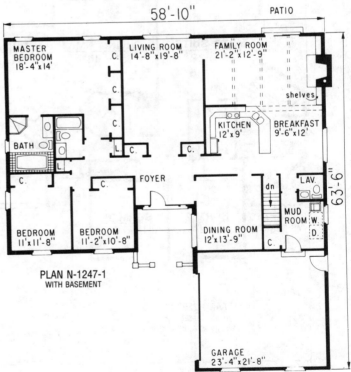

PLAN N-1247-1
WITH BASEMENT

Contemporary Exterior, Light-filled Interior

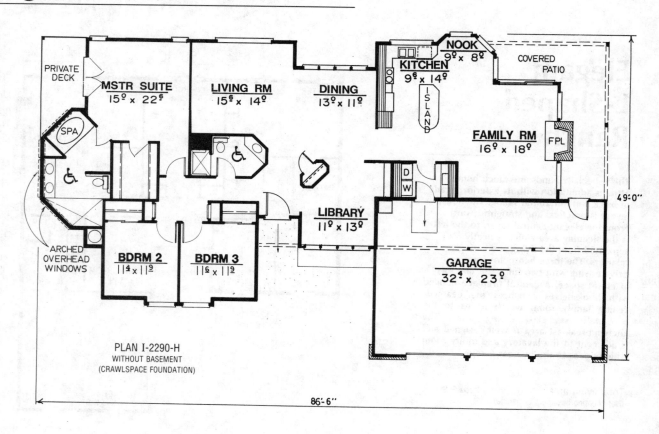

PRIVATE DECK

MSTR SUITE
15⁰ x 22⁶

SPA

LIVING RM
15⁶ x 14⁰

DINING
13⁰ x 11⁰

KITCHEN
9⁶ x 14⁰

NOOK
9⁰ x 8⁰

COVERED PATIO

ISLAND

FAMILY RM
16⁰ x 18⁰

FPL

ARCHED OVERHEAD WINDOWS

BDRM 2
11⁴ x 11⁹

BDRM 3
11⁶ x 11⁹

LIBRARY
11⁰ x 13⁰

D W

GARAGE
32⁴ x 23⁰

49'-0"

PLAN I-2290-H
WITHOUT BASEMENT
(CRAWLSPACE FOUNDATION)

86'-6"

Total living space: 2,290 sq. ft.
(Not counting garage)

TO ORDER THIS BLUEPRINT,
CALL TOLL-FREE 1-800-547-5570
156 (prices and details on pp. 12-15.)

Blueprint Price Code C
Plan I-2290-H

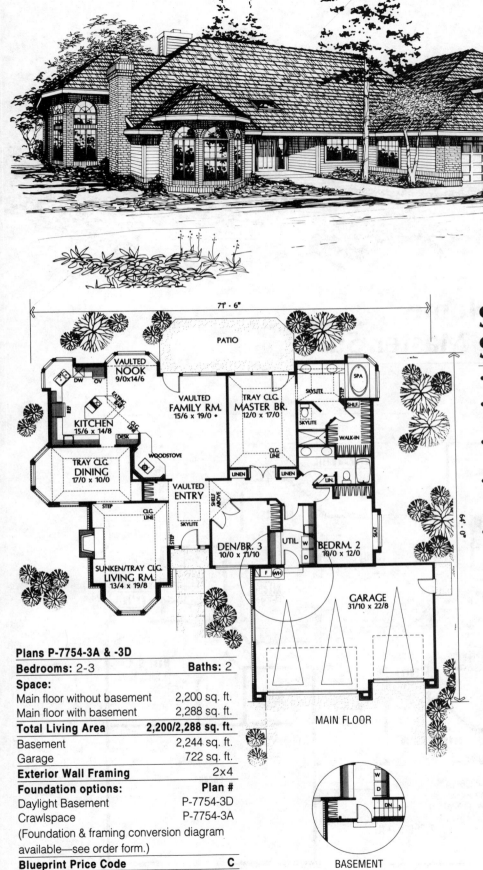

Plans P-7754-3A & -3D

Bedrooms: 2-3	**Baths:** 2

Space:

Main floor without basement	2,200 sq. ft.
Main floor with basement	2,288 sq. ft.
Total Living Area	**2,200/2,288 sq. ft.**
Basement	2,244 sq. ft.
Garage	722 sq. ft.
Exterior Wall Framing	**2x4**

Foundation options:	**Plan #**
Daylight Basement	P-7754-3D
Crawlspace	P-7754-3A

(Foundation & framing conversion diagram available—see order form.)

Blueprint Price Code	**C**

MAIN FLOOR

BASEMENT

Stunning One-Story Design

- The recessed front entry opens to a vaulted, skylighted foyer.
- The sunken living room has a tray ceiling, a fireplace and a turret-like bay with high arched windows.
- The dining room, one step up, also features a tray ceiling and a large bay window.
- The unusual kitchen includes a built-in desk, a corner sink surrounded by lots of counter space and windows, and a cooktop island with eating bar.
- The adjacent nook and family room boast vaulted ceilings and an abundance of windows facing the rear patio. A woodstove tucked into one corner of the family room radiates heat.
- Double doors topped by an overhead plant shelf provide an elegant introduction to the den or third bedroom.
- The master bedroom is also entered through double doors. A tray ceiling and a rear window wall add light and height to the sleeping area. Note the private access to the patio.
- The magnificent master bath includes a step-up garden spa tub, a large dressing area with double-sink vanity, a separate shower and a large walk-in closet. Two skylights shower the bath with light.
- Another full bath, a bedroom with a window seat and a walk-through utility room complete this stunning one-story design.

TO ORDER THIS BLUEPRINT, CALL TOLL-FREE 1-800-547-5570 (prices and details on pp. 12-15.) 157

Four-Bedroom Home
Includes Deluxe Master Suite

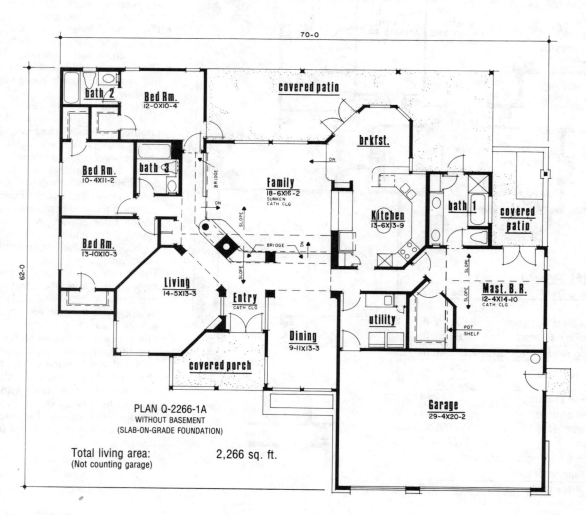

PLAN Q-2266-1A
WITHOUT BASEMENT
(SLAB-ON-GRADE FOUNDATION)

Total living area: 2,266 sq. ft.
(Not counting garage)

Blueprint Price Code C
Plan Q-2266-1A

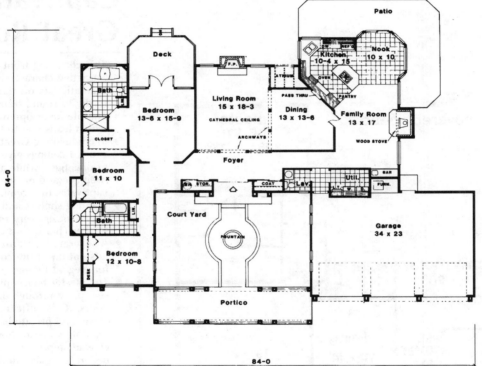

Southwestern Flavor

- A spectacular fountain courtyard, eye-catching portico and tile roof display a unique Southwestern flavor.
- The U-shaped interior and three-car garage surround the courtyard; three bedrooms along one side include the master with double doors to the entrance and private deck, plus a large bath with dual vanities, luxury bath and separate shower.
- Columned archways adorn entrances to the central living room with cathedral ceiling, fireplace and adjoining atrium and the dining room with pass-thru to the kitchen.
- The kitchen also offers a lovely corner sink window, pantry, merging, bayed nook with surrounding patio and adjacent family room with wood stove and wet bar.

Plan NW-391-M	
Bedrooms: 3	**Baths:** 2 ½
Space:	
Main floor	2,207 sq. ft.
Total Living Area	**2,207 sq. ft.**
Garage	782 sq. ft
Exterior Wall Framing	2x6
Foundation options:	
Crawlspace	
(Foundation & framing conversion diagram available—see order form.)	
Blueprint Price Code	C

Plan NW-391-M

Captivating Great Room

- This charming front has many attractive characteristics from a dramatic bay off the dining room to the ½ round transoms above.
- The tile foyer opens up to an arch which leads you to the overwhelming Great Room. The vaulted ceilings give you a feeling of openness, while a centered fireplace and media center captivates the room.
- Planting shelves and soffits are abundant in every room, adding further charm.
- A separate breakfast nook with bay juts out on to the covered porch for elegant dining.
- The master bedroom overlooks the rear patio through double French doors. It also offers a large walk-in closet and private bath with separate walk-in shower and an elegant step-up spa tub with a decorative glass block window viewing a private solarium.

Plan HDS-90-807

Bedrooms: 4	Baths: 3

Space:

Total living area:	2,171 sq. ft.
Garage:	405 sq. ft.

Exterior Wall Framing: 2x4 & concrete

Foundation options:
Slab.
(Foundation & framing conversion diagram available — see order form.)

Blueprint Price Code: C

Floor plan

bedrm 2 12⁰ · 10⁸

covered patio

master bedrm 18⁸ · 13⁰

brkfst

lin

w.i.c.

bedrm 3 10⁸ · 10⁶

fireplace

sink

dress

tub

family room 17⁰ · 20⁰

kit

dw

rng

ref

w

d

wh

ac

bedrm 4 10⁴ · 10⁸

foyer

dining 11⁶ · 14⁰

19⁰ · 21⁴

living 10¹⁰ · 14⁸

double garage

51'-4"

60'-0"

Plan HDS-90-807

REAR VIEW

Spacious Western Ranch

- A three-bedroom sleeping wing is separated from the balance of the home, with the master suite featuring a raised tub below skylights and a walk-in dressing room.
- Sunken living room is enhanced by a vaulted ceiling and fireplace with raised hearth.
- Family room is entered from the central hall through double doors; a wet bar and a second fireplace grace this gathering spot.
- Kitchen has functional L-shaped arrangement, attached nook, and pantry.

Plan H-3701-1A

Bedrooms: 4	Baths: 3½
Total living area:	3,735 sq. ft.
Garage:	830 sq. ft.
Exterior Wall Framing:	2x4

Foundation options:
Crawlspace only.
(Foundation & framing conversion diagram available — see order form.)

Blueprint Price Code:	F

110'-0"

DECK

BEDROOM 16'-6" x 20'-0"

BATH 12'-7" x 12'-2" skylights

WC

SUNKEN LIVING ROOM 30'-0" x 20'-0"

DINING 15'-9" x 14'-0"

raised tub

Shower

steps down

vaulted ceiling

clerestory window

linen

dresser

raised hearth

WALK-IN DRESSING ROOM 11'-3" x 7'-6"

furnace

WET BAR

KITCHEN 15'-4" x 11'-6"

folding screen

PANTRY

ref

CLOSET

LINEN

STOR

POWDER ROOM

ENTRY 15'-3" x 15'-3"

BEDROOM 12'-0" x 14'-6"

BATH

BEDROOM 12'-0" x 14'-6"

CLOSET

CLOSET

NOOK 11'-6" x 10'-0"

DECK

LAV

wdw. seat

wdw. seat

FAMILY ROOM 15'-0" x 24'-0"

Shower

BATH

LAUNDRY skylight

D W

THREE CAR GARAGE 31'-10" x 23'-8"

64'-0"

BEDROOM 19'-0" x 13'-0"

CLOSET

furnace

STORAGE

wdw. seat

Plan H-3701-1A

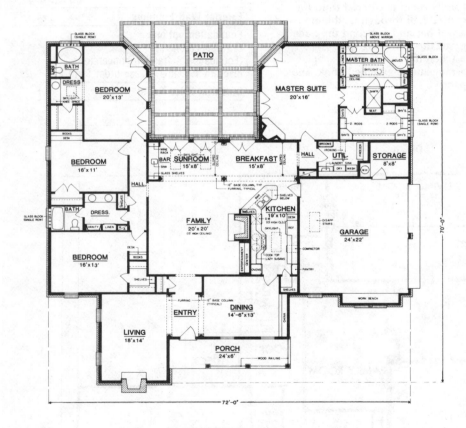

PLAN E-3102
WITHOUT BASEMENT

Exterior walls are 2x6 construction.
Specify crawlspace or slab foundation.

Ranch-Style Designed for Entertaining

- This all-brick home offers both formal living and dining rooms.
- The family room is large scale with 13' ceilings, formal fireplace and an entertainment center. An adjoining sun room reveals a tucked away wet bar.
- The master suite has private patio access and its own fireplace. An adjoining bath offers abundant closet and linen storage, a separate shower and garden tub with glass block walls.
- The home contains three additional bedrooms and two baths. Each bath has glass block above the tubs and separate dressing rooms.
- The master bedroom ceiling is sloped to 14' high. Both the sun room and the breakfast room have sloped ceilings with skylights. Typical ceiling heights are 9'.
- The home is energy efficient.

Heated area:	3,158 sq. ft.
Unheated area:	767 sq. ft.
Total area:	3,925 sq. ft.

Blueprint Price Code E
Plan E-3102

Southern Colonial with Authentic Style

- Porch columns, brick siding, and shuttered windows all contribute to this classic facade.
- This spacious home features large but detailed rooms, including a formal dining room and grand-sized family room and living room, each with fireplaces.
- King-sized closets, large baths, and generous bedrooms make up the sleeping quarters, well separated from the main living areas.

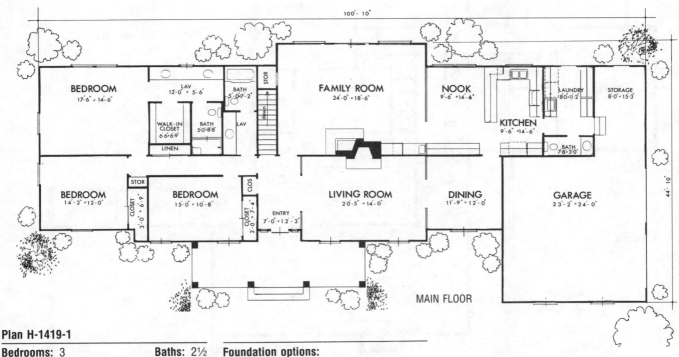

MAIN FLOOR

Plan H-1419-1

Bedrooms: 3	Baths: 2½

Total living area:	2,558 sq. ft.
Basement:	approx. 2,558 sq. ft.
Garage:	556 sq. ft.
Exterior Wall Framing:	2x6

Foundation options:
Standard basement only.
(Foundation & framing conversion diagram available — see order form.)

Blueprint Price Code: D

"Down-Home" Country Flavor

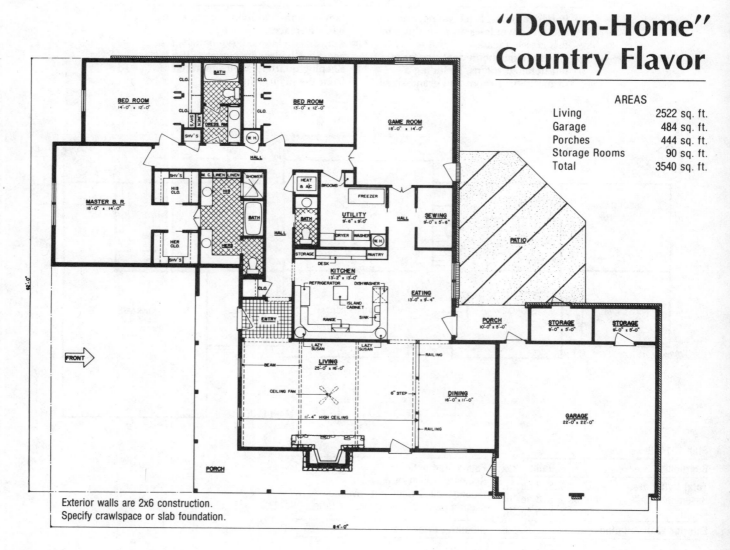

AREAS

Living	2522 sq. ft.
Garage	484 sq. ft.
Porches	444 sq. ft.
Storage Rooms	90 sq. ft.
Total	3540 sq. ft.

Exterior walls are 2x6 construction.
Specify crawlspace or slab foundation.

Blueprint Price Code D

Plan E-2502

High Luxury in One-Story Plan

- 12′ ceilings are featured in the entryway and living room.
- 400 sq. ft. living room boasts a massive fireplace and access to the rear porch.
- Corridor-style kitchen has angled eating bar and convenient nearby laundry facilities.
- Master suite incorporates unusual bath arrangement consisting of an angled whirlpool tub and separate shower.
- Secondary bedrooms are zoned for privacy and climate control.

Plan E-2302	
Bedrooms: 4	**Baths:** 2

Space:	
Total living area:	2,396 sq. ft.
Garage and storage:	590 sq. ft.
Porches:	216 sq. ft.

Exterior Wall Framing:	2x6

Foundation options:
Standard basement.
Crawlspace.
Slab.
(Foundation & framing conversion diagram available — see order form.)

Blueprint Price Code:	C

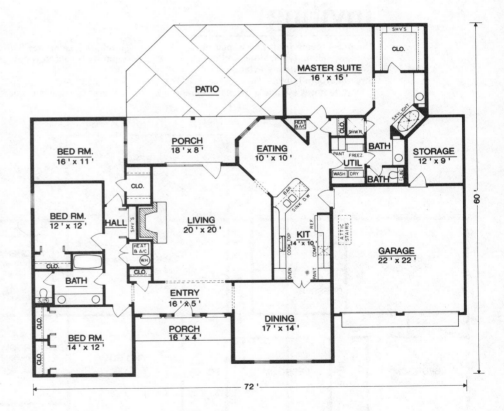

Plan E-2302

Spacious and Inviting

The four-column front porch, picture window, siding, brick, stone and cupola combine for a pleasing exterior for this three-bedroom home.

Extra features include a fireplace, screen porch, deluxe master bath and a large separate breakfast room.

Total living area: 2,306 sq. ft.
(Not counting basement or garage)

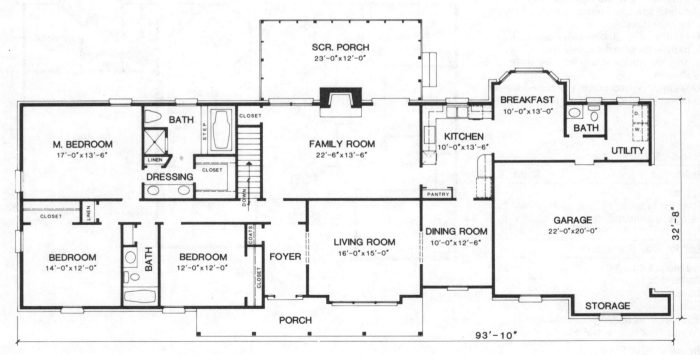

Specify basement, crawlspace or slab foundation.

Photo by Gil Ford

Luxury Living on One Level

- Exterior presents a classic air of quality and distinction in design.
- Spacious one-story interior provides space for family life and entertaining.
- The large central living room boasts a 13′ ceiling and large hearth.
- A roomy formal dining room adjoins the foyer.
- The gorgeous kitchen/nook combination provides a sunny eating area along with an efficient and attractive kitchen with eating bar and abundant counter space.
- The master suite is isolated from the other bedrooms for more privacy, and includes a luxurious bath and dressing area.
- Three additional bedrooms make up the left side of the plan, and share a second bath.
- The garage is off the kitchen for maximum convenience in carrying in groceries; also note the storage space off the garage.

**NOTE: The above photographed home may have been modified by the homeowner. Please refer to floor plan and/or drawn elevation shown for actual blueprint details.

Floor plan labels:
- MASTER SUITE 16' x 15'
- CLO.
- DRESS
- BED RM. 16' x 11'
- PORCH 18' x 8'
- EATING 10' x 8'
- HEAT & AC
- BRM STO LIN
- UTIL
- WASH DRY
- BATH
- STORAGE 8' x 8'
- W H
- SHV
- BED RM. 12' x 12'
- CLO.
- SHV'S
- HEAT & AC
- W H
- BAR
- SINK D W
- LIVING 20' x 18'
- KIT
- REF
- OVENS COOK TOP
- PANT
- COMP
- SHV'S
- ATTIC STAIRS
- GARAGE 24' x 22'
- CLO.
- DRESS
- BATH
- CLO.
- HALL
- ENTRY 16' x 6'
- BED RM 14' x 12'
- PORCH 16' x 4'
- DINING 14' x 14'

Dimensions: 60' / 72'

Plan E-2208

Bedrooms: 4	Baths: 2

Total living area:	2,252 sq. ft.
Garage:	528 sq. ft.
Storage:	64 sq. ft.

Exterior Wall Framing: 2x6

Typical Ceiling Heights:
8′ unless otherwise noted.

Foundation options:
Standard basement.
Crawlspace.
Slab.
(Foundation & framing conversion diagram available — see order form.)

Blueprint Price Code: C

Isolated Master Bedroom Suite

Exterior walls are 2x6 construction.
Specify basement, crawlspace or slab foundation.

AREAS

Living	2200 sq. ft.
Storage Rooms	96 sq. ft.
Garage	528 sq. ft.
Porches	200 sq. ft.
Total	3024 sq. ft.

TO ORDER THIS BLUEPRINT,
CALL TOLL-FREE 1-800-547-5570

Blueprint Price Code C
Plan E-2206

"Adult Retreat" in Master Bedroom Suite

- Exciting living room is virtually open on three sides.
- Wet bar lies between living area and large kitchen, which offers an eating bar and island cooktop.

- Elegant master suite features sitting area and attached bath with romantic angled tub covered with skylight and flanked by his 'n hers vanities.

Plan E-2106

Bedrooms: 3	Baths: 2

Space:

Total living area:	2,177 sq. ft.
Basement:	approx. 2,177 sq. ft.
Garage and storage:	570 sq. ft.
Porches:	211 sq. ft.

Exterior Wall Framing:	2x4

Foundation options:
Standard basement.
Crawlspace.
Slab.
(Foundation & framing conversion diagram available — see order form.)

Blueprint Price Code:	C

**NOTE:
The above photographed home may have been modified by the homeowner. Please refer to floor plan and/or drawn elevation shown for actual blueprint details.

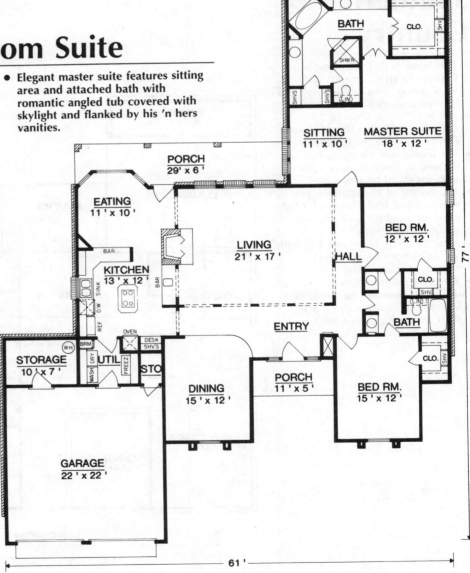

Plan E-2106

Southern Country

- This home is distinctly Southern Country in style, from its wide front porch to its multi-paned and shuttered windows.
- The living room boasts a 12' cathedral ceiling, a fireplace and French doors to the rear patio.
- The dining room is open, but defined by three massive columns with overhead beams.
- The delightful kitchen/nook area is spacious and well-planned for both efficiency and pleasant kitchen working conditions.
- A handy utility room and half-bath are on either side of a short hallway leading to the carport.
- The master suite offers his and hers walk-in closets and an incredible bath which incorporates a plant shelf above the garden tub.

Plan J-86140

Bedrooms: 3	Baths: 2½
Total living area:	2,177 sq. ft.
Basement:	2,177 sq. ft.
Carport:	440 sq. ft.
Storage:	120 sq. ft.
Porch:	233 sq. ft.
Exterior Wall Framing:	2x4
Ceiling Heights:	9'

Foundation options:
Standard basement.
Crawlspace.
Slab.
(Foundation & framing conversion diagram available — see order form.)

Blueprint Price Code:	C

STOR 18·6 x 5

CARPORT

PATIO

UTIL

w d

BKFST 12 x 12

LIVING 17 x 17

cathedral ceiling

MBR 17 x 14

KITCHEN 13 x 14

DINING 13·6 x 11·6

BR 13 x 11

BR 13 x 11

PORCH

62'—2"

36'—4"

TO ORDER THIS BLUEPRINT, CALL TOLL-FREE 1-800-547-5570

Plan J-86140

Soaring Spaces under Vaulted Ceilings

- A dignified exterior and a gracious, spacious interior combine to make this an outstanding plan for today's families.
- The living, dining, family rooms and breakfast nook all feature soaring vaulted ceilings.
- An interior atrium provides an extra touch of elegance, with its sunny space for growing plants and sunbathing.
- The master suite is first class all the way, with a spacious sleeping area, opulent bath, large skylight and enormous walk-in closet.
- A gorgeous kitchen includes a large work/cooktop island, corner sink with large corner windows and plenty of counter space.

Plans P-7697-4A & -4D

Bedrooms: 3	Baths: 2

Space:	
Main floor (crawlspace version):	2,003 sq. ft.
Main floor (basement version):	2,030 sq. ft.
Basement:	2,015 sq. ft.
Garage:	647 sq. ft.

Exterior Wall Framing:	2x4

Foundation options:
Daylight basement (Plan P-7697-4D).
Crawlspace (Plan P-7697-4A).
(Foundation & framing conversion diagram available — see order form.)

Blueprint Price Code:	C

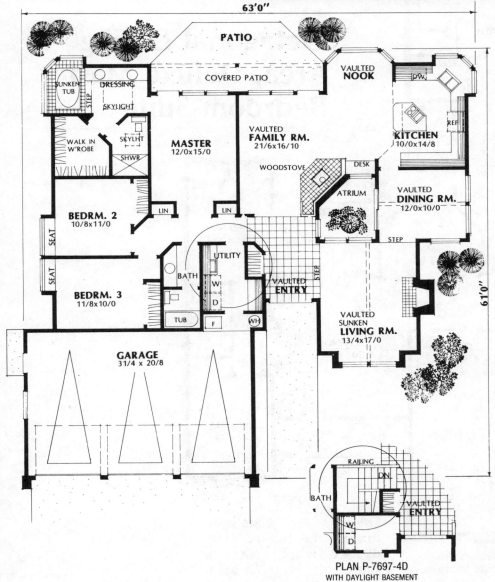

PLAN P-7697-4D
WITH DAYLIGHT BASEMENT

TO ORDER THIS BLUEPRINT,
CALL TOLL-FREE 1-800-547-5570
(prices and details on pp. 12-15.)

Plans P-7697-4A & -4D

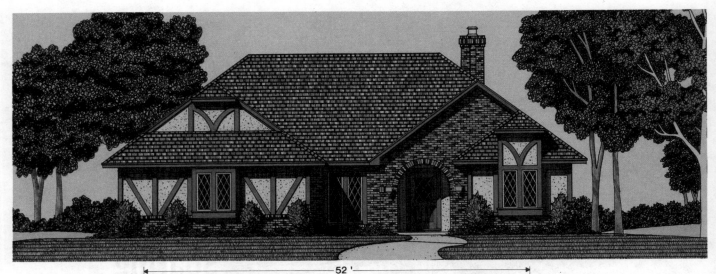

Octagonal Dining Area, Deluxe Master Bedroom Suite

52'

76'

BATH

STEP

LIN MC / LIN MC

SHV / CLO. / SHW'R / SEAT / CLO. / SHV

MASTER SUITE 18' x 16'

SLOPE CEILING

SKYLIGHT

SKKLIGHT

PLAN E-1912 (WITHOUT BASEMENT)

SLOPE CEILING

PORCH 14' x 10'

SKYLIGHT

CLO. / CLO.

BED RM. 14' x 12'

KITCHEN R.E.F. SLOPE CEILING

SINK

OVEN D W

COOK TOP

BAR

PANT.

SKYLIGHT

DINING 14' x 14'

SLOPE CEILING

BATH

LIN / VANITY / LIN

HALL

STOR

CLO.

STORAGE 10' x 6'

WH.

DRY WASH

UTIL 8' x 6'

STOR

CLO. / STOR

HEAT & A/C

LIVING 20' x 18'

SLOPE CEILING

SLOPE CEILING

ATTIC STAIRS

GARAGE 22' x 22'

PORCH 10' x 5'

BED RM. 14' x 12'

SEAT

AREAS

Living	1946 sq. ft.
Porches	282 sq. ft.
Garage & Storage	562 sq. ft.
Total	2790 sq. ft.

Exterior walls are 2x6 construction.
Specify crawlspace or slab foundation.

TO ORDER THIS BLUEPRINT, CALL TOLL-FREE 1-800-547-5570

172 (prices and details on pp. 12-15.)

Blueprint Price Code B

Plan E-1912

Ideal for Formal Entertaining

This lovely 1,940 sq. ft. French Provincial design features a formal foyer flanked by the living room on one side and the dining room on the other. A family room with a raised-hearth fireplace and double doors to the patio, and the L-shaped island kitchen with breakfast bay and open counter to the family room, allow for more casual living.

Adjacent to the breakfast bay is a utility room with outside entrance.

The master suite includes one double closet and a compartmentalized bath with walk-in closet, step-up garden tub, double vanity and linen closet. Two front bedrooms and a second full bath with linen closet complete the design. A recessed entry and circular porch add to the formal exterior.

Total living area: 1,940 sq. ft.
(Not counting basement or garage)

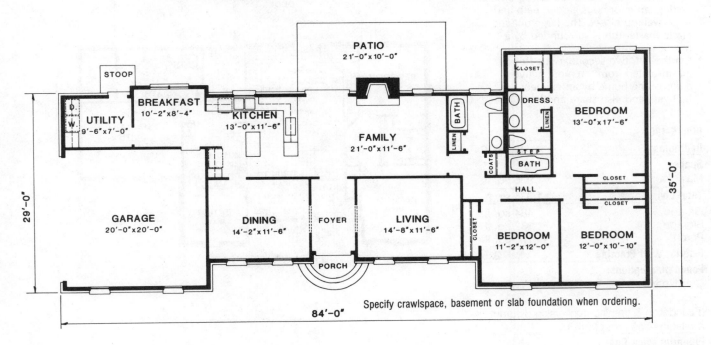

Specify crawlspace, basement or slab foundation when ordering.

Elegance Inside and Out

- The raised front porch of this brick home is finely detailed with wood columns, railings and moldings, and the transom French doors blend well with the stucco finish of the porch.
- The living room, dining room and entry have 12-ft. ceilings. Skylights illuminate the living room, which also includes a fireplace and easy access to a roomy deck.
- The master suite features a raised tray ceiling, an enormous garden bath and large walk-in closet. The large quarter-circle master tub is surrounded by a mirror wall.
- On the left, two secondary bedrooms are insulated from the more active areas of the home by an efficient hallway, and also share another full bath.

Plan E-1909

Bedrooms: 3	Baths: 2
Space:	
Main floor	1,936 sq. ft.
Total Living Area	**1,936 sq. ft.**
Garage	484 sq. ft.
Storage	132 sq. ft.
Porch	175 sq. ft.
Exterior Wall Framing	2x6

Foundation options:
Crawlspace
Slab
(Foundation & framing conversion diagram available—see order form.)

Blueprint Price Code	B

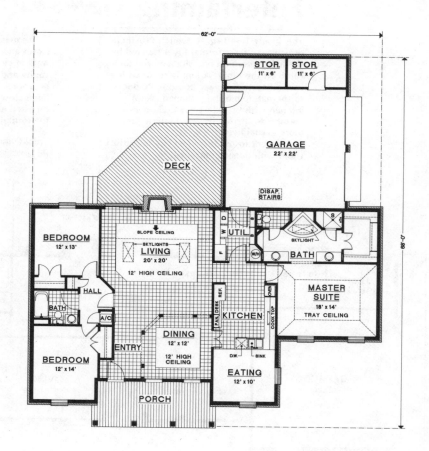

Plan E-1909

Country-Style Home with Welcoming Appeal

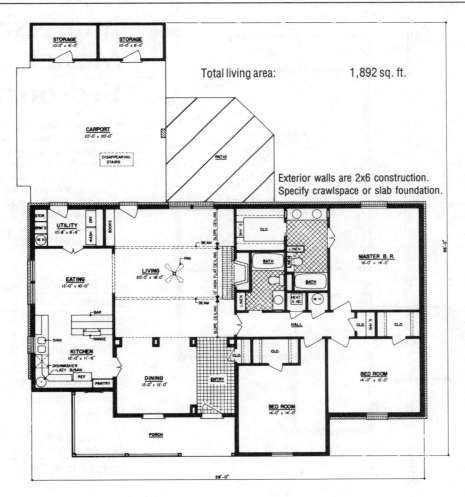

Total living area: 1,892 sq. ft.

Exterior walls are 2x6 construction.
Specify crawlspace or slab foundation.

STORAGE
10'-0" x 6'-0"

STORAGE
10'-0" x 6'-0"

CARPORT
22'-0" x 20'-0"

DISAPPEARING
STAIRS

PATIO

UTILITY
10'-6" x 6'-6"

EATING
12'-0" x 10'-0"

LIVING
20'-0" x 16'-0"

BATH

LINEN

HEAT
& AC

MASTER B. R.
16'-0" x 14'-0"

BATH

HALL

BAR

RANGE

SINK

KITCHEN
12'-0" x 11'-6"

DISHWASHER
LAZY SUSAN

REF

PANTRY

DINING
12'-0" x 12'-0"

ENTRY

CLO.

BED ROOM
14'-0" x 14'-0"

BED ROOM
14'-0" x 12'-0"

PORCH

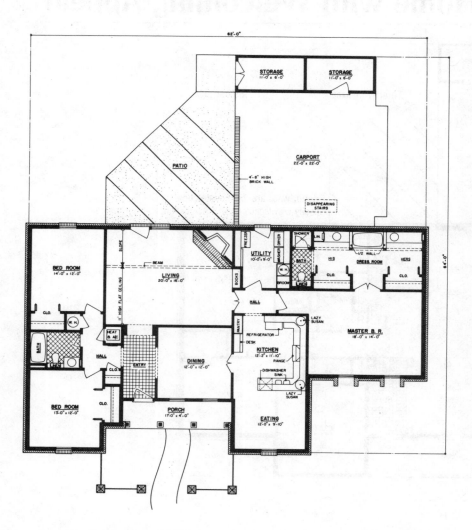

Impressive Master Bedroom Suite

- This updated ranch features an impressive master bedroom with separate dressing areas and closets.
- A lovely front porch opens into a formal dining room and rear-oriented living room with fireplace and attached patio.
- A roomy kitchen and eating area provide plenty of space for work and casual living.

Plan E-1818

Bedrooms: 3	Baths: 2
Space:	
Main floor:	1,868 sq. ft.
Total living area:	1,868 sq. ft.
Carport:	484 sq. ft.
Exterior Wall Framing:	2x6

Foundation options:
Crawlspace.
Slab.
(Foundation & framing conversion diagram available — see order form.)

Blueprint Price Code:	B

TO ORDER THIS BLUEPRINT,
CALL TOLL-FREE 1-800-547-5570
176 (prices and details on pp. 12-15.)

Plan E-1818

Sense of Elegance

- This stately three-bedroom one-story home displays a sense of elegance with its large arched windows, round columns, covered porch and brick veneer siding.
- An arched window in the clerestory above the entrance foyer allows penetration of natural light.
- The Great Room, with cathedral ceiling, fireplace, paddle fan, built-in cabinets and book shelves, has direct access to the sunroom through sliding glass doors with arched window above.
- The kitchen, with cooking island, services both the dining room and breakfast area, as well as the Great Room by means of a pass-thru.
- The master bedroom suite overlooks the rear deck with access through sliding glass doors.
- The master bath has a double-bowl vanity, shower, and garden tub.
- Two other bedrooms are located at the other end of the house for privacy.

Plan DG-231

Bedrooms: 3	Baths: 2

Space:	
Total living area:	2,099 sq. ft.
Basement:	1,947 sq. ft.
Garage:	410 sq. ft.
Storage area:	100 sq. ft.

Exterior Wall Framing:	2x4

Foundation options:
Standard basement.
Crawlspace.
(Foundation & framing conversion diagram available — see order form.)

Blueprint Price Code:	C

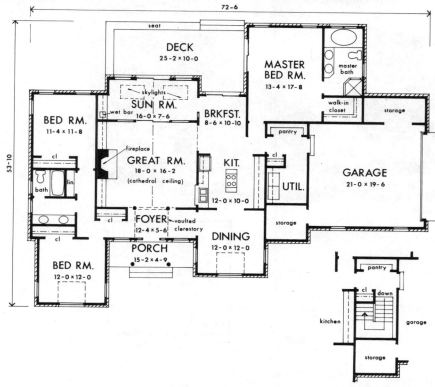

ALTERNATE PLAN
FOR BASEMENT

Plan DG-231

TO ORDER THIS BLUEPRINT, CALL TOLL-FREE 1-800-547-5570
(prices and details on pp. 12-15.)

REAR VIEW

Sunny Delight

- This three-bedroom country cottage home with a sunroom at the front takes advantage of south-facing lots.
- A generous entrance foyer allows direct access to Great Room, dining room, and sun room.
- A country kitchen with breakfast bar and cooking island provides an abundance of cabinet space and views into the Great Room.
- The Great Room, with direct access to deck and sun room, is oversized to offer a sense of spaciousness. Both the Great Room and the sun room have cathedral ceilings.
- The sun room also has four skylights to allow penetration of the sunlight.
- The master bedroom is on opposite side of house from other bedrooms for privacy. Note the double door entrance from the Great Room. Walk-in closets and a master bath with whirlpool tub, shower and double bowl vanity provide the latest in desired amenities.
- The garage is connected to the house by a covered breezeway.

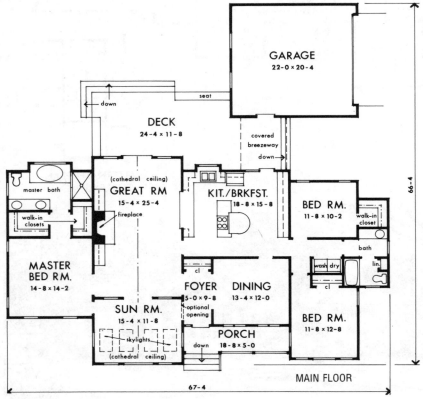

Plan DG-179	
Bedrooms: 3	Baths: 2
Space:	
Total living area:	2,053 sq. ft.
Garage:	447 sq. ft.
Exterior Wall Framing:	2x4
Foundation options: Crawlspace. (Foundation & framing conversion diagram available — see order form.)	
Blueprint Price Code:	C

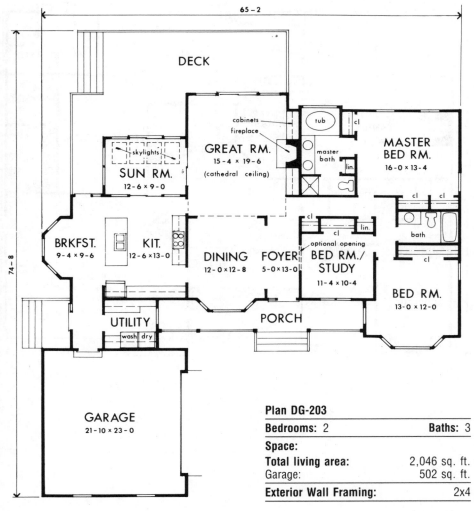

Intriguing Appearance

- This three-bedroom country cottage projects an intriguing appearance with its covered front porch, bay windows, dormers and L-shaped layout.
- The Great Room has a cathedral ceiling, along with a dramatic arched window above the exterior door leading to the deck.
- The sun room with operable skylights is accessible from the Great Room, kitchen, and deck for maximum exposure and enjoyment.
- The centrally located kitchen allows direct access to eating and living areas, and overlooks the breakfast bay.
- The master suite includes plenty of closet space and a private bath with double vanity and separate shower and tub under glass.
- The third bedroom can be opened to the foyer to be used as a study if desired.

Plan DG-203

Bedrooms: 2	Baths: 3
Space:	
Total living area:	2,046 sq. ft.
Garage:	502 sq. ft.
Exterior Wall Framing:	2x4

Foundation options:
Crawlspace.
(Foundation & framing conversion diagram available — see order form.)

Blueprint Price Code: C

TO ORDER THIS BLUEPRINT,
CALL TOLL-FREE 1-800-547-5570
(prices and details on pp. 12-15.)

Plan DG-203

Streetscape Interest

- Impressive rooflines with front gables, entry emphasis, and brick highlights give an interesting view of this one-story home from the street.
- The interior features two main, very open feeling living spaces.
- The formal space opens from the entry and reaches from the front to the rear of the house, opening to the lanai with sliders and windows.
- The informal living space includes an island kitchen overlooking the family room with fireplace and sunny breakfast eating area.
- The master suite is well separated from the secondary bedrooms. It has a dressing area, walk-in closet and exciting master bath with spa tub and glass shower.

Plan DD-2025

Bedrooms: 3	Baths: 2

Space:

Total living area:	2,025 sq. ft.
Garage:	494 sq. ft.

Exterior Wall Framing:	2x4

Foundation options:
Slab.
(Foundation & framing conversion diagram available — see order form.)

Blueprint Price Code:	C

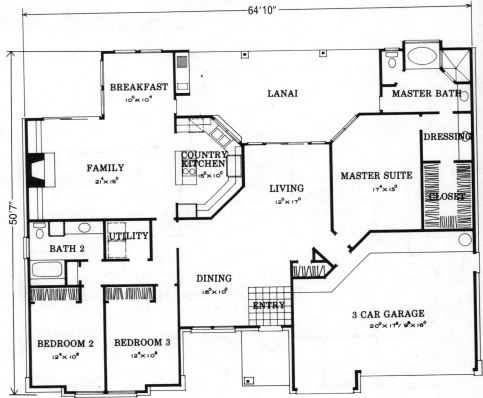

MAIN FLOOR

Plan DD-2025

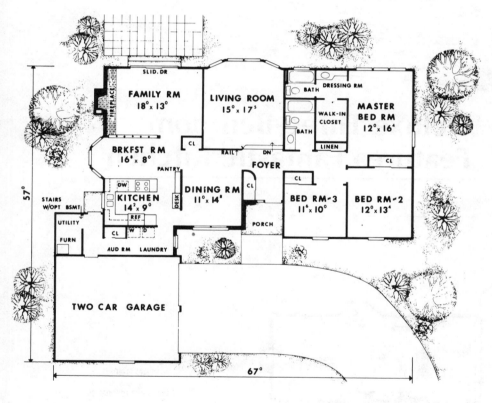

Country Classic

- A variety of siding materials blend together for a classic country exterior look.
- A dramatic sunken living room with bay window-wall is the view that greets arriving guests.
- A front-facing dining room completes the formal living area.
- The family room with fireplace is open to the kitchen and breakfast bay for informal family shared time.
- Three bedrooms and two full baths make up the sleeping wing of the home.

Plan AX-9762

Bedrooms: 3	Baths: 2

Space:	
Total living area:	2,003 sq. ft.
Basement:	2,003 sq. ft.
Garage:	485 sq. ft.

Exterior Wall Framing:	2x4

Foundation options:
Standard basement.
Slab.
(Foundation & framing conversion diagram available — see order form.)

Blueprint Price Code: C

Plan AX-9762

Deluxe Three-Bedroom
Features Fantastic Kitchen

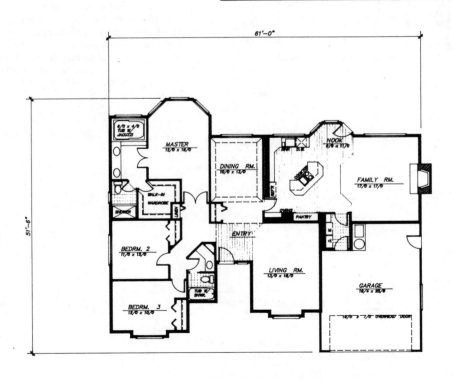

PLAN R-1080
WITHOUT BASEMENT
(CRAWLSPACE FOUNDATION)

Total living area: 1,990 sq. ft.

Blueprint Price Code B
Plan R-1080

Cozy L-Shaped Bungalow

This pleasing L-shaped design packs a smooth-flowing floor plan into 1,950 sq. ft. The master suite includes garden tub, shower, his and her vanities and separate walk-in closets. Two other bedrooms and a full bath complete the sleeping wing.

A large family room, foyer and separate living-dining room combine to form the center section. U-shaped kitchen, breakfast nook with bay window and separate utility complete the plan.

Total living area: 1,950 sq. ft.
(Not counting basement or garage)

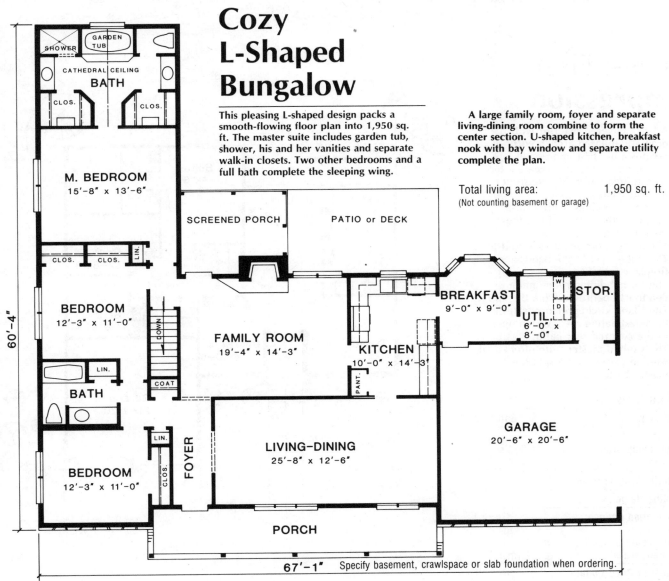

SHOWER · GARDEN TUB

CATHEDRAL CEILING
BATH

CLOS. · CLOS.

M. BEDROOM
15'-8" x 13'-6"

CLOS. · CLOS. · LIN.

BEDROOM
12'-3" x 11'-0"

DOWN

COAT

BATH

LIN.

BEDROOM
12'-3" x 11'-0"

LIN.

CLOS.

FOYER

60'-4"

SCREENED PORCH

PATIO or DECK

FAMILY ROOM
19'-4" x 14'-3"

KITCHEN
10'-0" x 14'-3"

PANT.

LIVING-DINING
25'-8" x 12'-6"

BREAKFAST
9'-0" x 9'-0"

UTIL.
6'-0" x 8'-0"

W

D

STOR.

GARAGE
20'-6" x 20'-6"

PORCH

67'-1"   Specify basement, crawlspace or slab foundation when ordering.

Blueprint Price Code B

Plan C-8620

TO ORDER THIS BLUEPRINT, CALL TOLL-FREE 1-800-547-5570
(prices and details on pp. 12-15.) **183**

A Big First Impression

- A brick covered exterior with dramatic pillared arched entry creates a big first impression.
- Open, flowing spaces create a big first impression inside the front door as well.
- Nine-foot ceilings, with a raised ceiling at the entry, add to the open feeling.
- The living room features a built-in TV center next to the handsome fireplace.
- The formal dining room and a den/fourth bedroom flank the entry.
- The island kitchen incorporates a breakfast eating area, which opens to the covered rear patio.
- The vaulted master suite offers dual walk-in closets and a splashing master bath.

Plan B-90039

Bedrooms: 3-4	Baths: 2
Space:	
Total living area:	1,806 sq. ft.
Garage:	427 sq. ft.
Exterior Wall Framing:	2x6
Ceiling Height:	9'

Foundation options:
Crawlspace.
(Foundation & framing conversion diagram available — see order form.)

Blueprint Price Code:	B

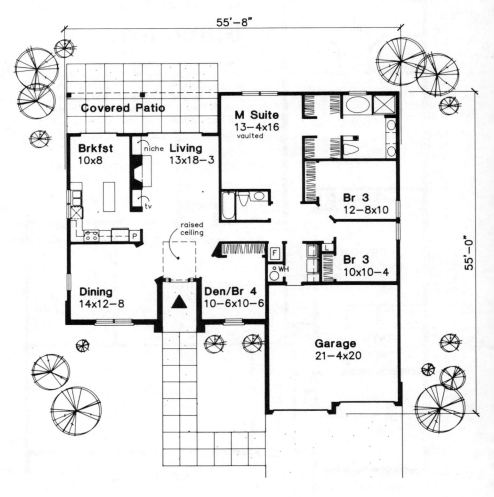

Plan B-90039

Classic Country-Style

- At the center of this rustic country home is an enormous living room with vaulted ceilings, a massive stone fireplace and entrance to a rear porch.
- The adjoining eating area and kitchen provide plenty of room for dining and meal preparation. A sloped ceiling with false beams, porch overlook, pantry, spice cabinet and counter bar are some attractions found here.
- Formal dining and entertaining can take place in the dining room off the entry.
- For privacy, you'll find the secluded master suite rewarding; it offers a private bath with dressing area, walk-in closet and isolated toilet and tub.
- The two additional bedrooms also have abundant walk-in closet space.

Plan E-1808	
Bedrooms: 3	**Baths:** 2
Space:	
Main floor	1,800 sq. ft.
Total Living Area	**1,800 sq. ft.**
Garage and storage	605 sq. ft.
Porches	354 sq. ft.
Exterior Wall Framing	2x4
Foundation options:	
Crawlspace	
Slab	
(Foundation & framing conversion diagram available—see order form.)	
Blueprint Price Code	**B**

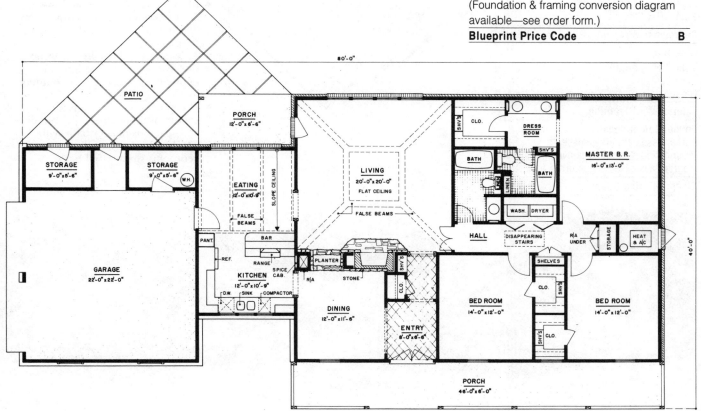

Plan E-1808

REAR

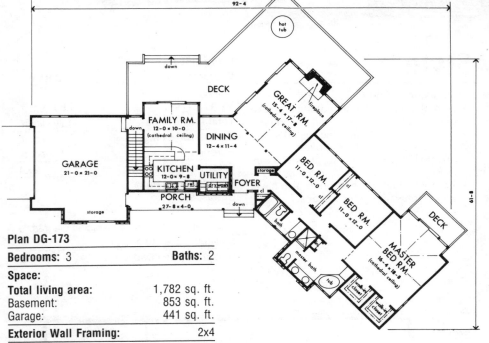

92-4

hot tub

down

DECK

FAMILY RM.
12-0 × 10-0
(cathedral ceiling)

GREAT RM.
15-4 × 17-8
(cathedral ceiling)

fireplace

DINING
12-4 × 11-4

down

GARAGE
21-0 × 21-0

KITCHEN
12-0 × 9-8

UTILITY

storage

BED RM.
11-0 × 12-0

FOYER

cl

storage

PORCH
27-8 × 4-0

ref.

drywash

cl

down

cl

BED RM.
11-0 × 12-0

DECK

bath

master bath

tub

MASTER
BED RM.
15-4 × 18-6
(cathedral ceiling)

cl

61-8

Plan DG-173

Bedrooms: 3	**Baths:** 2

Space:

Total living area:	1,782 sq. ft.
Basement:	853 sq. ft.
Garage:	441 sq. ft.

Exterior Wall Framing:	2x4

Foundation options:
Partial basement/crawlspace.
(Foundation & framing conversion diagram available — see order form.)

Blueprint Price Code:	B

Design Flexibility

- This country-style ranch generates visual excitement through its combination of exterior building materials and shapes. A covered front porch, with dormers above, adds to the country appeal.
- The angled ranch offers flexibility in design with the ability to lengthen the Great Room and/or family room to suit individual family space requirements.
- Both the family room and the Great Room have cathedral ceilings, and the Great Room also boasts a fireplace.
- An expansive deck area with hot tub wraps around the interior family gathering areas for outdoor living.
- The master bedroom has a cathedral ceiling, walk-in closet, private deck and spacious master bath with whirlpool tub. The other two bedrooms share a full bath.

FRONT

Plan DG-173

Rustic Home for Relaxed Living

A screened-in breezeway provides a cool place to dine out on warm summer days and nights, and the rustic front porch is ideal for relaxed rocking or a swing. A Great Room to the left of the entry has a fireplace and connects the dining area to the country kitchen.

The large master suite contains separate shower, garden tub, vanities and walk-in closets.

Total living area: 1,773 sq. ft.
(Not counting basement or garage)
(Specify basement, crawlspace or slab foundation)

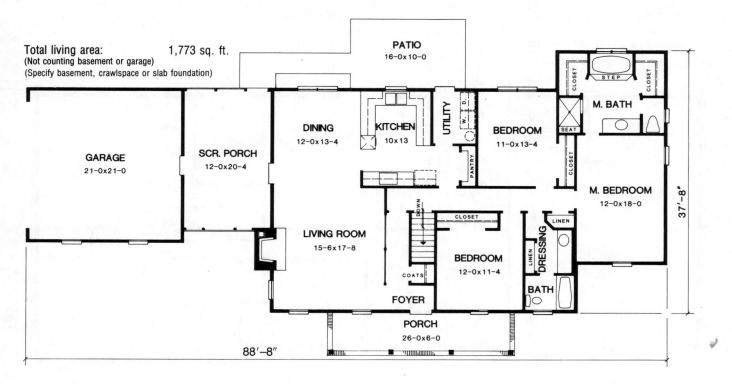

PATIO
16-0x10-0

DINING
12-0x13-4

KITCHEN
10x13

UTILITY

W. D.

PANTRY

BEDROOM
11-0x13-4

CLOSET

M. BATH

STEP

CLOSET

SEAT

CLOSET

M. BEDROOM
12-0x18-0

GARAGE
21-0x21-0

SCR. PORCH
12-0x20-4

LIVING ROOM
15-6x17-8

DOWN

CLOSET

COATS

BEDROOM
12-0x11-4

LINEN

DRESSING

LINEN

LINEN

BATH

FOYER

PORCH
26-0x6-0

88'—8"

37'—8"

Blueprint Price Code B

Plan C-8650

TO ORDER THIS BLUEPRINT, CALL TOLL-FREE 1-800-547-5570
(prices and details on pp. 12-15.)

Efficient Dining-Kitchen-Nook Combination

- Here's a four-bedroom design that is beautiful in its simplicity and ease of construction.
- All on one floor, it offers ample space for both family life and entertaining.
- A huge living room soars aloft with vaulted, beamed ceilings and features a massive fireplace to give a Great Room feel to the area.
- The roomy, efficient kitchen is flanked by a sunny informal eating

area protruding into the back yard and a front-facing formal dining room that is right off the elegant foyer.
- A deluxe master suite includes a dressing room, large closet and private bath.
- The three secondary bedrooms are larger than average and also offer ample closet space.
- Convenient storage and utility areas are segmented off the two-car garage.

Plan E-1702	
Bedrooms: 4	**Baths:** 2
Space:	
Total living area:	1,751 sq. ft.
Porch:	64 sq. ft.
Garage:	484 sq. ft.
Storage:	105 sq. ft.
Exterior Wall Framing:	2x4
Foundation options:	
Crawlspace.	
Slab.	
(Foundation & framing conversion diagram available — see order form)	
Blueprint Price Code:	B

77'-0"

EATING 11'-0"x 9'-6"

PATIO 21'-0"x12'-0"

STORAGE 13'-0"x 8'-0"

UTILITY 9'-0"x 8'-0"

WASH. DRYER

BRM'S. STOR.

PANTRY

DISHWASHER

KITCHEN 10'-0"x 9'-6"

SINK

SURF. UNIT

REF

OVEN

SLOPE

LIVING 19'-0"x16'-0"

BEAMS

SLOPE

BOOKS

SHV'S.

CLO.

POST ON 1/2 WALL

DRESS. ROOM

LINEN

LINEN

BATH

BATH

SHELVES

MASTER B. R. 16'-0"x13'-0"

GARAGE 22'-0"x22'-0"

BOOKS

DISAPPEARING STAIRS

HALL

CLO.

CLO.

DINING 11'-0"x10'-0"

ENTRY 10'-0"x5'-0"

CLO.

BED ROOM 12'-0"x10'-6"

CLO.

BED ROOM 12'-6"x11'-6"

BED ROOM 12'-6"x12'-6"

PORCH

32'-0"

Plan E-1702

Designed for Livability

- As you enter this excitingly spacious traditional home you see through the extensive windows to the back yard.
- This four-bedroom home was designed for livability of the maturing family with the separation of the master suite.
- The formal dining room expands spatially to the living room while being framed by the column and plant shelves.
- The bay that creates the morning room and sitting area for the master suite also adds excitement to this plan, both inside and out.
- The master bath offers an exciting oval tub under glass and separate shower, as well as a spacious walk-in closet and dressing area.

Plan DD-1696

Bedrooms: 4	Baths: 2
Space:	
Total living area:	1,748 sq. ft.
Garage:	393 sq. ft.
Exterior Wall Framing:	2x4

Foundation options:
Basement.
Crawlspace.
Slab.
(Foundation & framing conversion diagram available — see order form.)

Blueprint Price Code:	B

Floor Plan

54'10"

PATIO

SITTING

MORNING
9^8 x 9^4

BEDROOM 3
12^4 x 11^0

MASTER BEDROOM
14^4 x 18^0

KITCHEN
9^4 x 14^0

LIVING
15^0 x 19^8

BATH 2

50'5"

M BATH

UTIL

BEDROOM 4
10^0 x 10^4

DINING
11^4 x 11^4

GARAGE
19^8 x 20^0

BEDROOM 2
12^4 x 10^4

MAIN FLOOR

Plan DD-1696

TO ORDER THIS BLUEPRINT, CALL TOLL-FREE 1-800-547-5570
(prices and details on pp. 12-15.)

Grace and Finesse

A graceful brick arch sets off the entry to this beautiful one level home and complements the curve of the heightened windows found in the vaulted living room.

Measuring 1,685 sq. ft., this home has plenty of finesse but still manages to keep the square footage at an affordable level.

A barrel vaulted ceiling highlights the living room for a striking effect, while the adjoining dining room provides an added dimension of spaciousness.

The centrally located kitchen is spectacular. It not only has abundant counter and cabinet space, but is also designed as an integral part of the family room and nook. Note how the angled counter provides the cook a work area that encourages interaction with others in the adjoining living areas. The solarium windows that highlight the nook also provide plenty of natural light to brighten the kitchen as well.

The master bedroom doesn't skimp on any of the extras home buyers have come to expect. It boasts a private bath with dual vanities, illuminating skylight and a fantastic walk-in closet.

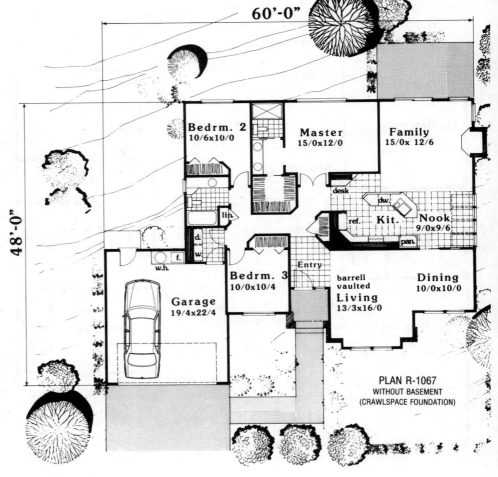

PLAN R-1067
WITHOUT BASEMENT
(CRAWLSPACE FOUNDATION)

Total living area: 1,685 sq. ft.
(Not counting garage)

TO ORDER THIS BLUEPRINT,
CALL TOLL-FREE 1-800-547-5570
190 (prices and details on pp. 12-15.)

Blueprint Price Code B
Plan R-1067

Great Room Featured

- In this rustic design, the centrally located Great Room features a cathedral ceiling with exposed wood beams. Living and dining areas are separated by a massive fireplace.
- The isolated master suite features a walk-in closet and compartmentalized bath.
- The gallery type kitchen is between the breakfast room and formal dining area. A large utility room and storage room complete the garage area.
- On the opposite side of the Great Room are two additional bedrooms and a second full bath.

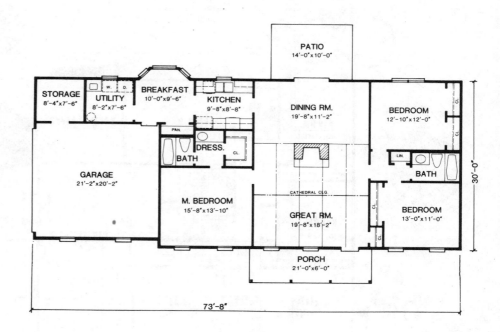

Plan C-8460

Bedrooms: 3	Baths: 2

Space:

Total living area:	1,670 sq. ft.
Basement:	approx. 1,600 sq. ft.
Garage:	427 sq. ft.
Storage:	63 sq. ft.

Exterior Wall Framing: 2x4

Foundation options:
Standard basement.
Crawlspace.
Slab.
(Foundation & framing conversion diagram available — see order form)

Blueprint Price Code: B

Plan C-8460

Designed for Casual Living

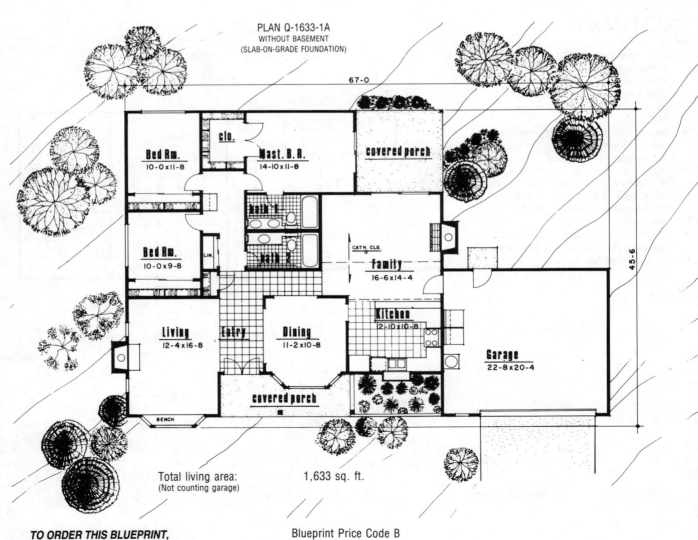

PLAN Q-1633-1A
WITHOUT BASEMENT
(SLAB-ON-GRADE FOUNDATION)

67-0

45-6

Bed Rm.
10-0x11-8

clo.

Mast. B.R.
14-10x11-8

covered porch

Bath 1

Bath 2

CATH. CLG.

family
16-6x14-4

Bed Rm.
10-0x9-8

LIN.

Kitchen
2-10x10-8

Garage
22-8x20-4

Living
12-4x16-8

Entry

Dining
11-2x10-8

covered porch

BENCH

Total living area:
(Not counting garage)

1,633 sq. ft.

Blueprint Price Code B

Plan Q-1633-1A

Appealing French Details

Authentic French details adorn the facade of this appealing one-story design. The slightly recessed doorway, arched windows, and curved shutters all add interest to this beautifully proportioned residence.

The vaulted ceiling of the Great Room makes this room appear much larger than its dimensions state. An oversized Palladian window creates a dramatic focal point and floods the room with natural light. The kitchen contains an unusual amount of cabinets and counter space.

Abundant closet space is provided for the inhabitants of the master bedroom. Also, note the convenient location of the laundry center, handy to both kitchen and bedroom areas.

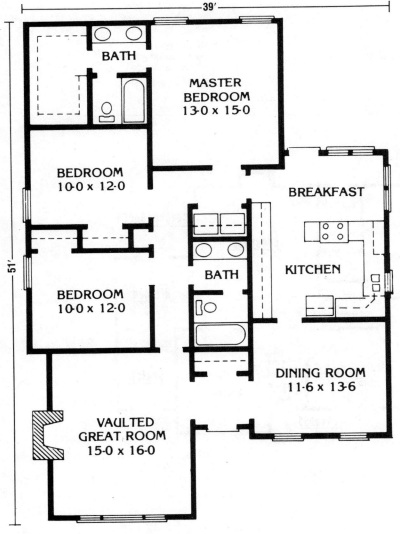

PLAN V-1586
WITHOUT BASEMENT
(CRAWLSPACE FOUNDATION)

Total living area: 1,586 sq. ft.

9'-0" CEILINGS THROUGHOUT

Blueprint Price Code B

Plan V-1586

Great Room Features Cathedral Ceiling

Total living area:
(Not counting garage)

1,559 sq. ft.

PLAN Q-1559-1A
WITHOUT BASEMENT
(SLAB-ON-GRADE FOUNDATION)

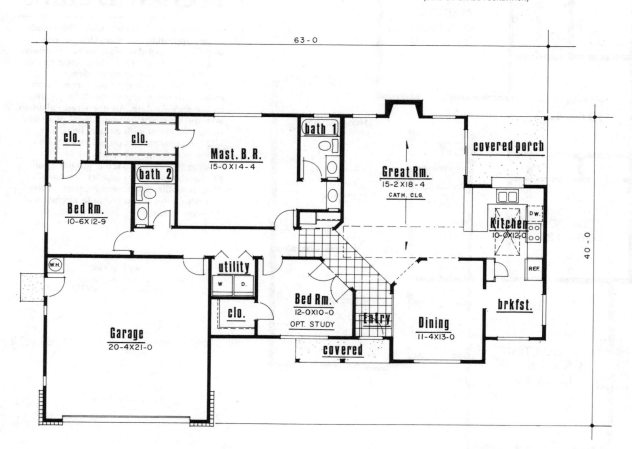

**TO ORDER THIS BLUEPRINT,
CALL TOLL-FREE 1-800-547-5570**
(prices and details on pp. 12-15.)

Blueprint Price Code B

Plan Q-1559-1A

Simple Plan for Economical Construction

Total living area:	1,522 sq. ft.
Carport:	397 sq. ft.
Storage:	39 sq. ft.
Front porch:	213 sq. ft.
Total area:	2,171 sq. ft.

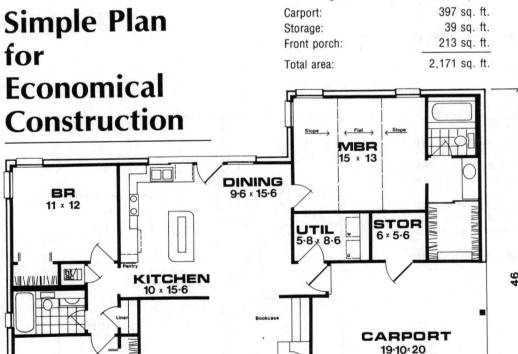

Specify basement, crawlspace or slab foundation.

Blueprint Price Code B

Plan J-8670

Cottage in the Country

- A nostalgic cottage exterior look would be appealing whether built in the country or the suburbs.
- The interior offers excitement and efficiency in its 1,497 sq. ft.
- A formal living room and interesting octagonal dining room greet guests from the entry.
- The kitchen overlooks the family room with cathedral ceiling, fireplace, and sliders to a covered patio.
- The master suite includes a vaulted ceiling, walk-in closet and private bath.

Plan Q-1497-1A

Bedrooms: 3	Baths: 2
Space:	
Total living area:	1,497 sq. ft.
Garage:	383 sq. ft.
Exterior Wall Framing:	2x4

Foundation options:
Slab.
(Foundation & framing conversion diagram available — see order form.)

Blueprint Price Code: A

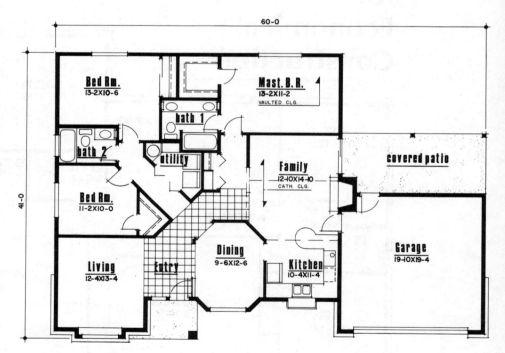

TO ORDER THIS BLUEPRINT, CALL TOLL-FREE 1-800-547-5570

Plan Q-1497-1A

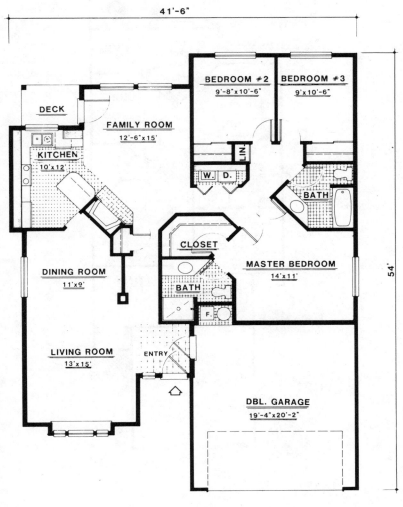

DECK

FAMILY ROOM
12'-6"x15'

BEDROOM #2
9'-8"x10'-6"

BEDROOM #3
9'x10'-6"

KITCHEN
10'x12

LIN.

W. D.

BATH

DINING ROOM
11'x9'

CLOSET

MASTER BEDROOM
14'x11'

BATH

F.

LIVING ROOM
13'x15'

ENTRY

DBL. GARAGE
19'-4"x20'-2"

41'-6"

54'

Angles Add Interior Excitement

- Eye-catching exterior leads into exciting interior.
- You'll find cathedral ceilings throughout the living and dining area.
- Angular kitchen includes eating bar, plenty of cabinet and counter space.
- Master suite includes angled double-door entry, private bath and large walk-in closet.
- Family room and kitchen join together to make large casual family area.
- Main bathroom continues the angled motif, and the washer and dryer are conveniently located in the bedroom hallway.

Plan NW-864

Bedrooms: 3	**Baths:** 2
Total living area:	1,449 sq. ft.
Garage:	390 sq. ft.
Exterior Wall Framing:	2x6

Foundation options:
   Crawlspace only.
(Foundation & framing conversion diagram available — see order form.)

Blueprint Price Code: A

**TO ORDER THIS BLUEPRINT,
CALL TOLL-FREE 1-800-547-5570**
(prices and details on pp. 12-15.)

Plan NW-864

Angular Interior Adds Spark

● **Mediterranean-style exterior encloses a creatively modern interior.**
● **Living and dining rooms form a "V", with the kitchen at the center.**
● **Master suite includes a triangular bath with separate tub and shower, which is in a five-sided enclosure.**
● **The study is also angled, and would make a great home office if needed for that purpose.**
● **A sunny breakfast nook adjoins the kitchen which is also angled for visual interest and efficiency.**
● **Laundry area is found in the garage entryway, next to the second bath.**

Plan Q-1449-1A

Bedrooms: 2	Baths: 2
Total living area:	1,449 sq. ft.
Garage:	387 sq. ft.
Exterior Wall Framing:	2x4

Foundation options:
  Slab only.
(Foundation & framing conversion diagram available — see order form.)

Blueprint Price Code:	A

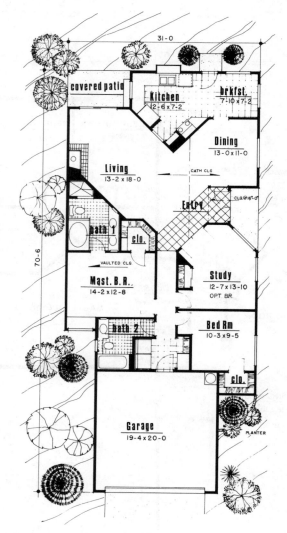

Plan Q-1449-1A

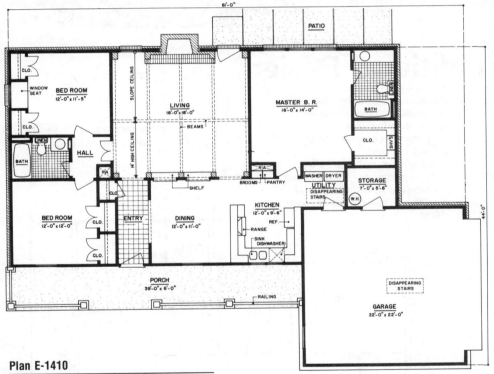

Vaulted Ceiling in Living Room

- This home packs a lot of grace and space into 1,418 square feet.
- Note the large living room with its beamed, vaulted ceiling and massive fireplace.
- The formal dining room lies off the foyer, and adjoins the efficient kitchen, which also includes a pantry and utility area.
- The master suite features a large walk-in closet and roomy master bath.
- At the other end of the home, two secondary bedrooms with abundant closet space share another full bath.
- The house-spanning porch invites guests to come in for a relaxing visit.

Plan E-1410

Bedrooms: 3	Baths: 2

Space:

Total living area:	1,418 sq. ft.
Garage:	484 sq. ft.
Storage:	38 sq. ft.
Porch:	238 sq. ft.

Exterior Wall Framing:	2x4

Foundation options:
Crawlspace.
Slab.
(Foundation & framing conversion diagram available — see order form.)

Blueprint Price Code:	A

Open Plan in Traditional Design

- This modest-sized design is popular for its simple yet stylish exterior, making it suitable for either country or urban settings.
- A covered front porch and gabled roof extension accent the facade while providing sheltered space for outdoor relaxing.
- Inside, the living room with a cathedral ceiling and fireplace is combined with an open dining area and kitchen with island to create one large gathering spot for family and guests.

- The master bedroom features a private bath, large closet and ample sleeping area.
- Two other bedrooms share a second full bath.
- A convenient utility area and walk-in pantry are found in the passageway to the carport; also note the large outdoor storage closet.

Plan J-86155

Bedrooms: 3	Baths: 2
Total living area:	1,385 sq. ft.
Basement:	1,385 sq. ft.
Carport:	380 sq. ft.
Exterior Wall Framing:	2x4

Foundation options:
Standard basement.
Crawlspace.
Slab.
(Foundation & framing conversion diagram available — see order form.)

Blueprint Price Code:	A

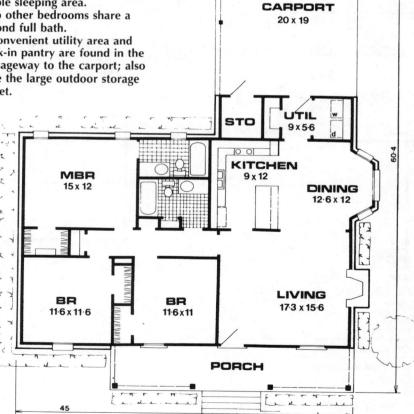

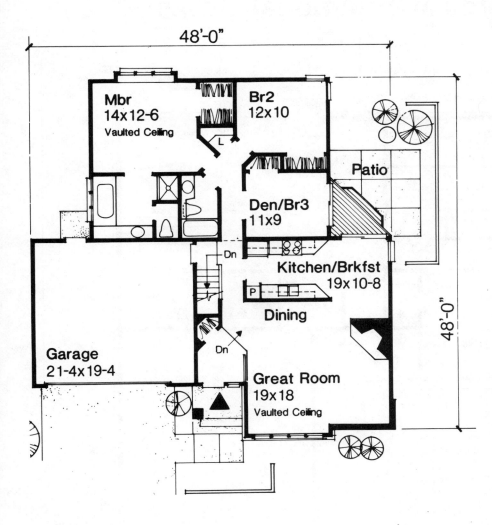

48'-0"

Mbr
14x12-6
Vaulted Ceiling

Br2
12x10

Patio

Den/Br3
11x9

Dn

Kitchen/Brkfst
19x10-8

P

Dining

Dn

Garage
21-4x19-4

Great Room
19x18
Vaulted Ceiling

48'-0"

Designed for Quiet, Private Sleeping Area

- This moderate-sized plan presents an impressive facade, with its large and interesting front window arrangement.
- An unusual Great Room plan allows for some separation of the kitchen/breakfast area from the dining/living section, but still makes them all part of one unit.
- The master bedroom includes a private bath with separate tub and shower, and another full bath serves the rest of the home.
- The third bedroom could serve as a den, study, or office if not needed for sleeping.
- The breakfast area offers easy access to an outdoor patio.
- Take special note of the unusual fireplace positioning in the Great Room.
- This plan comes with a full basement, which effectively doubles the space available.

Plan B-902

Bedrooms: 2-3	Baths: 2
Total living area:	1,368 sq. ft.
Basement:	1,368 sq. ft.
Garage:	412 sq. ft.
Exterior Wall Framing:	2x4

Foundation options:
Standard basement only.
(Foundation & framing conversion diagram available — see order form.)

Blueprint Price Code:	A

Plan B-902

Economical Traditional Design

PLAN E-1305
WITHOUT BASEMENT

Specify crawlspace or slab foundation.

54'-0"

PATIO

44'-6"

FLOOR RAISED 6"

MASTER B.R.
13'-6" x 13'-6"

KNEE SPACE

BATH

DRESS. ROOM

CLO.

SHV'S.

CLO.

BATH

VAULT

LIVING
17'-6" x 17'-0"

VAULT

DINING
12'-0" x 11'-0"

TURNED WD. POST DIVIDER

BAR

OVEN

SURF. UNIT

FALSE BEAMS

KITCHEN
11'-6" x 11'-0"

SINK

CLO.

R.A.

HALL

SHV'S

LINEN

DISAPPEARING STAIRS

CLO.

ENTRY

STOR.
6'-9" x 6'-6"

W.H.

UTIL.
6'-6" x 6'-3"

D.W.

BED ROOM
12'-0" x 11'-0"

BED ROOM
12'-0" x 11'-0"

CLO.

WASH. DRYER

REF.

PORCH

GARAGE
21'-0" x 21'-0"

AREAS

Living	1346 sq. ft.
Storage	44 sq. ft.
Garage	441 sq. ft.
Porch	61 sq. ft.
Total	1892 sq. ft.

Blueprint Price Code A
Plan E-1305

Compact Country Cottage

- A multi-paned bay window, dormers and a covered front porch dress up this compact, country cottage.
- The entrance foyer reveals a spectacular central Great Room with cathedral ceiling, fireplace and a view of the attached rear deck.
- The adjoining formal dining room is open to a U-shaped kitchen; both overlook a sheltered area of the expansive deck that has skylights.
- Convenient laundry facilities are near the two secondary bedrooms at the front of the home, one with front bay window.
- The master bedroom is secluded to the rear and offers its own deck access.

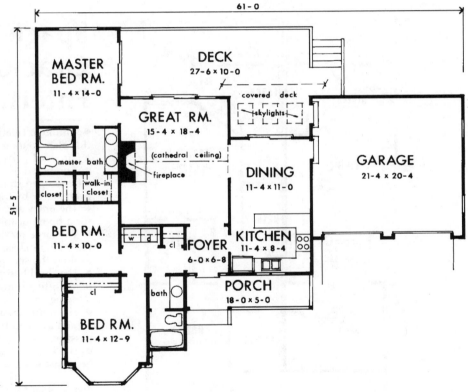

Plan DG-234	
Bedrooms: 3	**Baths:** 2
Space:	
Main floor	1,310 sq. ft.
Total Living Area	**1,310 sq. ft.**
Garage	434 sq. ft.
Exterior Wall Framing	2x4
Foundation options:	
Crawlspace	
(Foundation & framing conversion diagram available—see order form.)	
Blueprint Price Code	**A**

Plan DG-234

Space for Gracious Entertaining

- Although relatively modest in size, this plan contains abundant space for a fair-sized party or family gathering.
- Combined living/dining area creates a large open space, made to seem even larger by the vaulted ceiling.
- The entry area is also impressive for a home of this size.
- The large master suite includes a big walk-in closet and vaulted ceiling, as does the second bedroom.
- The third bedroom makes a nice home office if not needed for a sleeping room.
- The utility area is conveniently tucked away in the garage entry passage.
- The kitchen includes a cozy, sunny breakfast nook.

Plan Q-1300-1A

Bedrooms: 2-3	Baths: 2
Total living area:	1,300 sq. ft.
Garage:	374 sq. ft.
Exterior Wall Framing:	2x4

Foundation options:
Slab only.
(Foundation & framing conversion diagram available — see order form.)

Blueprint Price Code:	A

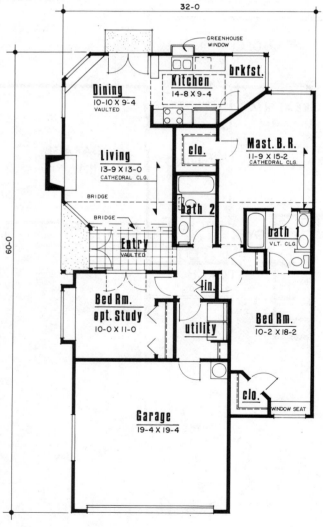

Plan Q-1300-1A

Affordable Country Charm

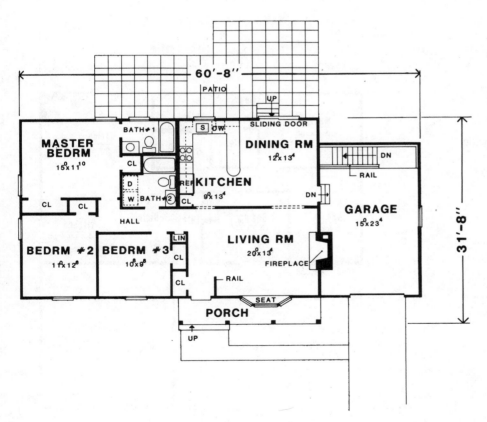

- A covered front porch, attached garage, and bay window add appeal to this efficient, affordable home.
- A spacious living room with fireplace and window seat offer plenty of family living space.
- The kitchen/dining room opens to a rear patio for indoor/outdoor living.
- The attached garage incorporates stairs for the optional basement.
- The plan includes three bedrooms and two baths on the same level, a plus for young families.

Plan AX-98602

Bedrooms: 3	Baths: 2

Space:	
Total living area:	1,253 sq. ft.
Basement:	1,253 sq. ft.
Garage:	368 sq. ft.

Exterior Wall Framing:	2x4

Foundation options:
Standard basement.
Slab.
(Foundation & framing conversion diagram available — see order form.)

Blueprint Price Code:	A

Plan AX-98602

Economical One-Level Design

- Great Room design concept creates large open area for living, dining rooms and kitchen.
- Large covered patio in rear extends entertaining area.
- Master bedroom includes walk-in closet and private bath.

Plan Q-1248-1A

Bedrooms: 3	Baths: 2
Total living area:	1,248 sq. ft.
Garage:	400 sq. ft.
Exterior Wall Framing:	2x4

Foundation options:
Slab only.
(Foundation & framing conversion diagram available — see order form.)

Blueprint Price Code: A

TO ORDER THIS BLUEPRINT,
CALL TOLL-FREE 1-800-547-5570

Plan Q-1248-1A

Secluded Entryway in Compact Design

AREAS

Living	1200 sq. ft.
Porches	60 sq. ft.
Utility & Storage	100 sq. ft.
Total	1360 sq. ft.

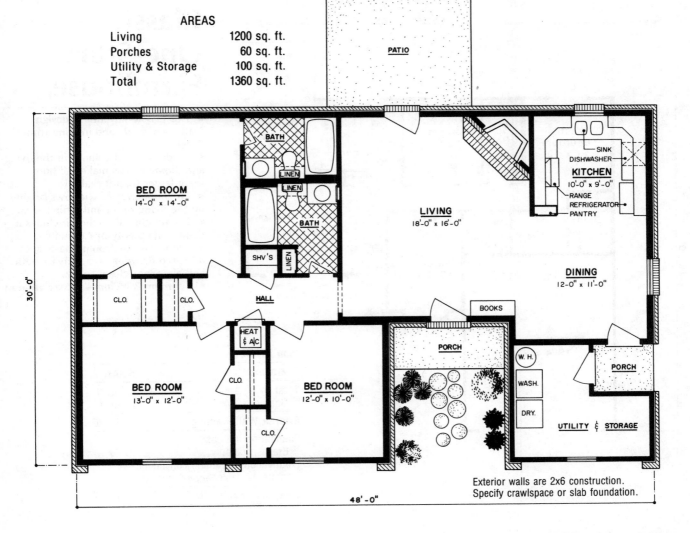

Exterior walls are 2x6 construction.
Specify crawlspace or slab foundation.

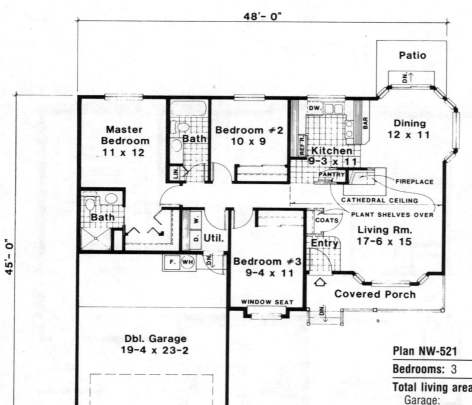

Master Bedroom 11 x 12

Bath

Bedroom #2 10 x 9

DW.

Kitchen 9-3 x 11

Dining 12 x 11

Patio

DN.

REFR.

BAR

PANTRY

FIREPLACE

CATHEDRAL CEILING

PLANT SHELVES OVER

COATS

Living Rm. 17-6 x 15

LIN.

Bath

D. W.

Util.

F.

WH

DN.

Bedroom #3 9-4 x 11

Entry

Covered Porch

WINDOW SEAT

DN.

Dbl. Garage 19-4 x 23-2

48'- 0"

45'- 0"

Classic One-Story Farmhouse

- This classic farmhouse design features a shady and inviting front porch.
- Inside, vaulted ceilings in the living and dining rooms make the home seem larger than it really is.
- An abundance of windows brightens up the living room and dining area.
- The functional kitchen includes a pantry and plenty of cabinet space.
- The master bedroom boasts a mirrored dressing area, private bath and abundant closet space.
- Bedroom 3 includes a cozy window seat.

Plan NW-521

Bedrooms: 3	**Baths:** 2
Total living area:	1,187 sq. ft.
Garage:	448 sq. ft.
Exterior Wall Framing:	2x6

Foundation options:
 Crawlspace only.
(Foundation & framing conversion diagram available — see order form.)

Blueprint Price Code:	A

TO ORDER THIS BLUEPRINT,
CALL TOLL-FREE 1-800-547-5570
208 (prices and details on pp. 12-15.)

Plan NW-521

Master Bedroom Suite Features "His 'n Hers" Baths

- A spacious and secluded master bedroom boasts a bath with separate his 'n hers dressing areas and closets.
- This traditional ranch also offers a huge central living room with fireplace and adjoining patio.
- A formal dining room is entered through double doors from the roomy kitchen and bayed eating room.
- Note the large and convenient utility area; also, the pantry in the kitchen.

Plan E-1812

Bedrooms: 3	Baths: 2
Space:	
Main floor	1,860 sq. ft.
Total Living Area	**1,860 sq. ft.**
Carport	484 sq. ft.
Exterior Wall Framing	2x6

Foundation options:
Crawlspace
Slab
(Foundation & framing conversion diagram available—see order form.)

Blueprint Price Code	**B**

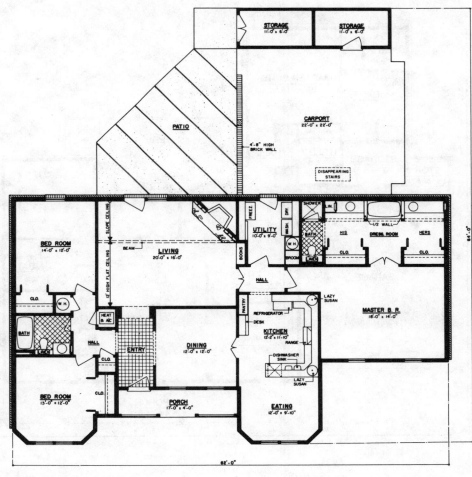

Plan E-1812

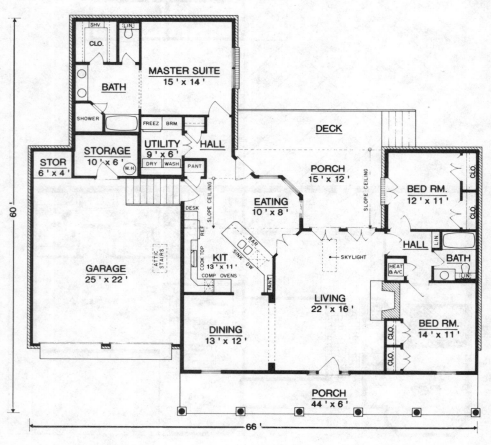

Raised Cottage Design Offers Large Covered Porches

- Twin dormers and covered porch add drama to this raised one-story.
- Large centered living room features 12' ceilings and built-in skylights.
- Kitchen has unusual but functional angular design, sloped ceilings, bar, and eating area that overlooks the adjoining deck.
- Elegant master suite is conveniently located near kitchen.

Plan E-1826

Bedrooms: 3	Baths: 2

Space:

Total living area:	1,800 sq. ft.
Garage:	550 sq. ft.
Storage:	84 sq. ft.
Porches:	466 sq. ft.

Exterior Wall Framing:	2x6

Foundation options:
Crawlspace.
Slab.
(Foundation & framing conversion diagram available — see order form.)

Blueprint Price Code:	B

Plan E-1826

Elegance and Convenience

- Exterior design presents a dignified, distinctive and solid look.
- Energy-efficient, 2 x 6 exterior walls are used.
- 15' ceilings and a beautifully detailed fireplace are part of the living room decor.
- Octagonal dining room has window walls on three sides to view adjacent porches.
- Master suite features access to a private porch and an attached bath with corner marbled tub and separate shower.

Plan E-1628

Bedrooms: 3	Baths: 2

Space:

Total living area:	1,655 sq. ft.
Garage and storage:	549 sq. ft.
Porches:	322 sq. ft.

Exterior Wall Framing: 2x6

Foundation options:
Crawlspace.
Slab.
(Foundation & framing conversion diagram available — see order form.)

Blueprint Price Code: B

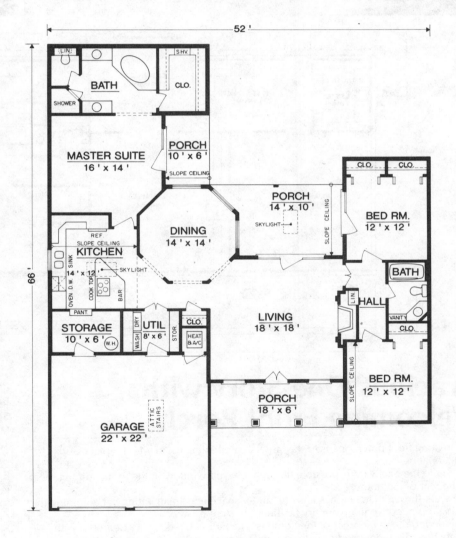

Plan E-1628

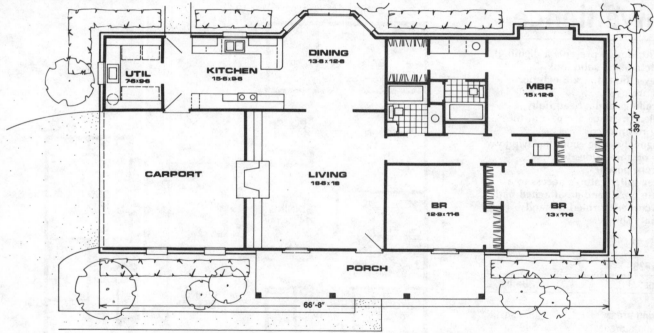

Gracious One-Story with Welcoming Front Porch

- An inviting front porch opens to the large, central living room with fireplace and functional built-ins.
- A view to the backyard is possible through a bayed window in the formal dining room at the rear of the home.
- The walk-through kitchen has lots of counter space and small eating bar adjoining the dining room; convenient laundry facilities are steps away.
- Secluded to the rear corner of the home is a generous-sized master bedroom with lovely boxed window and private bath with second walk-in closet, dressing area and isolated toilet and tub.
- Two additional good-sized bedrooms and a second full bath complete the floor plan.

Plan J-8692	
Bedrooms: 3	**Baths:** 2
Space:	
Main floor	1,633 sq. ft.
Total Living Area	**1,633 sq. ft.**
Carport	380 sq. ft.
Exterior Wall Framing	2x4
Foundation options:	
Basement	
Crawlspace	
Slab	
(Foundation & framing conversion diagram available—see order form.)	
Blueprint Price Code	B

TO ORDER THIS BLUEPRINT,
CALL TOLL-FREE 1-800-547-5570

Plan J-8692

(prices and details on pp. 12-15.)

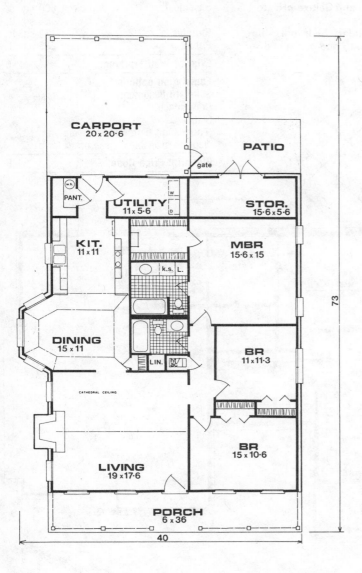

Traditional Design Fits Narrow Lot

- This compact, cozy and dignified plan makes great use of a small lot, while also offering an exciting interior design.
- Note the bay-windowed dining area, which joins the living room to provide a large space for entertaining.
- The living room features a warm fireplace and a cathedral ceiling.
- The master suite includes a deluxe private bath and large walk-in closet.
- Two secondary bedrooms share another bath in the hallway.
- Also note the pantry and utility space adjoining the kitchen, and the storage area off the rear patio.

Plan J-86161

Bedrooms: 3	Baths: 2
Space:	
Main floor	1,626 sq. ft.
Total Living Area	**1,626 sq. ft.**
Basement	1,626 sq. ft.
Carport	410 sq. ft.
Storage	104 sq. ft.
Porch	216 sq. ft.
Exterior Wall Framing	2x4

Foundation options:
Standard Basement
Crawlspace
Slab
(Foundation & framing conversion diagram available—see order form.)

Blueprint Price Code	B

Plan J-86161

Rustic Comfort

- While rustic in exterior appearance, this home is completely modern inside and loaded with the amenities preferred by today's builders.
- A large living room is made to seem immense by use of 16' ceilings, and an impressive fireplace and hearth dominate one end of the room.
- A formal dining room adds to the spaciousness, since it is separated from the living room only by a divider and a 6" step.
- The large U-shaped kitchen is adjoined by a convenient sewing and utility area, which in turn leads to the garage. A storage area is included in the garage, along with a built-in workbench.

- The sumptuous master suite features a sitting area, enormous walk-in closet and deluxe private bath.
- The two secondary bedrooms share another full bath and are zoned for privacy.

Plan E-1607

Bedrooms: 3	Baths: 2

Space:

Total living area:	1,600 sq. ft.
Basement:	approx. 1,600 sq. ft.
Garage:	484 sq. ft.
Storage:	132 sq. ft.
Porch:	295 sq. ft.

Exterior Wall Framing:	2x6

Foundation options:
Standard basement.
Crawlspace.
Slab.
(Foundation & framing conversion diagram available — see order form)

Blueprint Price Code:	B

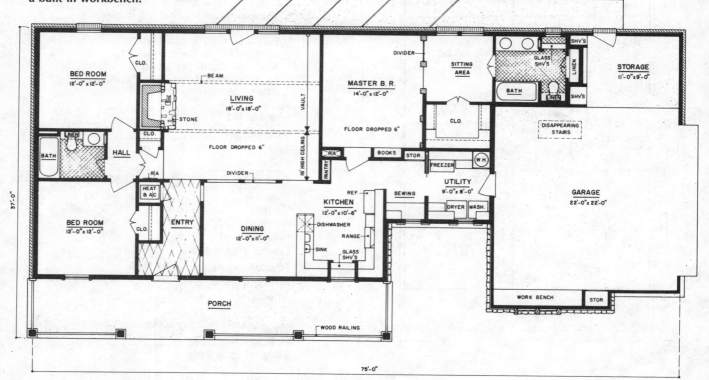

TO ORDER THIS BLUEPRINT, CALL TOLL-FREE 1-800-547-5570

Plan E-1607

Traditional One-Story Cottage

Shuttered windows, covered porch trimmed with Colonial style posts and fascia, small window panes that match the paneling of the garage doors, clapboard siding with corner board trim, and other Colonial touches combine to imbue this cottage with Early American charm.

An attractive and functional entrance hall with convenient closet space acts as a buffer between the casual and formal activity areas. At the rear of the house, the kitchen with dining space has sliding glass doors leading to a rear garden terrace.

Designed for family living, the plan features three bedrooms and two full baths, one of which serves the master bedroom privately. You will also note the master bedroom has an oversized walk-in closet. The central walkway that serves the bedroom wing is flanked on both sides by numerous storage and linen closets. Both bathrooms have built-in vanities.

Another interesting feature is the play room located at the rear of the attached garage. A utility room of generous proportions is also found in both versions of the plan. The plan with a basement provides for a family room that measures 17' x 11'. A convenient access to the garage connects with the hallway leading to the family room. A corner fireplace with a raised hearth opening is featured in both plans.

Overall width of the home measures 60' and the greatest depth including front and rear projections is 40'.

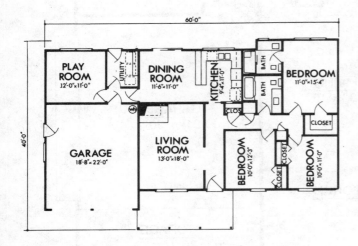

PLAN H-3707-1A
WITHOUT BASEMENT
(CRAWLSPACE FOUNDATION)

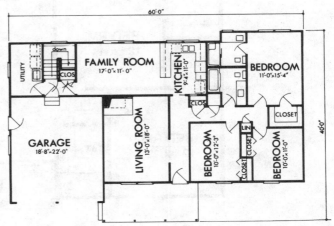

PLAN H-3707-1
WITH BASEMENT

Total living area: 1,486 sq. ft.
(Not counting garage)

Blueprint Price Code A

Plans H-3707-1 & -1A

Cozy, Compact One-Story Home

- Central living room and attached dining room feature 11′ ceilings.
- Cleverly positioned between the main living areas is a unique fireplace, wet bar, and book shelves combination.
- Isolated master suite boasts private bath and large walk-in closet.
- Secondary bedrooms have king-sized closets, and share a full bath.

Plan E-1427

Bedrooms: 3	Baths: 2

Space:

Total living area:	1,444 sq. ft.
Garage and storage:	540 sq. ft.
Porches:	160 sq. ft.

Exterior Wall Framing:	2x4

Foundation options:
Crawlspace.
Slab.
(Foundation & framing conversion diagram available — see order form.)

Blueprint Price Code:	A

Plan E-1427

The Solid Look of Permanence

- Exterior design lends an air of quality and elegance which is carried on throughout the home.
- Large, centered living room decor includes 10' ceilings, detailed fireplace, and ceiling fans.
- Side porch can be entered through living/dining area.
- Minimum halls generate maximum living space.
- Secluded master suite has romantic sitting area and designer bath.

Plan E-1435

Bedrooms: 3	Baths: 2
Space:	
Total living area:	1,442 sq. ft.
Garage and storage:	516 sq. ft.
Porches:	128 sq. ft.
Exterior Wall Framing:	2x4

Foundation options:
Crawlspace.
Slab.
(Foundation & framing conversion diagram available — see order form.)

Blueprint Price Code:	A

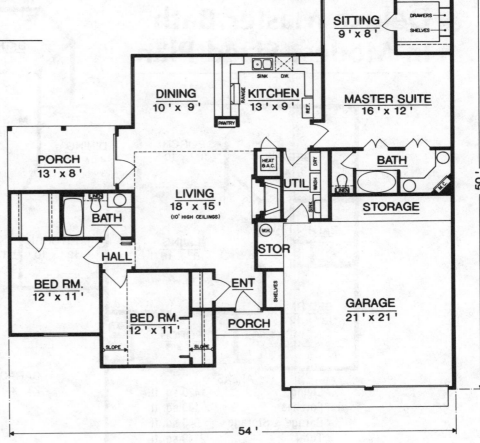

Plan E-1435

Deluxe Master Bath
In Modest-Sized Plan

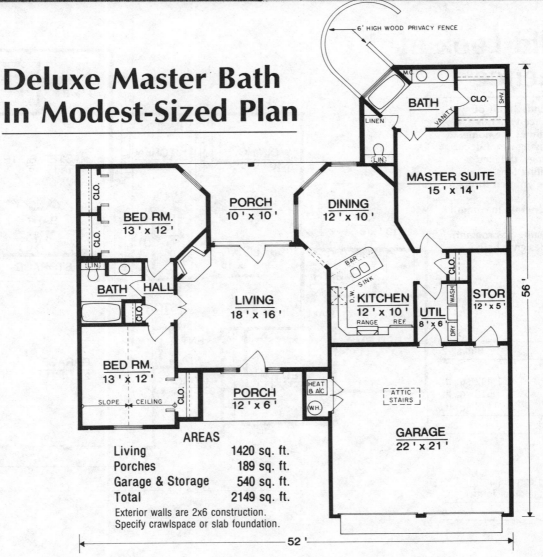

6' HIGH WOOD PRIVACY FENCE

BATH
CLO.
SHV.
LINEN
VANITY

MASTER SUITE
15' x 14'

BED RM.
13' x 12'
CLO.
CLO.

PORCH
10' x 10'

DINING
12' x 10'

BATH
HALL

LIN.
CLO.

LIVING
18' x 16'

BAR
SINK
D.W.
KITCHEN
12' x 10'
RANGE   REF.

CLO.
WASH
DRY
UTIL
8' x 6'

STOR
12' x 5'

BED RM.
13' x 12'

SLOPE   CEILING
CLO.

PORCH
12' x 6'

HEAT & A/C
W.H.

ATTIC
STAIRS

GARAGE
22' x 21'

56'

52'

AREAS
Living	1420 sq. ft.
Porches	189 sq. ft.
Garage & Storage	540 sq. ft.
Total	2149 sq. ft.

Exterior walls are 2x6 construction.
Specify crawlspace or slab foundation.

Blueprint Price Code A
Plan E-1426

Charming Traditional Design

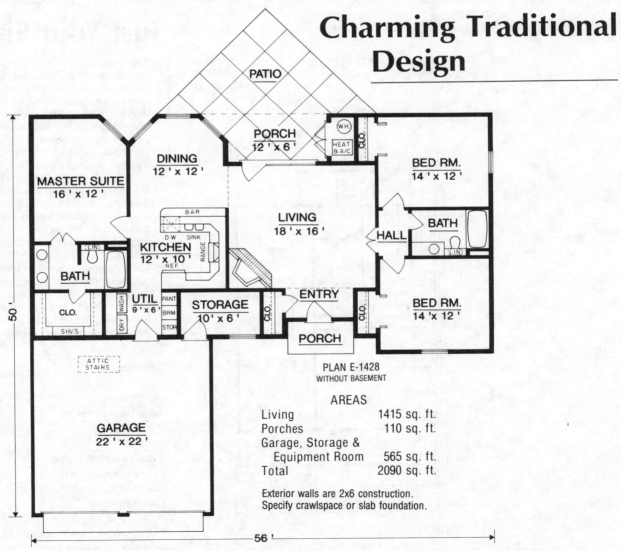

PATIO

PORCH
12' x 6'

WH

HEAT & A/C

CLO.

DINING
12' x 12'

BED RM.
14' x 12'

MASTER SUITE
16' x 12'

BAR

LIVING
18' x 16'

BATH

LIN

KITCHEN
12' x 10'

DW   SINK

REF   RANGE

HALL

LIN

BATH

CLO.

SHV'S

DRY   WASH

UTIL
9' x 6'

PANT

BRM

STOR

STORAGE
10' x 6'

CLO.

ENTRY

CLO.

BED RM.
14' x 12'

PORCH

50'

ATTIC
STAIRS

GARAGE
22' x 22'

PLAN E-1428
WITHOUT BASEMENT

AREAS

Living	1415 sq. ft.
Porches	110 sq. ft.
Garage, Storage & Equipment Room	565 sq. ft.
Total	2090 sq. ft.

Exterior walls are 2x6 construction.
Specify crawlspace or slab foundation.

56'

Just Your Size

- This country-style cottage will fit anywhere, even on a small, in-town lot. Its charming character and 35-ft. width make it an ideal choice for those who value vintage styling along with plenty of yard space. The large covered front porch further extends living space and contributes to the attractive facade.
- Vaulted ceilings in the dining room and living room lend a spacious feel to the home. The living room features a fireplace framed by windows, and bay windows brighten the dining room. A galley-style kitchen leads to the utility and storage rooms placed near the back entrance.
- The master bedroom has French doors opening onto a backyard patio, a private bath with lots of storage space, plus a walk-in closet. Another full bath is centrally located, just across the hall from the remaining two bedrooms.

Plan J-86119

Bedrooms: 3	Baths: 2
Space:	
Main floor	1,346 sq. ft.
Total Living Area	**1,346 sq. ft.**
Basement	1,346 sq. ft.
Carport	400 sq. ft.
Exterior Wall Framing	2x4

Foundation options:
Standard Basement
Crawlspace
Slab
(Foundation & framing conversion diagram available—see order form.)

Blueprint Price Code	A

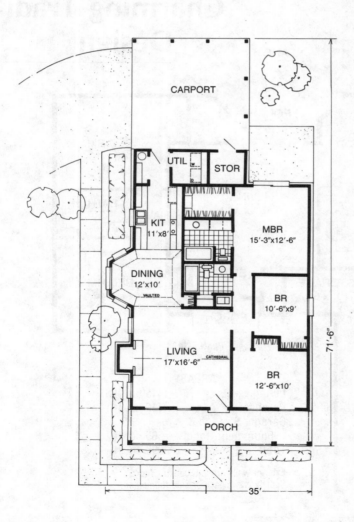

**TO ORDER THIS BLUEPRINT,
CALL TOLL-FREE 1-800-547-5570**

Plan J-86119

Photo courtesy of Barclay Home Designs

Angled Windows and Flowing Space

- This highly popular compact home proves that even smaller homes can be big on style and convenience.
- The bay-windowed living room and dining room combine to create a large space for entertaining.
- A sunny nook adjoins the kitchen, which includes a pantry.
- The master suite includes a private bath, roomy wardrobe closet and a double-door entry.
- The sheltered entry invites guests and family alike, and a convenient utility area is situated in the garage entry area.
- An optional third bedroom can be used for a den or TV room, open to the nook if desired.

**NOTE:
The above photographed home may have been modified by the homeowner. Please refer to floor plan and/or drawn elevation shown for actual blueprint details.

46'-0"

51'-11"

Nook 9/6x9/6
T.V./ Bdrm. 3 10/0x10/0
Bedrm. 2 12/6x10/0
Dining 10/0x10/0
Kit.
pantry
Master 14/0x14/0
Entry
Living 13/6x16/6
walk in wardrobe
Garage 19/6x22/0

Plan R-1028

Bedrooms: 2-3	Baths: 2
Total livng area:	1,305 sq. ft.
Garage:	429 sq. ft.
Exterior Wall Framing:	2x4

Foundation options:
Crawlspace only.
(Foundation & framing conversion diagram available — see order form.)

Blueprint Price Code:	A

Plan R-1028

Angles Open Rear of Home to More Sunshine

PATIO

PORCH
12' x 6'

WH

HEAT
& A/C

CLO.

BED RM.
14' x 12'

DINING
12' x 12'

MASTER SUITE
16' x 12'

BAR

DW   SINK

KITCHEN

LIVING
18' x 16'

HALL

BATH

LIN.

RANGE

REF.

BATH

LIN.

CLO.

WASH

DRY

UTIL
9' x 6'

PANT
BRM
STOR

STORAGE
10' x 6'

CLO.

ENTRY

CLO.

BED RM.
14' x 12'

SHLVS

SHLVS

50'

ATTIC STAIRS

PORCH
8' x 4'

GARAGE
22' x 22'

56'

AREAS

Living   1415 sq. ft.
Porches   114 sq. ft.
Garage, Storage
 Equip.   565 sq. ft.
Total   2094 sq. ft.

Exterior walls are 2x6 construction.
Specify crawlspace or slab foundation.

Blueprint Price Code A

Plan E-1424

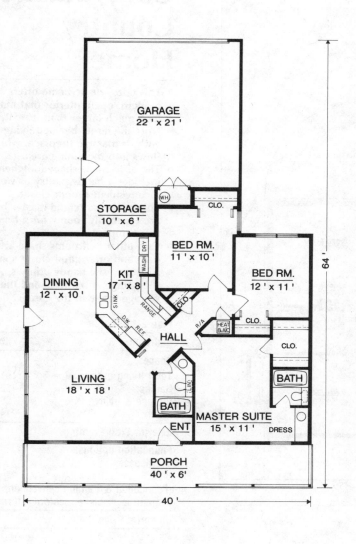

GARAGE
22' x 21'

STORAGE
10' x 6'

WH

CLO.

BED RM.
11' x 10'

BED RM.
12' x 11'

DINING
12' x 10'

KIT
17' x 8'

WASH DRY

SINK

RANGE

DW REF

CLO.

CLO.

CLO.

HALL

R/A

HEAT
&A/C

LIVING
18' x 18'

LIN

BATH

BATH

ENT

MASTER SUITE
15' x 11'

DRESS

PORCH
40' x 6'

64'

40'

Cozy Veranda Invites Visitors

- Large covered front porch has detailed columns and railings.
- Compact size fits small lots, yet facade gives illusion of larger home.
- Space-saving angular design minimizes hallway space.
- Master suite features walk-in closet, private bath, and separate dressing and sink area.

Plan E-1217

Bedrooms: 3	Baths: 2

Space:

Total living area:	1,266 sq. ft.
Garage and storage:	550 sq. ft.

Exterior Wall Framing:	2x6

Foundation options:
Crawlspace.
Slab.
(Foundation & framing conversion
diagram available — see order form.)

Blueprint Price Code:	A

Plan E-1217

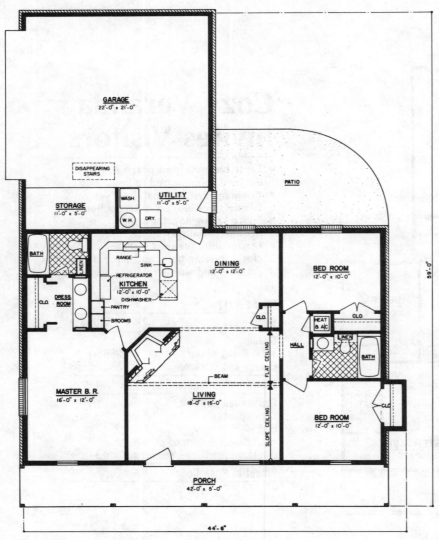

Cozy, Rustic Country Home

- This cozy, rustic home offers a modern, open interior that makes it look much larger than it really is.
- Note the large, beamed living room with its massive fireplace, which flows into the dining area.
- The efficient U-shaped kitchen includes a handy pantry as well as a convenient broom closet.
- The master suite and master bath are especially roomy for a home of this compact size.
- Two other bedrooms share a full bath and offer good closet space.
- Also note the handy utility space in the garage entry area, and the storage space in the garage.

Plan E-1109

Bedrooms: 3	Baths: 2

Space:	
Total living area:	1,191 sq. ft.
Garage:	462 sq. ft.
Storage & utility:	55 sq. ft.
Porch:	214 sq. ft.

Exterior Wall Framing:	2x6

Foundation options:
Crawlspace.
Slab.
(Foundation & framing conversion diagram available — see order form.)

Blueprint Price Code:	A

TO ORDER THIS BLUEPRINT, CALL TOLL-FREE 1-800-547-5570

Plan E-1109